CITY·SMART™
GUIDEBOOK

Nashville

Second Edition

by Susan Williams Knowles

John Muir Publications
Santa Fe, New Mexico

ACKNOWLEDGMENTS

My heartfelt thanks to the Nashville insiders whose quotes throughout the book made this city come alive in print.

John Muir Publications, P. O. Box 613, Santa Fe, New Mexico 87504

Printed in the United States of America.
Second edition. First printing April 1999.

ISBN 1-56261-459-2
ISSN 1091-3491

Editors: Marybeth Griffin, Elaine Robbins
Graphics editor: Tom Gaukel
Production: Rebecca Cook
Design: Janine Lehmann
Cover design: Suzanne Rush
Typesetter: Melissa Tandysh
Maps: Julie Felton
Printer: Publishers Press
Front cover photo: © John Elk III—Belmont Mansion, 1850s
Back cover photo: © Jean Higgins/Unicorn Stock Photos—Opryland Grounds

Distributed to the book trade by
Publishers Group West
Berkeley, California

While every effort has been made to provide accurate, up-to-date information, the author and publisher accept no responsibility for loss, injury, or inconvenience sustained by any person using this book.

CONTENTS

MAP CONTENTS

See Nashville the CiTY·SMaRT™ Way

The Guide for Nashville Natives, New Residents, and Visitors

In *City•Smart Guidebook: Nashville,* local author Susan Williams Knowles tells it like it is. Residents will learn things they never knew about their city, new residents will get an insider's view of their new hometown, and visitors will be guided to the very best Nashville has to offer—whether they're on a weekend getaway or staying a week or more.

Opinionated Recommendations Save You Time and Money

From shopping to nightlife to museums, the author is opinionated about what she likes and dislikes. You'll learn the great and the not-so-great things about Nashville's sights, restaurants, and accommodations. So you can decide what's worth your time and what's not; which hotel is worth the splurge and which is the best choice for budget travelers.

Easy-to-Use Format Makes Planning Your Trip a Cinch

City•Smart Guidebook: Nashville is user-friendly—you'll quickly find exactly what you're looking for. Chapters are organized by travelers' interests or needs, from Where to Stay and Where to Eat, to Sights and Attractions, Kids' Stuff, Sports and Recreation, and even Day Trips from Nashville.

Includes Maps and Quick Location-Finding Features

Every listing in this book is accompanied by a geographic zone designation (see the following pages for zone details) that helps you immediately find each location. Staying near Vanderbilt University and wondering about nearby sights and restaurants? Look for the Midtown label in the listings and you'll know that statue or café is not far away. Or maybe you're looking for the Ryman Auditorium. Along with its address, you'll see a Downtown label, so you'll know just where to find it.

All That and Fun to Read, Too!

Every City•Smart chapter includes fun-to-read (and fun-to-use) tips to help you get more out of Nashville, city trivia (Did you know that Andrew Jackson, the seventh president of the United States, is buried in Nashville's Hermitage garden cemetery?), and illuminating sidebars (in the Where to Stay chapter the Health and Fitness sidebar lists hotels with quality health club facilities). And well-known local residents provide their personal "Top Ten" lists, guiding readers to the city's best places to stop for lunch in the middle of a busy work day, tastiest barbecue joints, most popular attractions for kids, and more.

Sights and attractions noted with a ♿ are wheelchair accessible.

GREATER NASHVILLE

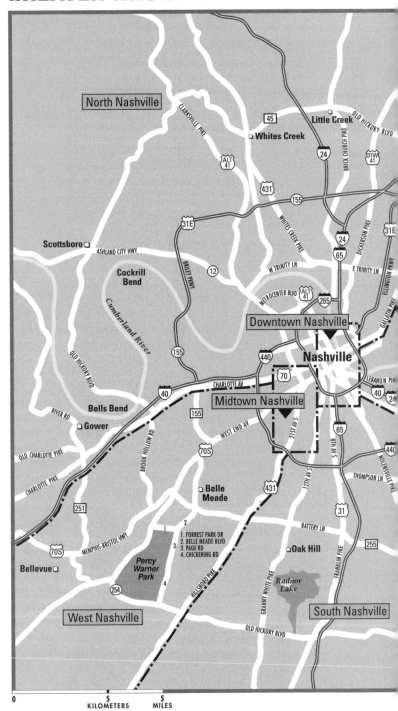

North Nashville

45
Little Creek
Whites Creek
CLARKSVILLE PIKE
OLD HICKORY BLVD
BRICK CHURCH PIKE
ALT 41
24
31W 41
431
155
Scottsboro
ASHLAND CITY HWY
31E
WHITES CREEK PIKE
24
31E
Cockrill
Bend
BRILEY PKWY
12
W TRINITY LN
65
DICKERSON PIKE
E TRINITY LN
ELLINGTON PKWY
Cumberland River
METROCENTER BLVD
ALT 41
265
Downtown Nashville
GALLATIN PIKE
OLD HICKORY BLVD
155
Nashville
440
LEBANON PIKE
RIVER RD
Bells Bend
Gower
40
CHARLOTTE AV
70
Midtown Nashville
40
24
OLD CHARLOTTE PIKE
155
BROOK HOLLOW RD
WEST END AV
70S
21ST AV S
65
440
CHARLOTTE PIKE
70S
THOMPSON LN
NOLENSVILLE PIKE
251
Belle
Meade
431
12TH AV S
8TH AV S
BATTERY LN
31
255
Bellevue
70S
MEMPHIS-BRISTOL HWY
Percy
Warner
Park
1. FORREST PARK DR
2. BELLE MEADE BLVD
3. PAGE RD
4. CHICKERING RD
Oak Hill
FRANKLIN PIKE
254
HILLSBORO PIKE
GRANNY WHITE PIKE
Radnor
Lake
West Nashville
South Nashville
OLD HICKORY BLVD

0   5   5
KILOMETERS   MILES

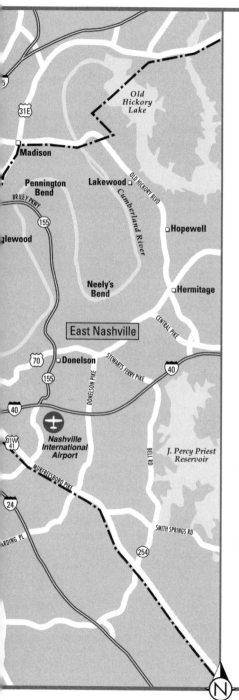

NASHVILLE ZONES

Downtown Nashville (DN)

Midtown Nashville (MN)
Includes the West End, Vanderbilt University area, and Hillsboro Village.

North Nashville (NN)
Includes all areas in north Nashville bounded by I-40 in the west and Gallatin Pike in the east.

East Nashville (EN)
Includes all areas in east Nashville bounded by Gallatin Pike in the north and Murfreesboro Pike in the south.

South Nashville (SN)
Includes all areas in south Nashville bounded by Murfreesboro Pike in the east and Hillsboro Pike in the west.

West Nashville (WN)
Includes all areas in west Nashville bounded by Hillsboro Pike in the south, I-40 in the north, and 440 in the east.

Mary Entrekin

1

WELCOME TO NASHVILLE

Nashville is the current boomtown of the upper South. It is a mixture of old-South tradition, grassroots popular culture, and new-South financial and political prowess. In the midst of growth and change, Nashville has managed to hold on to its characteristic demeanor of Southern hospitality. New residents are arriving daily from New York and Los Angeles to join the music and entertainment industries. Others come from cities and towns in Tennessee, Kentucky, and Alabama to take positions in healthcare, sales, publishing, and computer programming. By the year 2000, state capital Nashville, whose population (metro Davidson County only) is currently around 550,000, is expected to have secured its place as the center of the state's most populous metropolitan area.

The presence of powerful WSM Radio, which broadcasts the Grand Ole Opry on the AM band every Saturday night to listeners in surrounding states and truckers passing through Tennessee, has carved an aural jurisdiction for Nashville that has no doubt been a major contributing factor in spreading the gospel of country music far and wide.

Nashville is, literally, a crossroads of the upper South, with three major interstates passing through the city. First the steamboat trade and then the expansion of the railroads made the city an ideal center for distribution of goods. That function continues today on the highways, railways, and airspace passing through, under, and over the city. Truckstops of America is headquartered here, and rail freight is still loaded and unloaded daily on Nashville tracks.

Trucks and railcars laden with commodities are not all that passes through Nashville. The Nashville International Airport sees as many as 21,000 passengers every day, many of whom are engaged in burgeoning service-industry businesses, such as healthcare, publishing, electronic communications, banking, and entertainment. Privatized healthcare companies began clustering around Nashville's Hospital Corporation of America (HCA) in the early 1980s. With the merger of Columbia Health Care and HCA, Nashville remains the country's managed medical care headquarters. A pioneering fiber-optic telecommunications infrastructure has made the city a prime interchange on the information superhighway, and spin-off businesses are being started here daily. The exponential growth in popularity of country music over the past 20 years has generated not only an influx of management-level music-industry personnel—label heads, talent agents, intellectual property lawyers, business managers—but also recording engineers, camera operators, and production staff. The arrival of creative artists of all kinds—songwriters, singers, record and video producers, set designers and decorators, photographers, and graphic designers—has added immeasurable vitality to Nashville's cultural scene.

GETTING TO KNOW NASHVILLE

Downtown Nashville, located just west of the Cumberland River, is approximately eight blocks square. North Nashville, which includes historic Germantown and Fisk University, stretches out behind the State Capitol

---

Small Town/Big City

Cindy Wall, vice president of Cheekwood: Nashville's Home of Art and Gardens, says, "Despite its tremendous growth, Nashville still has the heart of a small town. We've got chic restaurants and hip coffeehouses, but some of the best food in town is at family-run 'meat 'n' threes.' We've got a new NFL football team, but you'll still find most of Nashville at a high school game every Friday during the fall. You can shop for designer labels or cowboy boots. You can take in a symphony performance, an opera, a Shakespeare play, or see an avant-garde exhibit that rivals anything you'll find in SoHo—or spend your evening in a local club, where every night talented musicians play only for drinks and tips. Best of all, Nashvillians are truly nice. Southern hospitality really does exist here, and visitors are treated like neighbors. And, just like any small town, I run into someone I know just about everywhere."

TIP

The Tennessee State Museum has an impressive collection of tools, weapons, pottery, and even a carved shell gorget (chest pendant) dating from the Paleo-Indians and representing the entire span of native habitation of the Middle Tennessee area.

Building, which is oriented north/south. The best views of Capitol Hill are from the north. The numbered avenues begin with First Avenue at Riverfront Park and run west to 32nd Avenue, just past Centennial Park. Numbered streets are on the other side of the river in East Nashville, once Nashville's prime residential neighborhood. Only a few East Nashville homes survived a devastating 1916 fire. The Hillsboro/West End area of Nashville, home to Music Row, Centennial Park, and Vanderbilt and Belmont Universities, is the location of residential neighborhoods that were once at the end of the streetcar line. Nashville stretches westward into classic large-lawned suburbia and, ultimately, into rolling farmland along the Harpeth River to the southwest. The city is growing in every direction toward I-840, a circumferential highway now under construction approximately 20 miles out from the city center.

A BRIEF HISTORY OF NASHVILLE

The Early Days

Not far north of the Metro Courthouse, near what is now the Tennessee Bicentennial Mall, were a salt lick and a sulfur spring that ran into the Cumberland River. Because the area was frequented by bison and deer, it was a hunting ground for the early peoples of the area whose stone tools and pottery fragments have been found there. There is also evidence that just across the Cumberland River was a ceremonial burial site with as many as four mounds. The early days of Nashville are intertwined with the fortunes of brave young men like James Robertson as well as those a generation older, such as Colonel Donelson, a Revolutionary War hero.

The Civil War in Nashville

Although the slave-holding citizens of Nashville were a minority and the city's wealth would certainly be threatened by the onset of war, the majority of citizens voted in 1861 (after an extended period during which leaders urged a neutral stance) for secession from the Union, making Tennessee the 11th and last state to do so. Nashville, protected only by Fort Donelson on the Cumberland River to the north, fell within months

NASHVILLE TIME LINE

1765 Hunters Henry Skaggs, Joseph Drake, Kaspar Mansker, Isaac Bledsoe, the first people of European descent to "discover" the area north of Nashville, visit the "Great Salt Lick."

1769 Jacques-Timothe DeMontbrun, a Quebecois fur trader, is the first non-Indian to inhabit the site of Nashville, on bluffs above the Cumberland River.

1779 James Robertson and his party, traveling overland from the Wautauga settlement in East Tennessee, reach the same site on the Cumberland River by crossing the ice on Christmas Day.

1780 John Donelson and the wives and children of Robertson's party arrive via flatboat on April 24. The Cumberland Compact, requesting self-government from the state of North Carolina, is signed in June by 256 men, and the town is named after Revolutionary War hero Francis Nash.

1790 Bob Renfroe, a free black who had come with the Donelson party, opens the popular Black Bob's Tavern on public square.

1796 Maj. Wm. T. Lewis opens the Nashville Inn. Tennessee is admitted as the 16th state of the United States of America.

1803 Lucinda "Granny" White establishes a tavern four miles west of the Natchez Trace.

1807 The Nashville volunteer fire department is established.

1819 *General Jackson*, the first steamboat to serve the city, arrives in Nashville.

1833 Nashville waterworks is established.

1835 Nashville is named the state capital.

1848 The first church for free blacks is established, with Nelson Merry as pastor.

1850 The first steam locomotive, ordered by the Nashville & Chattanooga Railroad, arrives by boat from Cincinnati.

1851 The first streetlights illuminate Nashville.

1862 The Union Army occupies Nashville.

1864 The Battle of Franklin and the Battle of Nashville, both severe defeats for the Confederates, were the last major Civil War activities in Middle Tennessee.

1866 Fisk University is founded.

1873 Vanderbilt University is founded by Cornelius Vanderbilt.

1885 The Watkins Institute for Adult Education is founded with a bequest left by Samuel Watkins. Meharry Medical College, the only private African American medical school still in existence, is founded.

1888 Electric streetcars define the first Nashville suburbs.

The Tennessee Centennial Exposition creates lasting legacies with construction of Centennial Park and the Parthenon.	**1897**
The Nashville YWCA is founded.	**1898**
The Marathon Motor Car is built in Nashville by Southern Motor Works.	**1910-14**
Portions of East Nashville are almost totally razed by fire.	**1916**
Blackwood Field, Nashville's first airfield, is built. The Nineteenth Amendment (women's suffrage) is ratified by the state legislature.	**1920**
WSM (We Shield Millions) Radio is founded by National Life and Accident Insurance Company.	**1925**
Harmonica player Deford Bailey, the first African American musician to join the Grand Ole Opry, is part of first-ever recording session in Nashville (RCA Victor).	**1928**
William Edmondson, a self-taught stone carver, is the first African American artist to have a one-person show at New York's Museum of Modern Art.	**1937**
Wilma Rudolph, an African American track star, and five teammates from Tennessee State University participate in the Olympic Games.	**1956**
The Life and Casualty Insurance Company builds Nashville's first skyscraper.	**1957**
Nonviolent lunch-counter sit-ins take place at three downtown Nashville sites.	**1960**
Metro Government is formed, uniting city and county.	**1962**
East Nashville's Edgefield district founds Nashville's first neighborhood association.	**1976**
The Tennessee Performing Arts Center opens. Nashville's two daily newspapers change hands. The morning *Tennessean* is purchased by Gannett, and the afternoon *Banner* is sold by Gannett to local investors.	**1979**
Vice President Al Gore hosts the first "Family Reunion" issues conference in Nashville.	**1993**
The Ryman Auditorium is remodeled and reopened as a concert venue.	**1994**
The Tennessee Bicentennial Mall and adjacent new buildings for Nashville Farmers Market open in north Nashville.	**1996**
Nashville Arena opens with Amy Grant's Christmas Show.	**1996**
Ground is broken for NFL football stadium on the east bank of the Cumberland River.	**1997**
The *Nashville Banner* (afternoon daily newspaper) closes its doors after 122 years in operation.	**1998**

The Rhythm of Nashville

"The community of peers in Nashville is critical," according to master songwriter and singer Tom Kimmel, who has had three albums of his own, songs recorded by artists from Joe Cocker to Johnny Cash, and hits in Australia and Germany.

"Publishing deals come and go, even for writers who have had number-one hits. There comes a time in almost everyone's career when it seems like you can't get arrested. I've been there, and I realized how much I need the support and inspiration of peers like Don Henry, Mark Germino, Dave Olney, Buddy Mondlock, [the late] Walter Hyatt, and many others in this town who will always give their audience something of substance and never resort to writing the lowest common denominator. The challenge is to find an individual at a publishing company who loves the heart of your work—someone who believes they can find a seam in the marketplace where the work can be exploited, rather than whipping the life out of you trying to satisfy someone else's notion of what could be a hit song. I believe that true talent holds up, and real substance outlasts and outshines the market-inspired trendy stuff."

and was occupied by Union troops by February 1862. Governor Isham G. Harris fled to Memphis, Confederate General Albert Sidney Johnston moved his command to Murfreesboro, and Confederate General Nathan Bedford Forrest led his troops into town to take all remaining Confederate supplies for his troops. As they left they burned the railroad bridge over the Cumberland and cut the cables on the suspension bridge, abandoning the city to its fate. For three years Nashville remained a city divided, with sympathizers on both sides of the conflict living in close proximity. East Tennessean Andrew Johnson was dispatched to Nashville by President Abraham Lincoln to become the military governor of Tennessee. Only newspapers committed to preserving the Union were allowed to continue publishing, and both the Methodist and Baptist publishing houses were enlisted in printing publications favoring the federal government. The life of the city, interrupted by occasional Confederate raids, continued almost as before, but crime and corruption were in the air. The scarcity of goods and supplies made the influx of population, including African American former slaves and other rural refugees, all the more difficult for Nashville residents.

Finally, in December 1864, the final showdown between General John B. Hood's army of Confederates and the occupying Federal forces of General George H. Thomas took place at Shy's Hill, just south of the city. Hood's troops, having fled Sherman's advancing troops in Georgia, had hoped to use Nashville as a rallying point for the war in the upper South. But Thomas' men, outnumbering them more than two to one, and the bitter cold weather, spelled a bloody defeat.

Nashville's recovery was the product of a combination of many different forces, from prominent citizens returning from both armies, to Union officers staying in Nashville to take advantage of economic opportunities sure to come during the city's rebuilding, to arriving northern industrialists hoping to cash in on the creation of a new infrastructure for Nashville and its environs. Reconstruction saw the founding of Fisk and Vanderbilt Universities, Meharry Medical College, and several decades of progress as Nashville reestablished its economic hegemony. Civil War reconstruction efforts ended with the fabulous Tennessee Centennial Exposition, celebrated in 1897 with a "city of lights" in the newly created Centennial Park, and paid for almost entirely by the railroads.

Modern Times

Early-twentieth-century Nashville saw the rise of banking, insurance, and education, and the continued growth of religious publishing. Nashville's insurance industry was led by National Life and Accident, whose primary market was the rural farmer. NLT's stroke of genius was to use the radio station they acquired in 1925 as a means to cater to their market. The story of WSM

Electric lights on display at the Tennessee Centennial Exposition

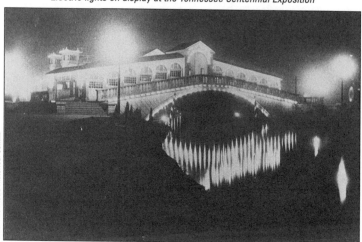

Nashville Metro Historical Comm.

(We Shield Millions, NLT's motto) Radio and the first broadcast of the Grand Ole Opry, so dubbed by announcer John D. Hay when a hillbilly music show came on immediately following a program of "grand opera," is now legend. The Opry, which featured the old-time music preferred by Tennesseans at the time, was an immediate hit. Weekly performances, still conducted as a radio show with commercials read aloud from the stage, continue to delight audiences over the radio and in person at the Opry House.

Nashville's publishing and printing industries owe a great deal to the longtime prominence of such major religious institutions as the Baptist Sunday School Board, the National Baptist Convention, the United Methodist Publishing House, the Church of Christ denomination, and the Gospel Music Association. The Southwestern Company, still a major force in turning out reams of Bibles and textbooks, is now surpassed by the international Thomas Nelson Company as the world's largest Bible publisher.

Both Nashville, a noted center of education, and the state of Tennessee have had their share of ups and downs in progressive thinking. Nashville women, led by Anne Dallas Dudley, took the fight for women's suffrage to the state capitol steps until the ratification of the Nineteenth Amendment by the Tennessee state legislature in 1920. Even though speakeasies were common in Nashville throughout the '20s and '30s , Prohibition was not repealed until 1939.

The two world wars had significant impact on Nashville in economic terms, with Du Pont building a massive gunpowder plant in Old Hickory in 1918, and AVCO (airplane parts), Nashville Bridge (barges and trusses), and Genesco (combat boots) all gearing up to peak production in the 1940s. Massive government programs such as the Works Progress Administration (WPA), the Tennessee Valley Authority (TVA), and the interstate highway system also benefited Nashville. From 1927 to 1930 the WPA helped to create the majestic Warner Park system in West Nashville, and in 1939 WPA workers built Berry Field, Nashville's first airport. In the 1940s TVA made it possible for Nashvillians to begin using electricity to heat their homes instead of the coal fires that had caused a thick cloud of smoke to almost constantly shroud the city for most of the century. Major federal highway building projects focused around Nashville have helped maintain the city's identity as a transportation hub.

During the late '30s and especially in the postwar years, Nashvillians moved to the suburbs in droves, causing a disproportionate demand for city services on Davidson County. A system of consolidated "Metro" government was proposed as early as 1952 in order to solve the problem and unite the city. It took 10 years to secure its final passage, but the 1962 Metropolitan Nashville Charter still serves as a symbol of progressive thinking by Nashville voters. Metro Nashville is governed by a 41-member elected city council whose monthly meetings are televised live over WDCN public television.

In 1951 two African Americans, Robert Lillard and Z. Alexander Looby, were elected to the city council. Both were prominent attorneys and, in

Nashville's Roots

Ann Reynolds, executive director of the Metro Historical Commission, gives her thoughts on the rich history of Nashville and its continuing influence on the city's major attractions. See Sights and Attractions chapter for descriptive listings.

"Even as Nashville is changing rapidly, there are still places here which speak of where we came from as a city and what has been important in establishing our sense of place. These are some of those":

1. **Hatch Show Print**—This nineteenth-century blockprint poster shop has merged Nashville's printing and music industries since 1879. Today it is recognized as Nashville's best print souvenir shop.

2. **Downtown Presbyterian Church**—The sedate exterior of this National Historic Landmark doesn't prepare a visitor for the interior's colorful decorative painting and stained-glass windows depicting Egyptian symbols and scenes.

3. **The Arcade**—A great place for lunch and a shoeshine. Don't miss the Peanut Shop.

4. **Richland-West End Neighborhood**—This is the quintessential early-twentieth-century neighborhood—mature trees, pleasant sidewalks for strollers, beautiful gardens, and houses with front porches.

5. **Davis-Kidd Booksellers**—This bookstore is more than a bookstore. It's a gathering place for Nashvillians, a restaurant, and a music venue.

6. **The Parthenon**—It is the Parthenon that most visitors ask to see. While some put it in the category of kitsch, I know no one who hasn't been impressed with its dignity on seeing it.

7. **Radnor Lake**—In the early 1970s, Nashvillians raised money to buy adjacent land when it was threatened with development. Today this 85-acre lake attracts migrating birds, fauna, Nashville residents, and visitors.

8./9. **Edgefield and East End**—These East Nashville neighborhoods date from the mid- to late nineteenth century and contain the city's largest sampling of architecture from that period. They are survivors—fire, tornado, and urban decline haven't destroyed them.

10. **Fisk University**—Jubilee Hall on the north end of the campus is a national historic landmark.

1955, along with Avon Williams Jr., were parties to one of the earliest school desegregation lawsuits in the country. While the school board approved integrated schools in principle in 1957, only 44 African American students actually enrolled in mixed schools due to widespread intimidation. (It would not be until court-ordered busing was put into effect in 1970 that Nashville schools would be fully integrated.) Nashville was the site of some of the earliest nonviolent racial protests in this country. Led by James Lawson, John Lewis, and others, lunch-counter sit-ins were staged by students at Fisk University during the early 1960s. Mayor Ben West,

Civil-rights advocates gather at the First Baptist Church

who exited with the formation of Metro government in 1962, is remembered as one who publicly acknowledged the civil rights of African American marchers in a 1962 confrontation.

The creation of the Metro Historical Commission in 1967 and its support by Mayor Richard Fulton in the 1970s have helped Nashville steer away from the effects of an urban-renewal plan that almost went too far in the late 1950s and early 1960s. Neighborhood associations, numbering as many as 20, have been formed by citizens wishing to preserve and maintain historic neighborhoods at the edges of potential urban blight.

Recommended Reading

African American Historic Sites (Metro Historical Commission, 1991).

Andrew Jackson Slept Here: A Guide to Historical Markers in Nashville and Davidson County (Metro Historical Commission, 1993).

Cities Under the Gun: Images of Occupied Nashville and Chattanooga, by James A. Hoobler (Rutledge Hill Press, 1996, second edition). A pictorial history by the curator of art and architecture, Tennessee State Museum.

Civil War Battle of Nashville: A Self-Guided Driving Tour (Metro Historical Commission, 1983).

The Country Reader: Twenty-five Years of the Journal of Country Music, by Paul Kingsbury (Vanderbilt University Press, 1996). A compilation of writings on all aspects of country-music history from the most authoritative source, Nashville's Country Music Foundation.

Finding Her Voice: The Saga of Women in Country Music (NY: Crown

Publishers) by Mary A. Bufwack and Robert K. Oermann (1993). Groundbreaking research by a sociologist and the longtime music critic for the *Nashville Tennessean.* Bufwack and Oermann also produced a spin-off television special on the same theme.

I'll Take My Stand: The South and the Agrarian Tradition, by Twelve Southerners (Louisiana State University Press, 1977 [reprint of Harper Brothers, 1930]). The agrarian "manifesto," a book of essays by (mostly) conservative Southerners who taught at Vanderbilt in the 1920s and '30s.

Nashville City Walk: Tracing Urban History (Metro Historical Commission, 1994).

Nashville in the New South, 1880–1930 and *Nashville Since the 1920s,* by Don H. Doyle (University of Tennessee Press, 1985). The Metro Historical Commission considers Doyle's books to be authoritative.

Nashville: The Face of Two Centuries, 1780–1980, by John Egerton (Plus-Media Inc., 1979). A highly-readable history of Nashville containing photos, reproductions of paintings, and other helpful graphics.

Red Grooms' Carousel:
Art for the People and of the People

A life-size revolving circus carousel in Riverfront Park, featuring humorous portraits of historical figures like Andrew Jackson and W.C. Handy instead of horses, will soon be the city's first major piece of permanent public art. The creation of native son Red Grooms, the "Tennessee Foxtrot" carousel owes its existence to the vision of many civic-minded arts supporters, including contractor Walter Knestrick, music promoter Will Byrd and his wife, Trudy, an arts activist, cookie entrepreneur Christie Hauck, and museum director Lois Riggins-Ezzell. Riggins-Ezzell, whose Tennessee State Museum mounted the huge Grooms retrospective in 1986, planted the idea of state historic figures as a theme for a major work more than 10 years ago. "My son Nicky (a Nashville musician) and I took Red and his wife, Lysiane, to the Grand Ole Opry on the eve of the exhibit opening," she says. "Not that Red ever needs inspiration, I just wanted to reacquaint him with some of the fabulous characters we call our own—from Minnie Pearl to Davy Crockett, and Cornelia Fort to Elvis."

Classical Nashville

"Nashville's classical dreams are most obvious not in its name but in its architecture. With the exception of the vernacular gothic of the Ryman Auditorium—and not even Captain Ryman expected his gospel hall to become a landmark—the symbols of our city are buildings in the classical style. Nashville has its own acropolis: The most topographically prominent site in the central city is crowned by a civic temple in the Greek Revival style—the Tennessee State Capitol (1845–1859). By the end of the nineteenth century, the identification of Nashville with Athens, Greece, was so ingrained in the popular imagination that choosing a full-scale replica of the Parthenon for the centerpiece of Tennessee's Centennial Exposition seemed a natural."

—Christine Kreyling, architecture and urban planning critic, *Nashville Scene*; coauthor, *Classical Nashville* (Vanderbilt University Press, 1996).

The People of Nashville

Nashville's original settlers were primarily Protestants from Scotland, Northern Ireland, and England who came down into Tennessee via the Virginia and North Carolina settlements. Early trappers and "long hunters" (who stayed away from home for years at a time, like Daniel Boone) included French Canadians like Jacques-Timothe DeMontbrun, Dutchman Kaspar Mansker, and a number of Revolutionary War veterans venturing westward, in many cases to claim land-grant territory. In the 1840s German, Irish, and Jewish immigrants from many parts of Europe arrived as part of a westward expansion that required a skilled labor force. Although at this same time there were slaves working the large plantations all around the city, "free blacks" in Nashville had voting and property rights and some opportunity for education. Religion played an important part in the lives of early Nashville citizens, as it does today. Downtown's Church Street held major Presbyterian, Baptist, and Methodist churches by the 1830s; St. Mary's Catholic Church was completed in 1847; the First Baptist Church, Capitol Hill (for free blacks) was built in 1848, and the impressive Vine Street Temple, with its nine onion-shaped domes, was erected in 1876.

The African American population of Nashville, which remains at around 20 percent today, amounted to at least a third of the population in the city from around 1870 to 1960. Nashville's African American community has a long, proud history. Two of the first private institutions of higher learning were established here for African Americans. Leaders of the African American intellectual community, like W.E.B. Du Bois, James Weldon Johnson, and Charles S. Johnson, were affiliated with Fisk University in the late nineteenth and early twentieth centuries. One of the first African American architectural firms in the country, McKissack and McKissack, began in Nashville and is still run by descendants of its founders. During the 1950s and '60s significant events associated with the Civil Rights movement took place in Nashville. Fisk University is home to the still-active Center for Race Relations, established by Charles S. Johnson, the university's first African American president.

The Native American population in Nashville and the surrounding area is relatively small, probably less than 1 percent, and is composed primarily of the Cherokee who managed to escape being expelled during the 1838 Indian removal on the infamous Trail of Tears. The Alliance for Native American Indian Rights holds several annual events in Lebanon, Tennessee, designed to reunite descendants and create public awareness of important traditions and ceremonies that should not be lost to history.

Nashville's fastest-growing population segments are Asians from Thailand, Vietnam, Cambodia, and Laos. There is a small but significant Korean community in Nashville. Japanese industry, which began with the arrival of Nissan's first American plant in nearby Smyrna, Tennessee, now forms a large sector of the Middle Tennessee economy and has brought a number of Japanese sales and management personnel to the area over the past 10 to 15 years. All told, Asians account for about 5 percent of Nashville's population.

The onion-shaped domes of the Vine Street Temple

Judging from the influx of Mexican eateries and Spanish-language signs appearing around town, the Hispanic population may soon rise above its current 2 to 3 percent. While some Mexican workers still travel through this agricultural region during harvest season, the majority of the Nashville Hispanic community has found work in manufacturing and service industries. At least one branch of the public library holds bilingual story hours, and special Cinco de Mayo celebrations are increasingly popular all over town.

Members of Nashville's gay and lesbian communities can be

found across almost all segments of the population and are growing in visibility. Annual events like the Artrageous Evening, a standing-room-only progressive gallery hop that benefits Nashville Cares, an AIDS advocacy organization; and Pride Week, which begins with a parade in Centennial Park, are contributing to the widespread acceptance of alternative lifestyles among Nashville's more conservative citizenry.

Nashville Weather

Nashville's climate is temperate, so all seasons are bearable. The nicest seasons are spring and fall, when there are a plethora of sunny days with blue skies and low humidity. Summers, especially July and August, can be very hot and humid. June can be either pleasant, sunny, and cool, or blasting hot. Since Nashville is located in a bowl-like valley, breezes are a rare commodity. The sky tends to look hazy whenever there is a lot of moisture in the air or if it has been a while since a front has passed through to clear it. The area tends to be high in pollens and other airborne irritants that vary from season to season.

Snow is usually a one- or two-time occurrence every year. Serious accumulations may occur in January or February, although there have been a few notable early-March blizzards in Nashville. Freezing rain and occasional ice storms are the fearsome foe of the Nashville driver. Often occurring in December and January, such storms can knock down power lines and bring interstate traffic to a standstill.

Dressing in Nashville

Nashville's professional community dresses formally: traditionally-cut suits with tailored shirts and conservative ties for men, suits or dresses with stockings and heels for women. These women and men—lawyers, bankers, accountants, real-estate developers, healthcare management, and insurance executives—do business on the national level and look the part. Employees of large downtown firms, as well as those in service industries tied directly to them, tend to dress in a fashion similar to that of their clients.

While the heads of the major record labels on Music Row are certainly players on the same level, their dress varies according to the situation. Music executives turn out in similarly formal business attire when necessary but are just as often spotted in jeans, starched shirts, and sport coats. During Country Music Week, tuxedos are required for the Country Music Awards and the four to six straight nights of formal evening functions put on by the record labels, the licensing agencies (BMI, ASCAP, SESAC), and the various associations (country, gospel, disk jockeys).

Nashville's Weather

	Average Daily High / Low Temperatures (degrees Fahrenheit)	Average Monthly Precipitation (inches)
January	46 / 28	4.5
February	51 / 30	4.0
March	60 / 38	5.6
April	71 / 48	4.5
May	79 / 57	4.6
June	87 / 65	3.7
July	90 / 69	3.8
August	89 / 68	3.4
September	83 / 61	3.7
October	72 / 48	2.6
November	59 / 38	3.5
December	50 / 31	4.6

Source: U.S. Department of Commerce, National Oceanic and Atmospheric Administration.

Evening dress is also a prerequisite for events on the lively Nashville social scene. At least 20 formal fundraising events, ranging from balls to wine auctions to concerts, are held here yearly, benefiting organizations like the Nashville Symphony, Cheekwood, the American Cancer Society, the Nashville Institute for the Arts, and the W.O. Smith Music School.

Elsewhere around town dress is less proscribed, and the casual approach—men without ties, women clad in pants or skirts without stockings—is pretty much the norm. Of course, fashion is a consideration, and any aspirations to "hipness" generally earn notice in Nashville. Most of those who work in the creative community (music, entertainment, art) tend toward informal dress with artistic touches (collarless shirts, boots with everything, lots of black), but there are also lots of self-assured or financially independent types in Nashville who dress strictly for comfort.

Essentially, if one looks well-heeled and confident in Nashville, one can go almost anywhere in any sort of attire. Woe be it to the unaware maitre d' who turns away a powerful L.A. entertainment-industry executive wearing casual clothing.

Grunge attire is still the rage for Generations X and Y, and for those bold enough to carry it off. And biker culture has come into major vogue as more and more of Nashville's successful are buying bikes instead of second cars—classic black leather and a genuine Harley-Davidson cycle just never really seem to go out of style.

When to Visit

The city is at its best in spring and fall, with lovely weather and gardens blooming all over town. Dogwoods and forsythia, daffodils and tulips put on magnificent displays. In autumn the red and yellow maples are spectacular all over town. In summer, the air, warm and heavy though it might be, is laden with the dusky sweetness of the magnolia grandiflora, which grows especially well here and is planted along many streets in the Hillsboro Village area of town, as well as in parks and gardens. Summer evenings find Nashville diners seated on patios and restaurant porches, cheering the Nashville Sounds baseball team, or enjoying a wide variety of outdoor concerts—many of which are free. Winter weather almost always permits outdoor exercise, so Nashville is not a cabin-fever town.

The Written Word

"Although Steven Womack's mystery series about a private eye named Harry James Denton (*Dead Folks' Blues*, *Torch Town Boogie*, and *Way Past Dead*) features murder and mayhem in Music City, his descriptions offer an insider's view of the city and its places. Well-known Nashville landmarks like the Bluebird Cafe show up in his books, but so do places where locals get good and cheap Chinese food.

The late Peter Taylor, who won a Pulitzer Prize for his novel *A Summons to Memphis*, set most of his works in Nashville. Taylor's works evoke people and places long gone and manage to capture the Southern traditions of familial honor and duty—and the very modern conflicts that those traditions provoke.

New York Times reporter Peter Applebome's book, *Dixie Rising: How the South Is Shaping American Values, Politics, and Culture* is just as it sounds—an overview of Southern culture city by city. The book caused an uproar among music-business folks when it was released because many had problems with Applebome's chapter on Nashville. Whatever you think about the music industry, his piece on Nashville explains just how much it permeates the social fabric of the city."

—*Galyn Glick Martin, Southern Festival of Books*

Andrea Conte, businesswoman and wife of Mayor Bredesen, has taken up the cause of domestic violence in her "You Have the Power" campaign. Conte, who fought off a would-be carjacker a few years back, has joined forces with social service agencies and law enforcement officials to create an atmosphere of citizen empowerment around the issue.

A word to the wise: Football games at Vanderbilt and Tennessee State University often draw so many out-of-town fans that they cause lodging problems, although many hotels offer special money-saving weekend packages. College graduations can create problems of the same kind in early May (there are five major universities and colleges here), as can Country Music Fan Fair (early June) and Country Music Week (usually the first week in October). Rather than offering discount packages during Fan Fair and CMA week, however, some hotels raise rates to whatever the market will bear, so it's best to get a guaranteed rate in advance.

Calendar of Events

January
Battle of New Orleans Anniversary Celebration, the Hermitage; Martin Luther King Jr. Parade and Commemorative Event, Downtown

February
Annual local African American History Conference, Metro Historical Commission and TSU downtown campus; Cheekwood's Antique and Garden Show, Nashville Convention Center; Heart of Country Antique Show, Opryland Hotel

March
Andrew Jackson Birthday Celebration, the Hermitage; Tennessee Old Time Fiddler's Contest, Clarksville

April
Main Street Festival, Franklin; Mule Day, Columbia; World's Biggest Fish Fry, Paris

May
Iroquois Steeplechase, Warner Park; Tennessee Crafts Fair, Centennial Park; Tennessee Renaissance Festival, Triune

June

American Artisan Craft Fair, Centennial Park; Balloon Classic, Warner Park; Country Music Fan Fair International, Tennessee State Fairgrounds; Sewanee Music Festival, Sewanee; Sinking Creek/Nashville International Film Festival

July

Folk Medicine Festival, Red Boiling Springs; Old Time Fiddler's Jamboree, Smithville; Uncle Dave Macon Days, Murfreesboro

August

Franklin Jazz Festival, Franklin; International Grand Championship Walking Horse Show, Murfreesboro; Italian Street Fair, Downtown; Tennessee Walking Horse Celebration, Shelbyville

September

African Street Festival, TSU campus; Alliance for Native American Indian Rights Pow Wow, Lebanon; Jack Daniel's Barbeque Cook-Off, Lynchburg; Tennessee State Fair, Fairgrounds

October

NAIA Pow Wow, Nashville; Oktoberfest, Germantown, North Nashville; Southern Festival of Books, Downtown; TACA (Tennessee Association of Craft Artists) Fall Fair, Centennial Park; Country Music Week, Opry House and Music Row

November

Country Christmas (through December), Opryland Hotel; Victorian Thanksgiving, Belle Meade Plantation; Artrageous Evening, galleries around town

---

TRIVIA

Coal Miner's Daughter (Michael Apted, director), starring Sissy Spacek as Loretta Lynn and Tommy Lee Jones as Mooney Lynn, 1980.

High Lonesome (Rachel Liebling, director), documentary about bluegrass music featuring Bill Monroe, 1991.

Nashville (Robert Altman, director), starring Lily Tomlin and Keith Carradine, 1975.

Sweet Dreams (Karel Reisz, director), starring Jessica Lange as Pasty Cline and Ed Harris as husband Charlie Dick, 1985.

A Thing Called Love, starring River Phoenix and Sandra Bullock, 1993.

December

Dickens of a Christmas, Franklin; Trees of Christmas, Cheekwood; Yulefest, Historic Mansker's Station, Goodlettsville; Travellers Rest Twelfth Night Festival, South Nashville

Cost of Living

Nashville, while not one of the most expensive cities in the country, is no bargain either. The prices below give an idea of the median price for desirable goods and services.

five-mile taxi ride:	$15–$18
hotel double room:	$85–$125
dinner for one, with tip:	$20–$25
movie admission:	$8
daily newspaper:	50 cents
16 oz. tube of brand-name toothpaste:	$2.49
admission to music venue for songwriters' night:	$3–$8

Business and Economy

Located in the midst of rural farmland, Nashville has always been a market center. Some of its earliest businesses were banks, insurance companies, granaries, feed and supply stores, distilleries, tobacco factories, taverns, restaurants, and hotels. Railroads, banks, insurance companies, and publishing houses prospered in the late nineteenth century, as their monumental downtown buildings testify.

Many of Nashville's hometown banks are now parts of large bank conglomerates like NationsBank and SunTrust. But local banks such as First American, Bank of Nashville, and Citizen's Bank, one of the first African American banks in the country, remain headquartered here, as does nationwide securities firm J.C. Bradford.

The American General Life Insurance Company subsumed Nashville's old National Life and Accident Company as well as Life and Casualty Company. Long intertwined with the country-music industry through its WSM Radio broadcast of the Grand Ole Opry, American General is now part of the Gaylord Entertainment Network megacorporation that owns Opryland, which includes the Opryland Hotel and the current Opry House, and the Ryman Auditorium, which was home to the Grand Ole Opry from 1941 to 1974.

The economic growth of the city over the past two decades has been accompanied by the ascendance of both country music into the prosperous pantheon of American pop music and the rise of privatized medical care, beginning with Hospital Corporation of America in Nashville in 1968. Since the mid-1970s, when stars like Dolly Parton began having crossover hits on country, pop, and adult contemporary radio, the country-music industry has become a worldwide phenomenon. As the entertainment industry grows and publishing and media become one, so Nashville, with its players already in place— major talent agencies like CAA and William Morris, its battery of intellectual property lawyers, its multi-faceted record labels that are often subsidiaries of larger companies such as CBS/ Sony and MCA/ Time-Warner Communications— will begin to diversify as well, poised for the challenges of the twenty-first century.

Wightman Chapel, where local musicians often perform

The private healthcare industry, which continues to take over hospitals across the country, has created spin-offs in both the child care and prison management industries. Not only is Nashville-based Columbia/HCA the largest healthcare firm of its kind, but Corrections Corporation of America, Healthtrust, Equicorp, and many other related firms are also located in Nashville.

The manufacturing sector has gained considerable ground in the region surrounding Nashville over the past several decades, from the arrival of Nissan's first American plant in outlying Smyrna in the early 1980s, to the relocation of Bridgestone/Firestone to LaVergne, to the building of GM's Saturn car plant just south of the city in Spring Hill, Tennessee.

BellSouth's headquarters building in the center of downtown Nashville signals the city's critical position on the information super-highway. Nashville is poised to become a key player in the electronic communication revolution that is exciting the entertainment, publishing, and business worlds. Ingram Industries, a massive book, periodicals, and electronic media distribution firm, has its world headquarters just outside of Nashville, and Thomas Nelson leads a long list of religious publishing houses that also have interests in the burgeoning Christian music recording industry.

Nashville's current mayor, Phil Bredesen, a Harvard-educated businessman who came to Nashville to run a private healthcare company in the late 1970s, has stayed to lead a city that has its eyes on a bright future. With the recent completion of Nashville's downtown indoor concert and sports arena, the city has hopes of one day drawing the Grammy Awards to town. Just across the Cumberland River, the Nashville stadium will open with the Tennessee Oilers' 1999 season.

Taxes

Since Tennessee is one of the few states with no state income tax, it falls to the municipalities to impose sales and property taxes in order to collect revenue sufficient to run city and county services. Nashville sales tax is 8.25 percent, which applies to all purchases, from basic necessities such as food to such luxury items as works of art. This can change a $50 dinner for two to $65 with tax and tip. One restaurant menu in Nashville lists the combined state and local taxes on wine as 23.25 percent!

Housing

Boomtown housing costs are the name of the game right now, with students and service industry workers keeping apartment rentals at an all-time high—starting around $500 for a barely decent one-bedroom. The price of homes here has gone through the roof because of great recent demand. One of the great selling points of Nashville used to be big houses and big lawns not affordable elsewhere, but now formerly lower middle-class neighborhoods are taking on the telltale signs of overgrooming that come with price hikes.

Schools

Nashville's public schools are currently adjusting to a new core curriculum imposed on them by the city school board—one of the first major city systems to revert to the goal of students acquiring a specific "canon of knowledge." With 44 private schools, including many with religious affiliations,

TRIVIA

Mark Deutschmann, owner of Village Realty, who has earned Nashville's Best Realtor honors for five of the past six years, on Nashville's current real estate boom: "Nashville is moving both in and out, with new housing construction in outlying areas being created at a record pace, and with some very interesting urban redevelopment beginning to bring the residential component to the city's urban center. High-rise apartment projects, the General Hospital site, and continued redevelopment in Nashville's inner loop are in the works as many decide to live closer to their work and social scene. Small urban neighborhood commercial districts are being revitalized, as the need for the urban neighborhood infrastructure is fulfilled. It is wonderful to experience a city revitalizing its core. . . ."

Nashville's public school system faces some stiff competition. And a growing population of parents intent on relocating to the city that's relatively sedate and "good for raising children" has upped the ante in recent years. Mayor Bredesen, an advocate of school reform and improvement, instituted a property tax hike in his first years in office and, with the proceeds, has managed to place art and music specialists in every secondary and most elementary schools in the Metro system (Nashville and Davidson County). A strong tax base in outlying counties such as Williamson (southwest) and Sumner (northeast) has allowed their public school systems to prosper as well, much to the benefit of suburban students.

2

GETTING AROUND NASHVILLE

The settlement of Fort Nashborough was sited on the bluffs of the Cumberland River, near a well-known salt lick. James Robertson's party is said to have crossed a frozen-solid Cumberland to reach its west bank on Christmas Day, 1779. Today downtown Nashville sits atop limestone bluffs on the west bank of the Cumberland, and the river remains the city's primary means of orientation. Nashville grew to the west and could still be considered "west heavy." In fact, until the building of a suspension bridge in the 1850s, there was little settlement on the east bank. The East End neighborhood, which today has the most intact grouping of Victorian homes in the city, was not founded until 1853. Nashville and Davidson County form the official metropolitan area, but the surrounding counties of Sumner, Robertson, Cheatham, Williamson, Rutherford, and Wilson can all be considered commuter communities for an urban center whose population is nearing 1 million and whose economy is on the upswing.

Nashville's Layout

While Nashville's layout may look like a jumble to the innocent visitor, order appears if one orients oneself at the river. From there one can see a basic downtown grid, with the named streets running east-west and the numbered streets north-south. The whole grid is tilted slightly northwest on its axis (First Avenue runs parallel to the riverbank). First Avenue was once crossed primarily by planks and ramps so that cargo being unloaded from the steamboats could be rolled directly into block-deep brick warehouses lining the wharf. Goods were sold out of the front doors of the

same warehouses on Second Avenue, also known as Market Street. The main street of town was also its widest, known fittingly as Broad (now Broadway), and began at the river. Broadway probably ran only as far as Hillsboro Pike (21st Avenue) until the advent of the electric streetcar in 1889. After the construction of the streetcar line extensions, it would continue as West End Avenue, past West Side Park (soon to be Centennial Park) toward Richland Park, Nashville's first "streetcar suburb."

FINDING YOUR WAY AROUND

Streets

Some of the named streets of downtown Nashville relate to what must previously have been their function, like Commerce, Capitol, Church, and Market Streets. Others honor early citizens, such as James Robertson Parkway, McGavock (Jacob), and Demonbreun (Timothe) Streets. Many of the streets that lead out of the downtown area are still referred to as "pikes" and also contain the names of towns for which they once served as main highways, such as Charlotte, Franklin, Gallatin, Nolensville, Lebanon, Murfreesboro, Clarksville, and Ashland City. To add to the confusion, the numbered avenues lead out to and connect with these out-of-town highways, so the same road often bears two and sometimes three names. For example, Eighth Avenue South becomes Franklin Pike; 12th Avenue South becomes Granny White Pike (after a tollhouse run by Granny White in the south part of the city outskirts); Broadway becomes West End Avenue , then becomes Harding Road (after William G. Harding, owner of Belle Meade Plantation, which is located on the western outskirts of town), and finally splits into Highways 70 and 100.

According to architectural historians, it is possible to judge the era in which parts of the city developed by looking at the street patterns. Nashville's downtown follows the early-nineteenth-century pattern of evenly spaced short blocks. This pattern continues in north Nashville's

Germantown neighborhood, founded in the 1840s, and in the aforementioned East End, which was called "Little Brooklyn" at one time. One begins to see longer blocks on the fringes of the downtown area that evolved during the later nineteenth century. These blocks are often oriented around a common space, bearing witness to the late-Victorian romanticism of boulevards, parks, and plazas. The streetcars, first pulled by mules, made possible the extension of city dwellings and city services such as electricity, gas, and water into the earliest neighborhoods (Eighth Avenue to 21st Avenue on the west side of town, Germantown to the north, and Edgefield and East End on the other side of the river). Once electric, the streetcar lines extended out to spacious suburbs with pastoral names like Woodmont and Glendale.

Highways

The arrival of the interstate highway system did not so much change the original layout of the city's roads as it did effectively underscore what was already in existence. I-65 south runs parallel to Franklin Pike, I-40 west parallels Harding Road, I-40 east parallels Lebanon Pike, I-24 parallels

Entrance of the Interstate

Peter Taylor wrote a moving short story called "The Throughway" about the coming of a road very like I-440 through Nashville. An elderly couple forced to move from the home they occupied since their marriage begins to question, on the final moving day, the rightness of everything that is familiar to them, including each other. I-440, which was started in the late 1960s and finally completed around 1985, was bitterly opposed by neighborhood groups, partly because it passed through some of Nashville's most settled middle-class neighborhoods. It took out family homes in the near suburbs of Nashville years before such measures were necessary for the completion of the road. By the time it was constructed, in fact, the city was so heavily populated near the road that large trucks were banned from using it, and the road bed had to be either lowered to stem noise and pollution or shielded by expensive sound-barrier walls. While it is widely used, it never was the sort of "by-pass" once envisioned by its designers. "The Throughway" can be found in In the Miro District and Other Stories [Knopf, 1977.]

TIP

For a nice view of downtown Nashville, the Vanderbilt University campus, and the surrounding green hills, climb or drive to the top of Love Circle (just off West End Avenue near Murphy Road). Standing on top of a grassy hillock housing an underground reservoir, you'll find a spectacular 360-degree view.

Clarksville Pike, I-24 south parallels Murfreesboro Pike, and I-440 (circumferential) follows the paths of Woodmont Boulevard, Thompson Lane, and White Bridge Road.

Circumferential Connector Highways

Ring highways seem always to have been useful ways to connect the three interstates that pass through the city like spokes on a wheel. Before I-440 was completed, there was an inner-city loop (I-265) and a periphery road Briley Parkway/Old Hickory Boulevard that made an almost complete circle on the outskirts of town. A final segment of that loop, just completed, connecting I-24 N with Opryland and the Airport on I-40 E, makes going from the north to east sides of the city much easier than having to go follow the Interstate highways as they merge at I-265. Parts of I-840, an outer loop approximately 25 miles out, are already in use, connecting I-24 S to I-40 E between Smyrna and Lebanon. This connector highway will eventually make bedroom communities out of what are now farmlands, ensuring Nashville's exponential growth well into the next century.

Public Transportation

Perhaps it's the do-it-yourself pioneer spirit of this former western frontier, but Nashville commuters seem very reluctant to let go of their automobiles or even to share them with others in a carpool arrangement. Ironically, the self-propelled vehicle demonstrated at Tennessee's 1897 Centennial Exposition was sponsored by the railroads, who were still trying to win public favor for rail transportation. Nashville's Union Station, which opened in 1900, was meant to herald a new century of rail travel, but in less than seven years, Nashville's own Marathon Motor Car Company began turning out vehicles only 1/2-mile away from the grand terminal.

Today HOV (High Occupancy Vehicle) lanes have appeared on the I-65 S, I-40 E, and there is talk of a high speed train for the I-245 corridor. While public transport is actually pretty efficient during business hours, it is still vastly underused by the majority of Nashvillians, and hardly a way

NASHVILLE TROLLEY

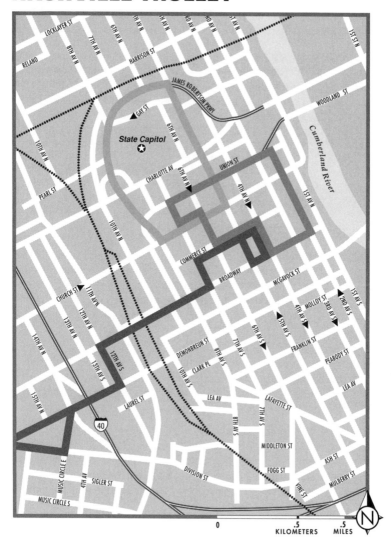

of life for those who do use it. Perhaps it is significant that the Metropolitan Transit Authority of Nashville (MTA) does not have a pronounceable acronym. This is probably because it is rarely mentioned in Nashville conversation.

The MTA's main transfer station is on both sides of Deaderick Street in the heart of downtown. Buses run hourly service to most parts of the

A paddleboat plies the Cumberland River

city, and the fares are $1.40 for adults, with a weekly pass for $14. MTA buses also serve the airport hourly from approximately eight in the morning to 10 every night. weekdays for the same fare (a bargain), leaving from Shelter C on Deaderick Street. The MTA's motorized trolley (bus) system runs from the heart of downtown's business district to lower Broadway to Music Row every 15 minutes during the day, at a cost of $1 per ride or $3 for the day. For questions about Metro Transit Authority services, call 615/862-5950. The new Landport behind Union Station now provides a place to park and ride the trolley into downtown. It will ultimately allow for an efficient switch from light rail (proposed from Murfreesboro to Nashville) to public transport.

Taxis and Airport Transfers

Taxis are easy to find at the airport, but must be scheduled in advance in other locations. It is also wise to double-check with the requested taxi to make sure you are on the schedule. Taxi service in Nashville is relatively expensive, and taxi drivers vary in helpfulness. A taxi ride from the airport will generally cost $15 or more. The Airport Shuttle, run by Gray Line Express, costs $9 one-way and $15 round-trip and serves major hotels in three areas: downtown, Vanderbilt, and Music Row. Most of the large hotels near the airport (Briley Parkway area) offer free shuttle service to the airport.

River-taxi services transport visitors from the Opry House and Opryland Hotel to the downtown Nashville riverfront. The "taxis" are more like ferries, since they carry up to 100 passengers at once. Although the service operates daily beginning in April, the schedule varies according to the season. Fares for adults are $13 round-trip; children ages 4 to 11 go for $10 round-trip. Tickets are available at the Opryland Hotel and the Ryman Auditorium. For information call 615/889-6611.

Driving in Nashville

The town is growing quickly into a large city, and at times the paved road infrastructure seems just barely adequate to accommodate the volume of local traffic and the ever-growing numbers of interstate transport vehicles moving through Nashville. Highway backups can happen quickly, and Nashville is beginning to have regular rush-hour traffic jams, not only on the freeways, but also on important corridors leading out to the suburbs. Be warned, I-440 in both directions, and West End Avenue and Hillsboro Pike are consistently slow during both morning and afternoon rush hour.

Driving Tips

Two words regarding driving in Nashville: Watch out! Downtown drivers are still getting used to the increasing pedestrian traffic in the lower Broadway and Music Row areas. Right turn on red is legal in Tennessee unless posted otherwise, but it still behooves both drivers and crosswalkers to look before moving, no matter whose turn it is to proceed. For some inexplicable reason, older Nashville drivers often turn left from the right-hand lane, so be wary when driving around neighborhood shopping centers in the older suburbs. While snow usually occurs in Nashville only once or twice per year, there are often sleet and ice storms that can throw traffic into disastrous straits. Because many drivers here have little experience with snow and icy driving conditions, it's always best to give them a wide berth.

Use I-440 to get around the west side of city from one side to the other. It links I-40 east to Knoxville with I-40 west to Memphis and has exits at I-65 south to Birmingham, Hillsboro Pike/21st Avenue South, and West End Avenue/Murphy Road. Many of downtown Nashville's one-way streets have been changed to accommodate the new lower Broadway/Fifth Avenue axis created by the Nashville Arena and its surrounding development.

TRIVIA

Glendale Park, opened in 1888 on 64 acres, was designed by the Nashville Railway Company to attract streetcar travelers. The trains turned around in Glendale Park, which even housed a small zoo by 1912. The park was closed in 1932, due not only to the Depression, but also to the rise in the automobile's popularity. The final run of electric streetcars in Nashville was on February 2, 1941, on the Radnor Line. The site of Glendale Park was developed into the graceful suburban neighborhoods located on either side of Lealand Lane (10th Avenue South, extended).

The transportation of a bygone era is displayed at the Belle Meade carriage house.

Parking Tips

Many parking meter lanes all over the city must be cleared during rush hours, seven to nine in the morning and 3:30 or four to six evenings. Read the signs carefully to make sure you don't get towed. By the same token, the loading zone areas that prevent parking during the business day usually expire at six in the evening, freeing desirable spots in front of busy restaurants at just the right moment. Downtown parking comes at a premium price these days, so visitors may wish to trolley in from the Music Row or Union Station areas. On-street parking is still pretty easily available elsewhere in town, with the exception of the Vanderbilt campus, where practically every student owns a car, making parking nearly impossible when school is in session. There are a few visitor spaces in front of the Administration, Fine Arts Gallery, and Sarratt Student Center buildings, but Vanderbilt is vigilant about parking spots, and visitors are likely to be towed if parked in loading zones and faculty spaces.

Biking in Nashville

It can be done, and intrepid commuters can be spotted daily heading to Vanderbilt and into the heart of downtown. A helmet is a must, and special attention must be paid to sewer grates whose openings go the same direction as bike tires. Sightseeing drivers along Music Row can pose a threat to bikers, as they may not notice the whereabouts of bikers or other drivers while swooning over a Garth Brooks look-alike. Some Nashvillians panic at the sight of a bicyclist at the edge of their lane and are loath to pass. Most bikers in Nashville would rather ride on quiet residential side streets and park roadways. Belle Meade Boulevard, a long, divided street leading to Percy Warner Park, is a favorite for bikers, walkers, and runners. Percy Warner Park and its companion park, Edwin Warner, have extensive paved roads that provide excellent five-or-more-mile rides. A Greenways Commission, 615/862-8400, established in 1992, is beginning to map bike and walk routes along the Cumberland River. In the meantime, stop in at Cumberland Transit, 2807 West End, or across the street at the Bike Pedlar, 2910 West End, to find out about sched-uled group rides in the local area and recommended biking routes around town.

Nashville International Airport

Nashville International Airport, operated by the Metropolitan Nashville Airport Authority, is surprisingly convenient, located just east of the city, at I-40 and Donelson Pike, within 10 miles of town. Its graceful and spacious architecture, divided by three ramped levels for easy access to departures, arrivals, and ground transportation, was designed by architect Robert Lamb Hart. The airport is arranged around a central core, with four concourses radiating out at roughly 30-degree angles. Departures are from the third level, which can be reached by escalators and elevators from parking on levels one and two. Baggage claim is on the second level. Four restaurants, two lounges, a coffee house, and a quiet waiting area can be found on the Departures Level. The Concourse Connector, inside the security gates, is a wide seating area overlooking the runways. Nashville International is served by all major U.S. airlines plus numerous regional and charter carriers. Direct service extends to more than 90 cities in the U.S., Canada, and Mexico.

Getting to the Airport

The airport is most easily reached from I-40 east, which has clearly marked exits in both directions. Donelson Pike, running along one side of the airport, provides another access point for those coming from Murfreesboro

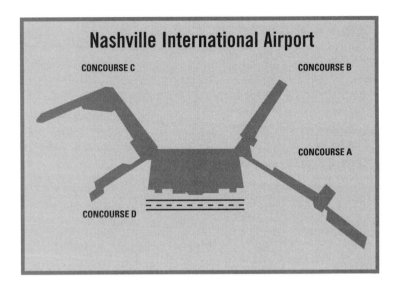

Nashville International Airport

CONCOURSE C

CONCOURSE B

CONCOURSE A

CONCOURSE D

Road or I-24. Coming in on I-24 from the south, there is a Nashville International Airport sign at Harding Place, which directs drivers to turn right onto Harding Place, a busy road that ultimately connects to Donelson Pike just before it crosses Murfreesboro Road.

Leaving the Airport

The ramp leaving the airport parking area leads directly onto I-40 west, which takes one past the exit for Briley Parkway (Grand Ole Opry House, Opryland Hotel) and provides access to I-440, a bypass to the south and west, on its way into downtown Nashville. Otherwise, exit left onto Donelson Pike, which provides access to I-40 eastbound (the Hermitage, which is in Donelson, is not far away). If you exit right you'll cross Murfreesboro

Airlines

Air Canada, 800/776-3000

American, 800/433-7300

Com-Air, 800/354-9822

Continental, 800/525-0280

Corporate Express, 800/ 555-6565

Delta, 800/221-1212

Delta Express, 800/325-5205

Mesa, 800/637-2247

Northwest, 800/225-2525

Skyway, 800/452-2022

Southwest, 800/435-9792

TWA, 800/221-2000

United, 800/241-6522

US Airways, 800/428-4322

Arts in the Airport

Since the opening of Nashville International Airport in 1987, the Airport Authority has sponsored Arts in the Airport, a program that includes a permanent collection of contemporary art by Tennessee artists, changing art exhibits in at least four locations throughout the airport, and live music every Friday at noon. When you arrive on the Departures Level (top level), be sure to look up into the glass-roofed rafters for The Airport Sun Project, *a light sculpture designed by internationally-known artist Dale Eldred. Eldred's sculpture has positioned panels of diffraction grating so that, as the earth turns on its axis, light strikes them and breaks into the colors of the spectrum. The sculpture changes throughout the day, casting ribbons of color onto nearby walls. For more information on Arts in the Airport, call MNAA's Communications Department at 615/275-1610.*

Road (take a right and it will lead you through south Nashville into downtown) or you may continue on Donelson Pike until you come to I-24 (south will take you toward Murfreesboro, Chattanooga, and Atlanta; north will lead you to I-440 or into downtown).

Train Service

Amtrak's closest passenger service is in Memphis, even though Nashville still has regular rail freight service coming through the Union Station yards. Amtrak reservations and information can be reached at 800/872-7245.

Interstate and Regional Bus Service

Greyhound Lines offers interstate bus service to Nashville from all over the country. The station is located downtown at 200 Eighth Avenue South, 615/255-3556 (local terminal) or 800/231-2222 (national reservations).

Local Charter Services

Perhaps because the tour bus has always been the preferred mode of travel for country-music performers, Nashville's country-music fans seem always to have preferred guided bus tours as a way to see Nashville. Parked curb-side at every shrine of country music are buses from one or more of Nashville's charter services. Many of them offer "homes of the stars" tours, which more often than not are merely drive-bys and not visits, so be sure to ask questions before signing up! A few charter services that are worth trying include: **Grand Ole Opry Tours**, 615/889-9490; **Johnny Walker Tours**, 800/722-1524 or 615/834-8585; **Orion Charters and Tours**, 800/333-5354; **Travelways Gray Line of Nashville**, 800/251-1864 or 615/883-0235.

Mary Entrekin

3

WHERE TO STAY

Nashville's hotels are, with a few exceptions, concentrated in the downtown area, near the airport, and in the "Music Valley" area near the Grand Ole Opry House. Motels ring the city, for the most part clustered around interstate exits. The neighborhood motel is pretty much a thing of the past, and those that do survive are generally located on city streets that have become commercial strips , which make staying there unappealing at best and unsafe at worst. The motels listed in this book are dependable, if not necessarily adventuresome, choices. Many belong to national chains that can vary widely, but have been selected here for their particular location. Some of the familiar hotel and motel names are now offering limited service, no-frills, or luxurious all-suite, residential-type lodgings for the independent traveler who wants to feel "at home." Outside of town, especially in the smaller cities around Nashville, there are local motels that one could choose with confidence. The bed-and-breakfast listings in this chapter reflect the trend towards personalized experience, replacing the mom-and-pop motels of yesteryear.

In the East Nashville zone, the gigantic Opryland Hotel reigns supreme, commanding the highest room rates in town year-round. There is never a "low season" at the Opryland Hotel, which has long been Nashville's primary convention hotel, and sits right next to the Opry House, where the Grand Ole Opry holds sway year-round.Visitors who come seeking the "Music City" experience may find it's worth paying the premium in order be at the center of the action. However, staying in the Midtown Nashville zone near "Music Row" or in the Downtown Nashville area near the nightlife of Second Avenue and lower Broadway might prove just as satisfying and certainly won't put as much of a strain on the wallet. Seasonal special events, like Country Music Week in October, Country Music Fan Fair in early June, or the many college and university graduation ceremonies in May will drive the rates up all over town.

Price rating symbols:

$	Under $50
$$	$50 to $75
$$$	$75 to $125
$$$$	$125 and up

DOWNTOWN NASHVILLE

Hotels

The few hotels downtown are primarily business/luxury hotels, so weekday rates are expensive. When weekend package deals are available, downtown Nashville, a walkable eight blocks square with historic buildings everywhere, can be a lovely place to stay. There's lots of nightlife downtown, as the Tennessee Performing Arts Center, the Ryman Auditorium, and the Nashville Arena are close at hand. New restaurants are opening up and down Second and Third Avenues, and honky-tonks still go all night on lower Broadway.

COURTYARD BY MARRIOTT
170 4th Ave. N.
Nashville 37201
615/256-0900 or 800/321-2211
$$$–$$$$
This 119-room hotel, opened in June 1998, is a renovation of the old Third National Bank Building right in the center of the downtown business district. The hotel, which features a marble-floored Art Deco lobby reminiscent of the bank's heyday, has 12 floors, a restaurant open for breakfast and lunch, and a workout facility featuring a fully equipped gym and whirlpool. Business travelers will welcome the familiar Marriott services in a location within walking distance of many downtown addresses and state and local office buildings. Parking, either valet or self-park in the hotel lot

across the street, is at additional charge. Room rates for doubles, kings with Jacuzzis, and suites are very competitive, even slightly less, than other downtown hotels, and weekend rates are offered. (Downtown)

CROWNE PLAZA
623 Union
Nashville 37219
615/259-2000 or 800/2-CROWNE
$$$–$$$$
The Crowne Plaza, a former atrium-style Hyatt with a revolving restaurant on the top level, is located directly across Legislative Plaza from the State Capitol. It's a well-appointed, friendly, convenient hotel with rooms that afford great views in all directions. There is an indoor pool and workout room on the lower level, and a nice casual restaurant on the mezzanine that looks out into the lobby. Persons under age 19 stay free in their parents' room. Parking garage available at extra charge. Discounts for AAA and AARP available if occupancy allows, but this hotel fills up when the state legislature is in town and during other downtown events such as the Southern Festival of Books. (Downtown)

DOUBLETREE HOTEL
315 4th Ave. N.
Nashville 37219
615/244-8200 or 800/222-8733
$$$–$$$$
In the heart of the central business district, the Doubletree is a quiet, elegant oasis. The building sits as a triangular wedge across a plaza from the NationsBank tower—as a result, some of the guest rooms are triangular in shape. Most rooms are fairly dark and only a few have good views, but as a result, this hotel is well laid-out for a quiet night's rest. The decor

DOWNTOWN NASHVILLE

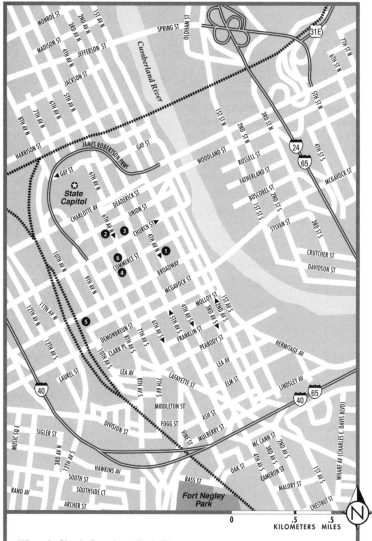

Where to Stay in Downtown Nashville

1 Courtyard by Marriott
2 Crowne Plaza
3 Doubletree Hotel
4 Renaissance Nashville Hotel
5 Union Station: A Grand Heritage Hotel
6 The Westin Hermitage Suite Hotel

is very nice and service is friendly (fresh-baked cookies are offered on check-in), although colleagues have reported that they are still working out the kinks in business services such as in-room voice mailboxes. Parking is available in the garage underneath for an additional charge. The lobby restaurant is always filled with business lunchers. Rates do not apply during Country Music Fan Fair. Inquire about seasonal packages and rates. (Downtown)

RENAISSANCE NASHVILLE HOTEL
611 Commerce
Nashville 37203
615/255-8400 or 800/468-3571
$$$$
A former Stouffer, this modern tower hotel connects to the Nashville Convention Center. One of the tallest buildings downtown, the hotel and its accompanying office building provide scenic views out over the city in all directions. Conventions often fill this hotel, which almost has the feel of a public building because of its proximity to the next-door Convention Center and the fact that its lobby serves as the lobby for the office building above. There is a public garage located across the street, accessible on your own or by the

TRIVIA

Pool player Minnesota Fats lived at the Hermitage for a number of years before its current incarnation as an all-suite luxury hotel, supporting himself by taking all comers at billiards.

valet parkers stationed out front. The health club includes an indoor pool, and guests are offered Legends Golf Club (private, located in Williamson County) access privileges, at a fee. Children under age 18 free with adult. AARP discount offered. (Downtown)

UNION STATION:
A GRAND HERITAGE HOTEL
1001 Broadway
Nashville 37203
615/726-1001 or 800/331-2123
$$$–$$$$
This Romanesque Revival–style train terminal was built in 1900 as a symbol of a new century of progress for Nashville (see Chapter 5). Freight trains still pass beside the station and the massive metal train shed behind, and the old timetable is posted over the reception desk. In 1985 the building was converted to a luxury hotel of 124 rooms.

Because it is such a unique setting, the Union Station hosts many special events—from music industry parties to free music showcases to weddings and other receptions of all kinds. The hotel lobby, where guests can enjoy a daily breakfast buffet or sip coffee and after-dinner drinks next to a massive limestone fireplace, was once the passenger waiting area—a large central court naturally lit by a Tiffany glass–paneled ceiling. An extensive program of symbolic sculptural decoration tells the story of the "union" of two railroad lines at Nashville. The rooms, most of which open onto the inner atrium, are priced according to level. While staying here can be a novelty, visitors should be aware that rooms opening onto the inner atrium can be quite noisy, freight trains still rumble under the building on a regular basis, and rooms on the lowest level are below street level and can be dark.

This hotel is undergoing a needed renovation and, it is hoped, a thorough review of hospitality and room-service standards. Valet parking is mandatory, and a discount is offered to AARP and AAA members if hotel occupancy permits. (Downtown)

THE WESTIN HERMITAGE SUITE HOTEL
231 6th Ave. N.
Nashville 37219
615/244-3121 or 800/WESTIN-1
$$$–$$$$

The only grand hotel remaining in the heart of downtown, the Hermitage was built in 1910. This fine hotel is my top choice, since all rooms are two-room suites and include amenities suited to both business and leisure travelers. It is Beaux Arts style, with a great deal of decorative architectural work in carved wood and plaster, gold detailing, marble floors, and stained-glass panels. The hotel was completely renovated in 1994, and its luxurious furnishings have been carefully groomed since it was acquired by Westin early in 1998. The staff is knowledgeable, friendly, and attentive.

A great place to meet, the Hermitage lobby bar with a mezzanine-level veranda opening off it, serves cocktails accompanied by grand piano music and a light menu during cocktail hour. The lower-level Oak Bar is a traditional club bar at its best. It overlooks the Capitol Grille, named in 1995 one of *Esquire* magazine's best new American restaurants, open for breakfast, lunch, and dinner. The Hermitage is listed on the National Register of Historic Places and is a member of Historic Hotels of America. The next-door parking garage that belongs to the hotel adds a

Robin Hood

Union Station

charge to your hotel room. There is no AAA discount here, but an AARP discount is available and so are special weekend rates according to availability. Foreign visitors should check with Westin's worldwide reservation service to secure special "bed-and-breakfast" or other promotional rates in advance. (Downtown)

MIDTOWN NASHVILLE

Hotels and Motels

COURTYARD BY MARRIOTT
1901 West End Ave.
Nashville 37203
615/327-9900 or 800/321-2211
$$$

With a convenient location near Music Row and Vanderbilt, this busy, limited-service hotel is aimed primarily at business travelers who appreciate Marriott's exacting management standards. The lobby is tiny, parking is at a premium, and this hotel is right on busy West End Avenue, so there is nothing inherently interesting about it, except

MIDTOWN NASHVILLE

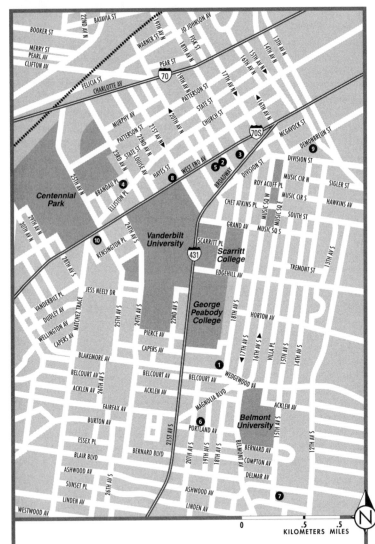

Where to Stay in Midtown Nashville

1 Commodore Inn & Guest House
2 Courtyard by Marriott
3 Days Inn Vanderbilt-Music Row
4 Hampton Inn & Suites
5 Hampton Inn Vanderbilt
6 Hillsboro House
7 Linden House
8 Loews Vanderbilt Plaza Hotel
9 Shoney's Inn
10 Vanderbilt Holiday Inn Select

for its proximity to midtown restaurants and public transportation (West End buses run frequently). It's convenient for tourists who want to be within walking distance to Music Row attractions, or parents visiting their college-age children at Vanderbilt. There is an exercise room and a restaurant on site, and early-morning runners might enjoy the run to and around Centennial Park, approximately one mile west of the hotel. AAA and AARP discounts are offered weekends only. (Midtown)

DAYS INN
VANDERBILT-MUSIC ROW
1800 West End Ave.
Nashville 37203
615/327-0922 or 800/325-2525
$$$

The Days Inn is an old standby located close to Music Row and Vanderbilt. It is a true motel, with rooms opening off outdoor walkways and an outdoor swimming pool just off the lobby. Service is friendly and accommodating and this motel has lots of repeat business visitors, from traveling salespeople to construction workers here to help meet the labor shortage in Nashville's booming economy. Rooms are very basic, with the cramped bathrooms common to Days Inn architecture, and small, thin towels, but you can ask for a quiet room away from the street and sleep comfortably here. An adequate continental breakfast (again, no frills) is included and served in the lobby. Room rates beginning at $79 per night may seem high but are competitive for this part of town. (Midtown)

HAMPTON INN & SUITES
2300 Elliston Pl.
Nashville 37203
615/320-6060 or 800/426-7866
$$$

Two blocks from the Vanderbilt campus, this new Hampton Inn features 35 one-bedroom suites as well as standard rooms. The hotel has one floor dedicated to nonsmokers, an outdoor pool, and a workout room. The rate includes a simple continental breakfast. It's within easy walking distance of Centennial Park, Vanderbilt University, and several nice midtown-area restaurants, as well as Nashville's excellent Tower Records store. Rates do not apply during the Country Music Fan Fair or during Vanderbilt University special events. (Midtown)

HAMPTON INN VANDERBILT
1919 West End Ave.
Nashville 37203
615/329-1144 or 800/426-7866
$$$

Near Vanderbilt and the Music Row area, the usually busy Hampton Inn is a dependable, if not luxurious, choice. The hotel has both an outdoor pool and a workout facility, and the room rate includes a very basic continental breakfast. Over 50 percent of the rooms are nonsmoking. Children under age 18 are free with parents, and there is a discount for seniors. Rates do not apply during the Country Music Fan Fair or during Vanderbilt University special events. (Midtown)

LOEWS VANDERBILT
PLAZA HOTEL
2100 West End Ave.
Nashville 37203
615/336-3335 or 615/320-1700 or
800/235-6397
$$$–$$$$

On the corner of 21st Avenue and West End Avenue, across from Vanderbilt University's main gates, the luxurious Loews Vanderbilt Plaza Hotel caters primarily to business travelers but offers occasional special rates, particularly on weekends, when Vanderbilt is not in session. Rooms are beautifully appointed and the hotel is kept in pristine order. A concierge level provides fax and dataports for computers and special hospitality. Although there is a small fitness center on the second level of the hotel, guests in search of a swimming pool or more extensive workout facility can have access to the nearby and very nice Baptist Health Center for a moderate fee. The garden piano bar in the lobby, where a well-known local jazz pianist entertains on Friday evenings, has entertainment daily and serves from 3 p.m. until midnight. The Plaza Grill restaurant is one of Nashville's "power breakfast" spots, and the food is good, featuring regional specialities for both lunch and dinner that can also be ordered up from room service.

Next door, on the lower level of the same building, is Ruth's Chris Steak House, where they will put your dinner on your hotel tab as an added convenience. Starbucks is the official coffee at Loews, which features in-room coffeemakers and a complimentary coffee bar set up in the lobby each morning. AAA and AARP discounts are honored. Parking in onsite garage is extra. (Midtown)

SHONEY'S INN
1501 Demonbreun
Nashville 37203
615/255-9977 or 800/222-2222
$$–$$$
This Shoney's Inn is right on the corner of Demonbreun and I-265 (inner loop of interstate system). It's on Music Row, in the center of the tourist action, about one long block from the Country Music Hall of Fame. This is a motel, with rooms looking out over the parking lot from two levels, and parking within sight of your

room. The rates are competitive and the rooms perfectly adequate. There's a Shoney's family-style restaurant next door and an outdoor swimming pool. Children under age 18 are free in their parents' room. Its location makes it a prime spot for families and major-league country-music fans. "Music on the Row," a free summertime concert series on Wednesday nights, takes place in the adjacent parking lot. AAA and AARP discounts are honored. Rates do not apply during Country Music Fan Fair. (Midtown)

VANDERBILT HOLIDAY INN SELECT
2613 West End Ave.
Nashville 37203
615/327-4707
$$$
In front of the Vanderbilt stadium and across from Centennial Park, this very nice Holiday Inn, now operated by Bristol Hotels & Resorts, is within walking distance of restaurants and the Elliston Place area. Rooms include such niceties as irons and ironing boards and are comfortably furnished with sitting areas and balconies. A 300-room, 10-story high rise, this hotel has an outdoor swimming pool, a restaurant, and a lounge. Children under age 18 stay free with parents, and AAA and AARP discounts are available. Rates do not apply during Country Music Fan Fair or other special events, particularly Vanderbilt-related. (Midtown)

Bed-and-Breakfasts
COMMODORE INN & GUEST HOUSE
1614 19th Ave. S.
Nashville 37212
615/269-3850
$$–$$$

A beautiful two-story stone house with a two-bedroom guest cottage behind, the Commodore Inn is located in the Hillsboro Village area, within walking distance of stores, restaurants, and the movie theater. Breakfast is included in the room rate. The house, built in 1925 by the owner of Nashville's finest stonecutting business, D.Y. Johnson, has intrigued owner Charles Whitnel, a historian by inclination, to learn its history. Furnished with antiques throughout, and surrounded by beautifully landscaped grounds, the Commodore Inn only rents rooms in the main house when the cottage, which has a fireplace, a loft bedroom, and a full kitchen, is full. Perfect for a several-day stay with family or if you are traveling with a group of friends or a wedding party. (Midtown)

HILLSBORO HOUSE
1933 20th Ave. S.
Nashville 37212
615/292-5501
$$
This 1904 antique-furnished Victorian cottage is located on a quiet street near Vanderbilt and Belmont Universities, within walking distance of Hillsboro Village restaurants and Watkins-Belcourt movie theater.

Two rooms with private baths, and a third with shared bath, are cozy with high ceilings and hardwood floors. Breakfast is included in the room rate. (Midtown)

LINDEN HOUSE
1501 Linden Ave.
Nashville 37212
615/298-2701
$$
This turn-of-the-century Victorian cottage is located in the quiet Hillsboro-Belmont neighborhood, not too far from the up-and-coming 12 South district, the revival of a historic shopping street. If you want to get a feel for a midtown neighborhood and enjoy walking on tree-lined streets, you'll enjoy Linden House. All rooms are nonsmoking, spacious, and furnished with antiques. Linden House has one large bedroom with shared bath upstairs, and a suite of two bedrooms downstairs, with a separate outside entrance. Breakfast is included in the room rate. Seniors receive a 10-percent discount. (Midtown)

NORTH NASHVILLE

This area of town is close to many historic sites related to the arrival of

---

TRIVIA

Hillsboro Village, with its three blocks of brick storefronts, is one of Nashville's oldest remaining shopping areas. Its Belcourt Cinema was originally built in 1925 as a silent movie house. By 1931 it had become the Nashville Children's Theater, and few Nashvillians know that it was for two years (1934–36) home to the Grand Ole Opry. In 1937 it became the Community Playhouse. The theater was remodeled in 1966 to create two auditoriums, and it became Nashville's first "art house," showing first-run foreign and American films.

the first settlers to the area. See Chapter 5: Sights and Attractions, North Nashville.

Hotels

HOLIDAY INN EXPRESS–BRICK CHURCH
2401 Brick Church Pike
Nashville 37207
615/226-4600 or 800/465-4329
$$
This small, five-story hotel has an exercise center with whirlpool and sauna and offers free continental breakfast. Half the rooms are non-smoking, children stay free, and AAA and AARP members receive discounts. (North Nashville)

HOLIDAY INN HENDERSONVILLE
615 E. Main
Hendersonville, TN 37075
615/824-0022
$$
This classic Holiday Inn, on the main street of the all-American town of Hendersonville, is a find. Family-oriented, well-kept, and friendly, with plenty of parking, free local calls, an outdoor pool, and a number of nonsmoking rooms, this seems like the Holiday Inn of yesteryear. It's off the beaten path for Music City tourists, yet close enough to many of the earliest historic sites in the area to be convenient for sightseeing. (North Nashville)

REGAL MAXWELL HOUSE
2025 MetroCenter Blvd.
Nashville 37228
615/259-4343 or 800/457-4460 or 800/222-8888 (Regal Hotels International)
$$$–$$$$
Located on the fringes of downtown, this modern hotel bears the name of Nashville's legendary grand hotel, the Maxwell House, which burned to the ground in 1961. The original hotel, begun in 1859 but not completed until 1869, was the city's business and social center for many years. It was one of the first establishments to offer Jack Daniel's Tennessee Whiskey. Teddy Roosevelt called the dining room's coffee "good to the last drop" on a visit to Nashville in 1907, and the rest is history.

The current hotel offers lots of amenities including extensive meeting rooms, a large free parking lot, an outdoor swimming pool, tennis courts and a health club featuring both sauna and steam room, and a rooftop restaurant. The hotel has a friendly air, and the good rates for the quality of amenities offered may be due to the fact that it's a little out

TRIVIA

The old Maxwell House hotel was one of the first establishments to offer Jack Daniel's Tennessee whiskey to its bar patrons as an alternative to true Bourbon, which can come only from Kentucky. The current hotel maintains a display case filled with historical memorabilia, which includes a 1907 letter from Lem Motlow to his Uncle Jack Daniel, in which he assures his uncle that the whiskey is being widely enjoyed by hotel patrons.

The Hancock House: A Bed-and-Breakfast Inn

of the way, just north of the I-265 loop from downtown. A special "club level" gives business travelers access to office services and hospitality. Current management evokes the hotel's historical ties by maintaining a display case filled with historical memorabilia, and placing menu items honoring the famed Maxwell House cuisine on the bill at J.D.'s Chop House. AAA discount available depending upon availability. (North Nashville)

SUMNER SUITES
330 E. Main St.
Hendersonville, TN 37075
615/826-4301 or 800/747-8483
$$$

They seem to have thought of everything at Sumner Suites. These fairly new hotel suites include kitchenettes with coffeemakers and microwave ovens. There is a fitness center as well as an outdoor pool, local calls are free, and so is a daily continental breakfast. Perfect for business travelers on extended-stay jobs as well as families traveling

with children, or budget travelers who don't wish to eat out at every meal. (North Nashville)

Bed-and-Breakfasts

All of the bed-and-breakfasts listed below are located about 15 miles north of Nashville in historic homes near the earliest settlements in the region.

THE HANCOCK HOUSE:
A BED-AND-BREAKFAST INN
2144 Nashville Pike
Gallatin 37066
615/452-8431
$$$

The 15-room inn, which is listed on the National Register of Historic Places, dates prior to 1878, when it was known as Avondale Station, a toll-gate and stage stop. The inn itself has five bedrooms, all with fireplaces and private baths. A separate two-bedroom log cabin, with fireplace, private bath, and Jacuzzi, is located several hundred yards away. The dining room serves a full or continental breakfast; lunch and

GREATER NASHVILLE

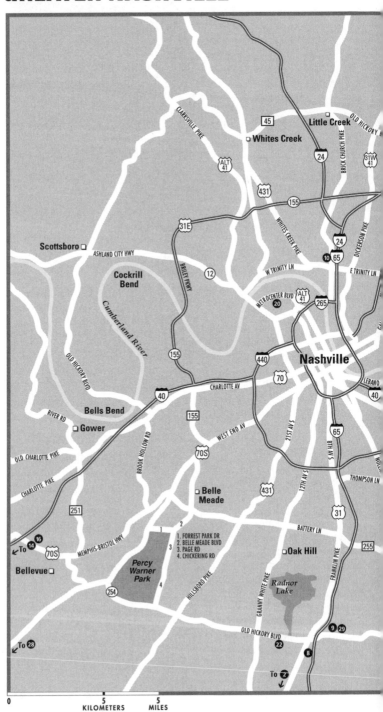

Little Creek

Whites Creek

Scottsboro

Cockrill Bend

Cumberland River

Bells Bend

Gower

Nashville

Belle Meade

Bellevue

Percy Warner Park

1. FORREST PARK DR
2. BELLE MEADE BLVD
3. PAGE RD
4. CHICKERING RD

Oak Hill

Radnor Lake

CLARKSVILLE PIKE
OLD HICKORY
BRICK CHURCH PIKE
31W 41
ALT 41
431
155
WHITES CREEK PIKE
DICKERSON PIKE
31E
ASHLAND CITY HWY
BRILEY PKWY
W TRINITY LN
E TRINITY LN
METROCENTER BLVD
ALT 41
OLD HICKORY BLVD
RIVER RD
OLD CHARLOTTE PIKE
CHARLOTTE PIKE
CHARLOTTE AV
WEST END AV
21ST AV S
8TH AV S
THOMPSON LN
LEBANON
BROOK HOLLOW RD
12TH AV S
BATTERY LN
MEMPHIS-BRISTOL HWY
HILLSBORO PIKE
GRANNY WHITE PIKE
FRANKLIN PIKE
OLD HICKORY BLVD

To 14
To 28
To 7

0   5   5
    KILOMETERS   MILES

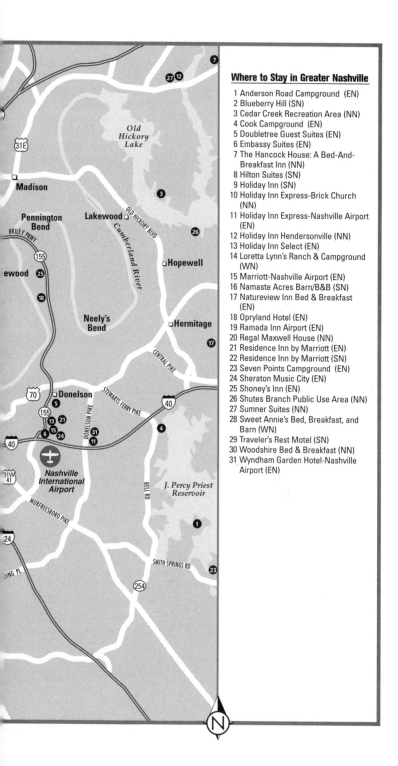

Where to Stay in Greater Nashville

1 Anderson Road Campground (EN)
2 Blueberry Hill (SN)
3 Cedar Creek Recreation Area (NN)
4 Cook Campground (EN)
5 Doubletree Guest Suites (EN)
6 Embassy Suites (EN)
7 The Hancock House: A Bed-And-Breakfast Inn (NN)
8 Hilton Suites (SN)
9 Holiday Inn (SN)
10 Holiday Inn Express-Brick Church (NN)
11 Holiday Inn Express-Nashville Airport (EN)
12 Holiday Inn Hendersonville (NN)
13 Holiday Inn Select (EN)
14 Loretta Lynn's Ranch & Campground (WN)
15 Marriott-Nashville Airport (EN)
16 Namaste Acres Barn/B&B (SN)
17 Natureview Inn Bed & Breakfast (EN)
18 Opryland Hotel (EN)
19 Ramada Inn Airport (EN)
20 Regal Maxwell House (NN)
21 Residence Inn by Marriott (EN)
22 Residence Inn by Marriott (SN)
23 Seven Points Campground (EN)
24 Sheraton Music City (EN)
25 Shoney's Inn (EN)
26 Shutes Branch Public Use Area (NN)
27 Sumner Suites (NN)
28 Sweet Annie's Bed, Breakfast, and Barn (WN)
29 Traveler's Rest Motel (SN)
30 Woodshire Bed & Breakfast (NN)
31 Wyndham Garden Hotel-Nashville Airport (EN)

dinner are by reservation only. Swimming, tennis, and horseback riding are available. A favorite site for country wedding receptions and dinner parties. (North Nashville)

WOODSHIRE BED & BREAKFAST
600 Woodshire Dr.
Goodlettsville 37072
615/859-7369
$$
The Woodshire Bed & Breakfast is in a well-groomed suburban neighborhood, just off the main street of Goodlettsville. Lodgings are in the main house, a handsome reproduction New England saltbox tastefully furnished with antiques and contemporary crafts. There are two guest bedrooms (each with a bath) in the house itself, and a charming mid-nineteenth-century log cabin, with private bath, behind. A lovely small garden in the backyard offers a peaceful retreat after a day of doing the town. Rates include a delicious country breakfast with your hosts, a friendly retired couple. No smoking. Moderate rates. (North Nashville)

Campgrounds

CEDAR CREEK RECREATION AREA
Resource Manager,
Old Hickory Lake
No. 5 Power Plant Rd.

Hendersonville 37075
615/754-4947
$
Located about 10 miles north of I-40 off Old Hickory Boulevard, this public camping area includes 60 sites, all with full hook-ups, and is operated by the U.S. Corps of Engineers. Amenities include a swimming area on the lake, boat ramps, and a bathhouse. Open Apr–Oct. (North Nashville)

SHUTES BRANCH
PUBLIC USE AREA
Old Hickory Lake
501 Weather Station Rd.
Old Hickory 37138
615/754-4847
$
Shutes Branch is a public campground with 35 sites, boat ramps, barbeque grills, and showers. Electric and water hook-ups are available. Open May–Sep. (North Nashville)

EAST NASHVILLE

A number of the establishments in this listing are located in and around the Opryland/Music Valley area which is northeast of downtown on a bend of the Cumberland River. Listings for the airport area and South Briley Parkway accommodations can also be found here.

TRIVIA

Nashville's first hotel was the Nashville Inn, opened in 1796 on the public square, very near where the Davidson County courthouse stands today. Major William T. Lewis operated the inn, which provided food and lodging as well as stabling for horses. In 1817 Andrew Jackson gave a dinner party for 16 gentlemen, ordering 17 bottles of Madeira wine and four dozen cigars for his guests. Total bill for the festivities, including a bottle of whiskey that cost 50¢, came to $61.

Hotels and Motels

DOUBLETREE GUEST SUITES
2424 Atrium Way
Nashville 37214
615/889-8889 or 800/222-8733
$$$–$$$$

Just off Briley Parkway, on a quiet hillside near the airport and Opryland, the Doubletree offers nicely furnished spacious living quarters, a well-equipped health club with a small indoor/outdoor pool, and a restaurant on site. Prices are moderate considering the appointments and size of rooms, and there are lots of special rates, depending upon availability. Ask about "extended stay" and weekend "Dream Deals" if these might fit into your travel plans. Seven suites are wheelchair-accessible. AAA and AARP members get discounts. (East Nashville)

EMBASSY SUITES
10 Century Blvd.
Nashville 37214
615/871-0033 or 800/362-2779
$$$

A bright pink building near the airport, this hotel looks like it was intended for some other city. The Embassy has close to 300 suites, the majority of which are nonsmoking and 14 of which are wheelchair-accessible. Room rates include a "cooked-to-order" breakfast. Children stay free with parents, and AARP discounts are honored. (East Nashville)

HOLIDAY INN EXPRESS–NASHVILLE AIRPORT
1111 Airport Center Dr.
Nashville 37214
615/883-1366 or 800/HOLIDAY
$$–$$$

Just off Donelson Pike, in a new industrial park near the airport, this very nice, limited-service Holiday Inn has the majority of its rooms designated as nonsmoking. Four are wheelchair-accessible. The rooms are clean and the front desk staff friendly and accomodating. Rooms are entered from inside the hotel, and there is plenty of parking out front. Holiday Inn Express has voice mail in each room, a shuttle to nearby restaurants, and a complimentary breakfast buffet on site. Children under age 12 are free with their parents, and AAA and AARP discounts are available. Weekend "great rates" and a "bed-and-breakfast" rate are good deals when available. Foreign travelers should note that Holiday Inns offer worldwide reservations, and this would be a good choice for a convenient first night's stay when arriving in Nashville by air. (East Nashville)

HOLIDAY INN SELECT
2200 Elm Hill Pike
Nashville 37214
615/883-9770 or 800/633-4427
$$$

This Holiday Inn, managed by Bristol Hotels and Resorts, has recently been renovated to include such amenities as data ports, voicemail, coffeemakers, and an iron and ironing board in every room. The Ivories piano bar has live music nightly and attracts a crowd. The lobby restaurant and an informal cocktail lounge overlook the Holidome recreation center, which has a swimming pool and Jacuzzi in plain sight of the lobby. (Parents of small children will probably appreciate this more than exercise seekers.) More than 50 percent of the rooms here are nonsmoking and a shuttle service is offered to the airport. Located just off Briley Parkway, very near the airport and close to the Opryland complex. AAA and AARP discounts are offered. Rates usually go

The Opryland Hotel and its marketing staff seem to have a knack for endlessly inventing "tradition." A new complex of rooms, shops, and restaurants called the Delta will feature a four-and-a-half-acre landscaped garden complete with a river and flatboats! Maybe Opryland's goal is to finally convince tourists that Nashville is in fact Memphis (many Europeans have long thought this anyway)—the King's presence is claimed here in more ways than just the simple possession of his gold Cadillac by the Country Music Hall of Fame.

up during Country Music Fan Fair in June. (East Nashville)

MARRIOTT–NASHVILLE AIRPORT
600 Marriott Dr.
Nashville 37214
615/889-9300 or 800/228-9290
$$$–$$$$

Located near the airport, just off Briley Parkway, this is a full-service Marriott hotel with a restaurant and 400 rooms, 175 of which are nonsmoking. This reliable hotel functions as a home away from home to many business travelers, including a colleague who comes to Nashville monthly and appreciates the well-outfitted workout facility and the excellent room service. Children under age 12 stay free. (East Nashville)

OPRYLAND HOTEL
2800 Opryland Dr.
Nashville 37214
615/889-1000
$$$$

With 2,800-plus rooms, the Opryland Hotel is a world unto itself. The hotel is a neo-plantation-style complex, with white-columned porches and porticos surrounding most of its red-brick structures. The Cascades, a glassed-in atrium, contains fountains, plants, restaurants, and shops. This is

a convention-center hotel, with extensive meeting rooms and display facilities. There are two outdoor pools at Opryland, heated so they can be enjoyed as long as the weather is reasonably mild. The room rates, among the highest in town, remain fairly constant, as this hotel is well-booked year-round. A fitness center is available on-site for a moderate charge of $4 per day, and parking costs $5 if you park yourself, $12 for valet service.

During the annual Country Music Week festivities each October, the hotel is alive with lavish formal events, as country stars and music executives walk under covered canopies from the Opry House next door. The Springhouse Golf Club is located nearby. Across from the front of the hotel is the Music Valley Drive area, where numerous country-music souvenir shops, family-style restaurants, and hotels and motels are located. (East Nashville)

RAMADA INN AIRPORT
837 Briley Pkwy.
Nashville 37217
615/361-6999
$$

This is your basic motel, with rooms entered from covered walkways outside. The rooms are standard issue but well-kept, and the management is friendly and helpful. There is an outdoor pool and visitors may wish to request a quiet room on the back of the motel, which is set against a wooded expanse. An expanded continental breakfast is served in the lobby. There is no restaurant on site, although a family-style Denny's is located next door.

A courtesy van to the airport runs between 6 a.m. and 11 p.m. and a "Park N Fly" program is available for those who wish to leave their car in secure parking for up to three days (after three days, the cost is $5/day. Discounted rates are available when occupancy allows, but moderate prices are the main incentive to stay here in any case. (East Nashville)

RESIDENCE INN BY MARRIOTT
2300 Elm Hill Pike
Nashville 37214
615/889-8600 or 800/331-3131
$$$-$$$$
This nicely landscaped Marriott looks like a condominium complex. Most of the suites have fireplaces, all have equipped kitchens and close access to a nice outdoor pool. VCR rentals are available, and a free continental breakfast is served daily. AAA and AARP discounts are honored. (East Nashville)

SHERATON MUSIC CITY
777 McGavock Pike, Century City
Nashville 37214
615/885-2200 or 800/325-3535
$$$$
This luxurious 400-plus-room hotel, located close to the airport just off Briley Parkway at Elm Hill Pike, sits on well-manicured grounds worthy of a country club. Its handsome brick exterior, white columns, and circular driveway bear out this first impression, as does the richly furnished, marble-floored, wood-paneled lobby. There is a Business Center, with computers and work stations; and a Club Floor with dataports, voicemail, fax machines, coffeemakers, and there are bathrobes in every room. Room service will even bring you wine by the glass—a first for Nashville hotels in my experience.

A health club with indoor and outdoor pools, sauna, and whirlpool, is accessible by a back elevator, so fitness mavens don't have to cross the lobby in bathrobes. The extensive grounds feature jogging trails and lighted tennis courts. Parking is free; there are two cocktail lounges, one with live entertainment; and there's a gourmet "Apples in the Field" restaurant and a coffee shop. Children under age 18 stay free with their parents, and AARP discounts are honored. The Sheraton Music City received a high rating in Zagat's most recent survey. (East Nashville)

SHONEY'S INN
2420 Music Valley Dr.
Nashville 37214
615/885-4030 or 800/222-2222
$$$
Nashville-based Shoney's is master of the home-style restaurant, and their hotel/motels are designed for "just folks." They've outdone themselves here in order to compete with the Opryland appeal by offering an indoor heated pool and outdoor Jacuzzi, a lounge with nightly live entertainment, and complimentary continental breakfast and shuttle service to Opryland Hotel. Shoney's Restaurant is right next door. Children under age 18 are free, and discounted rates are available for AAA and AARP members. (East Nashville)

WYNDHAM GARDEN
HOTEL–NASHVILLE AIRPORT
1112 Airport Center Dr.
Nashville 37214
615/889-9090 or 800/996-3426
$$$

Located in a small industrial park just off busy Donelson Pike at I-40, this hotel is within a mile of the airport. Always nicely furnished, with welcoming reading and sitting areas, the Wyndham hotel chain caters to both business and leisure travelers and offers reasonable rates weekdays as well as special weekend deals. The majority of this hotel's 180 rooms are nonsmoking, and all rooms come with coffeemakers and hairdryers. There's a casual restaurant and a swimming pool on site, and a fireplace in the lobby reading room. (East Nashville)

Bed-and-Breakfasts

NATUREVIEW INN
BED & BREAKFAST
3354 Old Lebanon Dirt Rd.
Mt. Juliet 37122
615/758-4439 or 800/758-7972
$$–$$$

One of the few bed-and-breakfast accommodations in this book that is not a historic house, the Natureview Inn is a neatly-kept ranch house with a warm atmosphere. It's located off a country road near the Hermitage and not far from the airport. There are four guest rooms, arranged in two apartment/suites with a shared bath in each suite. One suite has its own full kitchen—ideal for families or those who desire a several-day stay. There is a large deck for enjoying the outdoors during the warm months and an outdoor pool for the hot ones. The owner's son, a certified chef, creates full breakfasts

daily. Specialties include broiled grapefruit, fluffy mushroom omelets, and huevos rancheros, made with bonafide New Mexico peppers that hail from the owner's former home. Small dogs are allowed. Seniors receive a 10-percent discount. (East Nashville)

Campgrounds

ANDERSON ROAD CAMPGROUND
Percy Priest Lake
Nashville 37214
615/361-1980
$

Operated by the U.S. Corps of Engineers, this public campground has 37 sites (no hook-ups), a bathhouse, picnic tables and grills, boat ramps, and a laundry facility, and is open April through September. (East Nashville)

COOK CAMPGROUND
Percy Priest Lake
3737 Bell Rd.
Nashville 37214
615/889-1096
$

Operated by the U.S. Corps of Engineers, this public campground has 57 sites for primitive camping, a bathhouse with restrooms, and a small playground. Open April through September. (East Nashville)

SEVEN POINTS CAMPGROUND
Percy Priest Lake
Nashville 37214
615/889-5198
$

This U.S. Corps of Engineers property is a public campground that has 60 sites, all with hook-ups. It includes a swimming area, boat ramps, picnic tables, grills, bathhouse, and a Laundromat. Open April through October. (East Nashville)

Hillsboro House Bed-and-Breakfast, p. 43

SOUTH NASHVILLE

Hotels and Motels

HILTON SUITES
9000 Overlook Blvd.
Brentwood 37027
615/370-0111 or 800/445-8667
$$$–$$$$

Located at Old Hickory Boulevard and I-65 south, the Hilton suites each include two rooms with a refrigerator and microwave. Six suites are wheelchair-accessible. The restaurant serves free full breakfast, and there is a cocktail lounge on site. The fitness center has a nice indoor pool. Inquire about special family and weekend packages. (South Nashville)

HOLIDAY INN
760 Old Hickory Blvd.
Brentwood 37027
615/373-2600 or 800/465-4329
$$$

A mile from I-65 south, in the heart of Brentwood, this 248-room hotel has 140 nonsmoking rooms, seven wheelchair-accessible rooms, a swim-ming pool, a whirlpool, a restaurant, and in-room coffeemakers. Rates vary with special events. AARP discounts are available. (South Nashville)

RESIDENCE INN BY MARRIOTT
206 Ward Cir.
Brentwood 37027
615/371-0100 or 800/331-3131
$$$–$$$$

A suite hotel, with full kitchens in all and fireplaces in most suites. Six of 110 suites are wheelchair-accessible, and 60 are nonsmoking. The Residence Inn offers a heated outdoor pool, free continental breakfast, and a grocery shopping service. Discounts granted for AAA and AARP members. (South Nashville)

TRAVELER'S REST MOTEL
Exit 74B, 107 Franklin Rd.
Brentwood 37027
615/373-3033
$$

This small motel was here long before the Brentwood boom. It has 36 plain but perfectly adequate rooms and is located right on busy Franklin Pike,

Health and Fitness

Only a few Nashville hotels feature the kind of full-service health club facilities that today's traveler has come to expect. If fitness is important to your lifestyle, even while on vacation, you might wish to take my preference list into account:

1. **Sheraton Music City Hotel**—*Topping the list is this country club–like hotel, which features not only a workout room with bikes, treadmills, and weight machines, but an indoor/outdoor pool and lighted outdoor tennis courts.*

2. **Opryland Hotel**—*Two heated outdoor pools stay open as long as the weather allows. The gym facility is offered for a small additional daily charge.*

3. **Crowne Plaza**—*On the lower level of the hotel is a well-kept small gym and an indoor pool. The pool is usually not crowded.*

4. **Renaissance Nashville Hotel**—*The indoor pool is adjacent to an outdoor sundeck and a fully-equipped gym. Access to the outdoors makes this option the most attractive among the downtown hotels, but it's often full of kids.*

5. **Courtyard by Marriott, downtown**—*A fully-equipped workout room with a whirlpool bath will help you get pumped for an important meeting or soothe meeting-weary muscles after a long day.*

6. *Last but not least, if you don't mind an early-morning stroll, several non-equipped hotels have worked out agreements with nearby facilities for a moderate fee:* **The Westin Hermitage-McKendree Health & Fitness Center** *(three blocks away);* **Loews Vanderbilt Plaza-Baptist Fitness Center** *(two blocks away);* **Union Station Hotel-Cummins Station Fitness Center** *(two blocks away).*

but the price is right, the place is so unassuming as to escape notice, and the management is friendly and down-home. A continental breakfast is served in the lobby every morning, and there are lots of nearby restaurants, movie theaters, and places to shop. (South Nashville)

Bed-and-Breakfasts

BLUEBERRY HILL
4591 Peytonsville Rd.
Franklin 37064
615/791-9947
$

This beautiful house high on a hill is located approximately 25 miles from downtown Nashville. It is a replica Federal-style home built with old hand-hewn beams and floorboards of heart pine. There is a fireplace in every room, and great views out the windows, which face east toward the ring of hills surrounding Nashville. The two charming guest rooms furnished with antiques each have a private bath. A delicious full breakfast, often featuring blue-berry specialities made from berries grown just outside, is served every morning. (South Nashville)

NAMASTE ACRES BARN/B&B
5463 Leiper's Creek

Franklin 37064
615/791-0333
$$–$$$

This lovely ranch-like property, complete with horse barns, an exercise room, and a swimming pool, is located in a valley just outside of Leiper's Fork, a small community 25 miles southwest of town and about three miles from the Natchez Trace Parkway. Four suites are available, each with a bath, private entrance, in-room refrigerator, and coffee-maker. A hot tub is ready for guests year-round. (South Nashville)

WEST NASHVILLE

Bed-and-Breakfasts

SWEET ANNIE'S BED, BREAKFAST, AND BARN
7201 Crow Cut Rd., S.W.
Fairview 37062

T i P

There are a number of bed-and-breakfast accommodations to be found away from the immediate city center, both in historic neighborhood locations and out in the country. Centralized reservation services make it simple to call, write, or e-mail for Nashville-area accommodations:

Natchez Trace Bed and Breakfast Reservation Service, P.O. Box 193, Hampshire 38461. For more information call 615/285-2777 or 800/377-2770, or go to their web page *www.bbonline.com/natcheztrace/index.html.*

Tennessee Bed & Breakfast Inn-Keepers Association, 5341 Mountain View Rd., Ste. 150, Antioch 37013. For more information call 281/499-2735, fax 281/403-9335 or go to their web page *www.bbonline.com/tn.*
This Web site includes photographs, rates, descriptions, and one or two recipes from each bed-and-breakfast listed. *The Williamson County Bed & Breakfast Inns Association* publishes their own brochure. They can be reached at www.bbonline.com /tn/williamson/

615/799-8833
$$
Sweet Annie's is a contemporary home located 10 miles from the entrance to the Natchez Trace Parkway, offering stables, a swimming pool, and hot tub. Personal fitness and spa services, at an extra charge, can be arranged with your hosts, as can special yoga weekends. Bicyclists can arrange to be met at the airport. A full breakfast is included in the room rate. (West Nashville)

Campgrounds

LORETTA LYNN'S RANCH & CAMPGROUND
44 Hurricane Mills Rd.
Waverly 37078
931/296-7700
$–$$
Loretta's famous ranch is located 65 miles west of town (on I-40 toward Memphis), but a visit here, especially when Loretta is performing, will add just the right country-music adventure to your Nashville visit. Billboards posted around town tell when she'll be in residence. The campground has 200 sites for primitive camping at a moderate rate. RV sites and cabins are also available for early arrivals. (West Nashville)

Mary Entrekin/Bongo Java

4

WHERE TO EAT

Nashville has always been a "just-plain-good-food-and-lots-of-it" kind of town. Basic is the key word. To fully experience the vernacular cuisine of this area, visitors will want to sample more than one "meat and three" restaurant, more than one barbecue stand, and eat at least a bite of fried catfish. Because what's plentiful at the farmers market is their stock in trade, scanning the menus of plate-lunch restaurants all over town will serve as an informal guide to what foods are in season.

Tradition and loyalty are family values on the Nashville restaurant scene—the menus never change at the Loveless Café or Rotier's, and it is a rare day when there is not a waiting line at either.

The multitude of small ethnic eateries that has opened in Nashville over the past 10 years has added immensely to the city's culinary offerings. Because these restaurants are generally inexpensive, they have also begun to make inroads into the food vocabulary of a large segment of the population. The presence of many small Asian and Middle Eastern groceries have made formerly hard-to-find ingredients readily available to Nashville's small but growing coterie of professionally trained chefs.

This chapter begins with a list of restaurants organized by the type of food each offers. For details about each restaurant, dining spots are listed alphabetically within each geographic zone. Dollar-sign symbols indicate how much you can expect to spend per person for a meal (one appetizer, one entrée, and dessert) at each restaurant.

Price rating symbols:
$ Under $10/person
$$ $11 to $20
$$$ $21 and up

American/Contemporary

Cafe One Two Three (DN) p. 61
Cakewalk/Zola (MN) p. 62, 66
Capitol Grille (DN) p. 61
F. Scott's (WN) p. 81
Mad Platter (NN) p. 72
Midtown Café (MN) p. 68
Sasso (EN) p. 76
Sunset Grill (MN) p. 71
Tin Angel (MN) p. 71
Wild Iris (SN) p. 79

American/Traditional

Cherokee Resort & Steakhouse (EN)
    p. 73
Green Hills Grille (WN) p. 82
Houston's (MN) p. 66, 67
Ireland's (MN) p. 68
Jack Russell's: An American Cafe (SN)
    p. 78

Barbecue

Bar-b-Cutie (EN) p. 84
Center Point Pit Barbecue (NN) p. 84
Corky's Bar-B-Q (SN) p. 84
Hog Heaven (MN) p. 84
Mary's Kitchen and Catering (NN)
    p. 85
Ray's Bar-b-que (NN) p. 85
Tennessee's Best BBQ (MN) p. 85
Tex's World Famous BBQ (SN) p. 85
Whitt's Barbecue (all over town) p. 85

Breakfast

Capitol Grille (DN) p. 61
Corner Market (WN) p. 70, 81
Donut Den (WN) p. 81
Loveless Café (WN) p. 83
Meridee's Breadbasket (SN) p. 79
Pancake Pantry (MN) p. 68
Provence Breads & Café (MN) p. 69

Coffeehouses

Bongo Java (MN) p. 62, 80
Cafe Coco (MN) p. 80
Fido (MN) p. 80
J&J's Market/Broadway Coffee and
    Tea (MN) p. 80

Kijiji (NN) p. 80
Radio Cafe (EN) p. 80

Fast Food

Bro's (SN) p. 70, 77
Calypso Café (DN, MN) p. 61, 77
Kelley's Karry Out (EN) p. 73
San Antonio Taco Company (DN, WN)
    p. 63

Fine Dining

Capitol Grille (DN) p. 61
F. Scott's (WN) p. 81

Indian

Sitar (MN) p. 69

Italian

A Taste of Italy (WN) p. 62, 83
Basante's (MN) p. 62, 64
Sole Mio (DN) p. 64

Japanese

Asahi (WN) p. 81
Ichiban (DN) p. 62
Koto (DN) p. 62

Plate Lunch/Diners

Amy's at St. Cloud (DN) p. 59
Arnold's Country Kitchen (DN) p. 76
City Cafe (SN) p. 78
Dotson's (SN) p. 78
Elliston Place Soda Shop (MN)
    p. 67
Monell's (NN) p. 70, 73
Rachel's Garden (EN) p. 73
Satsuma Tea Room (DN) p. 63
Swett's Restaurant (WN) p. 66, 73
Sylvan Park Restaurant (MN) p. 71

Mexican

La Hacienda Taqueria (SN) p. 78
El Palenque (WN, SN) p. 78, 81

Middle Eastern

Ali Baba (EN) p. 76
Baraka Bakery and Restaurant (SN)
    p. 76

Neighborhood Bar & Grill
Green Hills Grille (WN) p. 82
Houston's (MN) p. 66, 67
Ireland's (MN) p. 68
Rotier's (MN) p. 69
Sportsman's Grille (MN,WN) p. 71, 83
Tin Angel (MN) p. 71

Pizza
Da Vinci's Gourmet Pizza (MN) p. 67
House of Pizza (DN) p. 61

Sandwiches
A Taste of Italy (WN) p. 62, 83
Bread & Co. (WN, SN) p. 77, 81
Corner Market (WN) p. 70, 81
Laurell's Central Market (SN) p. 79
Meridee's Breadbasket (SN) p. 79
Mosko's Muncheonette (MN) p. 68
Provence Breads & Café (MN) p. 69, 70
Vandyland (MN) p. 72

Seafood
Laurell's Central Market (SN) p. 79
Laurell's 2nd Avenue Oyster Bar (DN) p. 63

The Shack Seafood Restaurant (NN) p. 72

Thai
International Market (and International House) (MN) p. 66, 67
Siam Café (SN) p. 79

Vegetarian
Peaceful Planet (MN) p. 69
Windows on the Cumberland (DN) p. 64

DOWNTOWN NASHVILLE

AMY'S AT ST. CLOUD
500 Church St.
Nashville
615/242-2697
$

This welcome addition to downtown lunchtime restaurants serves changing daily specials as well as a nice sampling of sandwiches and salads. Yeast rolls here are scrumptious, and the specials lean toward comfort

Cafe One Two Three

Cafe One Two Three

DOWNTOWN NASHVILLE

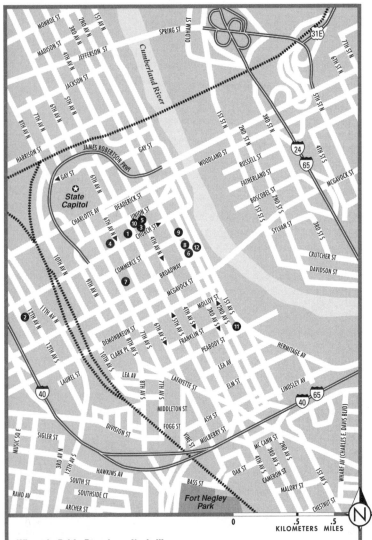

Where to Eat in Downtown Nashville

1 Amy's at St. Cloud
2 Cafe One Two Three
3 Calypso Café
4 Capitol Grille
5 House of Pizza
6 Ichiban
7 Koto
8 Laurell's 2nd Avenue Oyster Bar
9 San Antonio Taco Company
10 Satsuma Tea Room
11 Sole Mio
12 Windows on the Cumberland

foods like turkey and dressing or chicken pot pie. Service is quick, carryout is not a problem, the food is always good, and homemade desserts are featured. Lunch Mon–Fri. ♿ (Downtown)

CAFE ONE TWO THREE
123 12th Ave. N.
Nashville
615/255-2233
$\$–\$\$\$$

This beautiful restaurant in the "gulch," an industrial neighborhood next to the railroad tracks between downtown and West End, is an old storefront with brick walls, tile floors, tin ceilings, and a polished wood and brass bar. Comfortably formal, the white tablecloths and candlelit tables make this a perfect place for a romantic meal. The menu is one of the most innovative in town, with "new Southern" specialties that treat staples like grits and black-eyed peas with respect, pairing them with fresh fish, aged beef, and fine wines. One of the best restaurants to open in Nashville in years. Dinner Mon–Sat. ♿ (Downtown)

CALYPSO CAFÉ
21 The Arcade
Nashville
615/259-9631
$

The Calypso Café turns out consistently good food fast with carryout specialties like jerk chicken, black beans and rice, and calaloo (greens with seasonings). Chairs and tables are available out front in the Arcade, a fun place to watch passersby. Lunch weekdays. Additional locations: South and Midtown Nashville. ♿ (Downtown)

CAPITOL GRILLE
231 Sixth Ave. N., at the Westin Hermitage Hotel
Nashville
615/345-7116 or 615/244-3121
$$$

Preparing three meals daily, from delectable breakfast entrées such as eggs on smoked salmon with wild mushrooms and tomato béarnaise, to a pulled applewood-smoked pork sandwich (BBQ by another name) with pecan coleslaw and sweet potato fries, to nightly selections with suggested wines to accompany each course, this is one of Nashville's most interesting and accomplished kitchens. The dining room, located on the lower level of the historic Hermitage, Nashville's last grand hotel, is elegant, and the service is efficient and unpretentious. Chef Kevin Goodwin prepares imaginative dishes that rely alternately on Asian, New Mexican, Italian, and Cajun influences. The citrus-soy marinated seared tuna with crisp stir-fried vegetables and carrot ginger sauce takes sushi to an exciting crescendo, and the crème brûlée Napoleon with caramel sauce and roasted almonds is worth skipping lunch for. Breakfast, lunch, dinner daily. Reservations recommended for lunch and dinner. ♿ (Downtown)

HOUSE OF PIZZA
15 Arcade
Nashville
615/242-7144
$

A narrow restaurant with a large hot oven lining one wall, the House of Pizza offers a very simple menu that's hard to beat: fresh from the oven, thin-crust pizza by the slice and cold beer. This straightforward Italian-American restaurant could be found anywhere in the Northeast, but in Nashville it's a rare treat. Lunch Mon–Sat. ♿ (Downtown)

ICHIBAN
109 Second Ave. N.
Nashville
615/254-7185
$–$$

This friendly restaurant, with a full bar in front and a sushi bar in back, has two levels of dining and wonderful Japanese food ranging from "lunch box" meals, to *udon* and *soba* noodle dishes, to specials written only in Japanese. Their sushi is some of the best in town, and there is a handwritten menu on a small blackboard next to the sushi bar where those items not on the regular sushi bill of fare are explained. Ichiban, which has managed to survive the tourist explosion on Second Avenue so far, is usually crowded with Nashville residents even though parking downtown is getting tougher and tougher. Their special fried oysters in tempura are a treat, as is their cold steamed spinach with sesame sauce. Most telling is the fact that they have a very faithful Japanese clientele. Lunch and dinner daily. &
(Downtown)

KOTO
130 Seventh Ave. N.
Nashville
615/255-8122
$–$$

One-Hit Wonders

Architect Manuel Zeitlin, native Nashvillian and designer of some of Nashville's finest restaurant interiors, will drive a long distance for a fine meal:

"What I would give for a great Chinese restaurant, or even a noodle house. For now I have to be content with going to Chicago or Atlanta or New York or even Chattanooga for great complete meals. I guess it makes sense that in Nashville we are at least lucky to have one-hit wonders."

1. **Bi Bim Bap** at Arirang tops the list: bowl of rice, your selection of uniquely flavored Korean vegetables, and an egg on top (good as a hot lunch in winter)
2. **Sole Mio**'s mussels
3. **Arnold**'s fried oysters (Friday only)
4. **Varallo**'s chili with tamales and spaghetti and a side of turnip greens
5. **Basante**'s gnocchi
6. **The Barbecue** van at 18th and Charlotte (shoulder sandwich)
7. **Bongo Java**'s Juanita Burrita (for breakfast)
8. **A Taste of Italy**'s baked ricotta
9. **Cakewalk/Zola**'s Seafood Operetta
10. **East India Company**'s buffet

Koto's chef/owner is always visible behind the counter and is sometimes willing to invent new combinations on request. There are rolls here named after favored customers, and there's even a "Nashville Roll." All of the fresh fish is in sight on the long sushi counter, and the skilled chef is fascinating to watch. The service is efficient and graceful, and guests have a choice of regular or tatami-mat seating. Koto serves excellent tempura, rice, and noodle dishes as well. Lunch Tue–Fri, dinner Tue–Sun. &
(Downtown)

LAURELL'S 2ND AVENUE OYSTER BAR
123 Second Ave. N.
Nashville
615/244-1230
$–$$

Laurell's, in an old storefront with pressed-tin ceilings, offers Cajun-influenced food and features fresh oysters in season and a friendly bar. The red beans and rice is always done right and the gumbo can also be counted on. The service is unfailingly good, and daily specials are offered. Many artists have gotten their first Nashville visibility on the walls at Laurell's. This is a nice place to start an evening with oysters and beer or just have a cocktail at a table near the front and watch Second Avenue passersby. Lunch and dinner daily. (Downtown)

SAN ANTONIO TACO COMPANY
208 Commerce
Nashville
615/259-4413
$

SATCO, as this place is called by locals, serves up consistently good Tex-Mex selections in a huge dining room. Self-service ordering and pickup make

this a quick place for a cheap and filling meal to eat in or take out. Try a soft chicken taco with *pico de gallo*, and the *queso* and chips. A counter from which guests self-serve salsa and several versions of *pico de gallo* lets you doctor your food to your own taste. Started by two Vanderbilt law students from Texas, SATCO's original location right across from the campus (see Midtown zone for listing) has an outdoor patio where they serve buckets of iced-down beer. Lunch daily. &
(Downtown)

SATSUMA TEA ROOM
417 Union St.
Nashville
615/256-5211
$

Satsuma is Nashville's most beloved downtown lunchroom, so it's advisable to go either early or late in order to keep from having to stand in line (unless you're interested in eavesdropping on the local patois). This is a cozy dining room on two floors where the food is served on blue and gray stoneware from Louisville's famous Hadley pottery. The menu changes daily, but features homemade chicken noodle and other soups, old-fashioned hot dishes like chicken croquettes or turkey hash over cornbread paired with green peas and a congealed-cranberry salad. Regular daily specials like shrimp creole (Friday) keep their place on many business calendars. Satsuma's old-fashioned desserts and yeast rolls have no equal. The menu faithfully offers a low-calorie lunch, which I have never seen anyone order.

Satsuma is famous for box lunches of fried chicken, coleslaw, a ham roll and a pimento cheese sandwich, grapes, and Kentucky Derby pie, so if you are planning an all-day excursion take note. Homemade cakes and pies are available for takeout, as are the rolls. Lunch weekdays. Credit cards not accepted. Wheelchair-accessible only through the kitchen. (Downtown)

SOLE MIO
94 Peabody St.
Nashville
615/256-4013
$$

This contemporary Italian restaurant has lots of picture windows and a great view of downtown, overlooking Nashville from the heights of Rutledge Hill, a historic neighborhood located six blocks south of Broadway. Authentic Italian dishes (the herbs are grown right outside the door) at fair prices and a friendly atmosphere make this a lovely place for a quiet dinner for two on the deck or a large family meal at one of the round tables. Daily specials include mussels whenever they are available, and the chef does some kind of magic with tomato sauce with a touch of cream and vodka.

The Italian chef-owner and his wife are always much in evidence, and sometimes send tiny treats (appetizer nibbles before, a biscotti bite after the meal, or sometimes a really rich dessert for the table to share) just to show diners their appreciation. This is the sort of restaurant you are always hoping to find when you just go somewhere on instinct. Live music Fri and Sat evenings; brunch Sat and Sun; lunch, dinner Tue–Sun. & (Downtown)

WINDOWS ON
THE CUMBERLAND
112 Second Ave. N.
Nashville
615/251-0097
$

Located in the back of a Second Av-enue warehouse building, Windows on the Cumberland is a friendly and casual vegetarian restaurant whose dining area looks out over the Cumberland River. The simple fare at Windows always includes a daily pot of beans, steamed veggies and rice, and a great avocado sandwich. Several kinds of hot and iced tea are available, along with imported beers. Local musicians or poets often perform here at night. Lunch Tue–Sat, dinner Tue–Sun. No credit cards. (Downtown)

MIDTOWN NASHVILLE

BASANTE'S
1800 West End Ave.
Nashville
615/320-0534
$$–$$$

Don't be put off by this small restaurant's location in the Days Inn. Luis Fonseca is a talented chef and his terrific restaurant will send any gourmet diner away satisfied. The cuisine is Italian, but his approach, bringing unusual ingredients to old standards such as ravioli filled with seafood, or roasted chicken and spinach lasagna, breaks a few rules. The preparation is exquisite, the candelit, white-tableclothed ambience is romantic, and the service is well-informed and unpretentious.

A particularly nice touch is that Fonseca has prepared a wine list on which everything is available either by bottle or glass. Salads are tossed with a perfect and unusual lemon-dill vinaigrette, the grilled roasted pepper polenta appetizer has received raves from a number of friends, and the grilled pork tenderloin and portabella mushroom in port wine glaze is spectacular. The menu lists several vegetarian pastas and a number that

MIDTOWN NASHVILLE

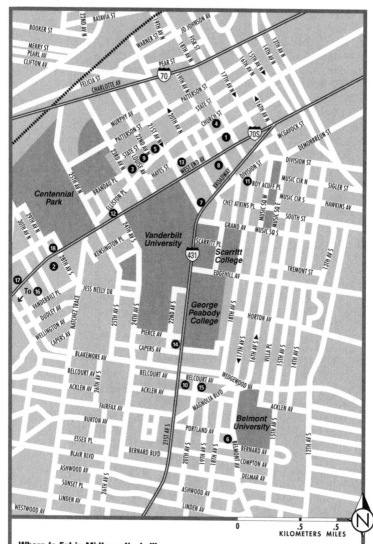

Where to Eat in Midtown Nashville

1 Basante's
2 Cakewalk/Zola
3 Calypso Café
4 Da Vinci's Gourmet Pizza
5 Elliston Place Soda Shop
2 Houston's
6 International Market (and International House)
7 Ireland's
8 Midtown Café
9 Mosko's Muncheonette

10 Pancake Pantry
11 Peaceful Planet
10 Provence Breads & Café
12 Rotier's
13 Sitar
14 Sportsman's Grille
15 Sunset Grill
16 Sylvan Park Restaurant
17 Tin Angel
18 Vandyland

0   .5   .5
KILOMETERS   MILES

include seafood or meat, including a melt-in-your-mouth gnocchi with tomato cream and pancetta. Chef Fonseca does not mind if diners break the cardinal rule and skip the entrée altogether. Lunch Mon–Fri; dinner Mon–Sat. & (Midtown)

CAKEWALK/ZOLA
3001 West End Ave.
Nashville
615/320-7778
$$–$$$

This small dining room has for many years been voted Nashville's best restaurant. The food is always exquisitely prepared and presented, the servers know something about wine, and the original chef, Debra Paquette, has recently returned as owner. The hybrid name reflects the restaurant's original name and Paquette's new muse, Zola, the spirit of the Mediterranean.

The seasonal menu features dishes that will always linger in the memory, such as veal Smen, shank grilled and marinated in Turkish chili paste with a dollop of yogurt feta cream and eggplant fries; or Moroccan lamb loin with Ras el Hanout spices served with pumpkin risotto and fall greens. Fresh fish, a variation on bouillabaisse, and three or four vegetarian entrées are always offered. The wine list has been carefully thought out, bread and rolls are made on the premises, and desserts include homemade sorbets and a baklava created from phyllo, pistachios, and brown sugar. Dinner daily. Reservations suggested. & (Midtown)

CALYPSO CAFÉ
2424 Elliston Pl.
Nashville
615/321-3878
$

For description, see listing in Downtown Nashville. A friend from Memphis stops in at this Calypso, just off West End Avenue, every time he passes

---

Favorite Dining Spots

Music Row insider and discerning diner Bobby Cudd, Talent Agent at Monterey Artists, takes his artists and out-of-town visitors to these favorite spots for good food and friendly service:

Lunch

   International Market *(order Thai Nam Sod or Kao Pao from the kitchen)*

   Swett's *(the original "meat and three" steam table)*

Dinner

   Shalimar *(chicken tikka masala with mango chutney, vegetable samosa)*

   Houston's *(Deluxe burgers in the closest thing Nashville has to an upscale London pub)*

---

through Nashville for a delicious, predictable, healthful, and cheap lunch. Lunch and dinner daily. (Midtown)

DA VINCI'S GOURMET PIZZA
1812 Hayes St.
Nashville
615/329-8098
$

Not too far from downtown, Vanderbilt, and Music Row, Da Vinci's is located in an attractive brick house that has tables outside in warm weather. Their pizza includes a range of toppings from grated vegetables piled high with three cheeses, to pesto and potatoes, to classic ingredients like Canadian bacon or aged pepperoni. The excellent house salad is big enough for two people. Da Vinci's, which serves a wide selection of imported beers, offers great service and cozy indoor seating. The bowl of big red-delicious apples offered free to diners at the cash register is symbolic of this restaurant's approach: Generous and healthy food is their top priority. Lunch Wed–Fri, dinner Tue–Sun. (Midtown)

ELLISTON PLACE SODA SHOP
2111 Elliston Pl.
Nashville
615/327-1090
$

Elliston Place is a classic soda fountain in what was once a drugstore—the octagonal tiles on the floor are original. There is seating at the counter for those who like to watch their milkshakes being prepared or who are just stopping by for a piece of homemade apple pie à la mode. One wall is lined with booths containing individual miniature jukeboxes, and the old Nashville Sound (George and Tammy, Loretta and Conway) wails continuously from the jukebox

at the rear. The waitresses have been here since these were top-10 hits, and the menu—fountain treats, hamburgers and grilled cheese sandwiches, and plate lunches with fried chicken on Tuesday and Saturday—has been the same for at least 20 years. Breakfast, lunch, and dinner Mon–Sat. Credit cards not accepted. (Midtown)

HOUSTON'S
3000 West End Ave.
Nashville
615/269-3481
$$

Hearty is the key word to describe the food at Houston's, a much-loved neighborhood bar and grill in the Vanderbilt University area. A well-stocked bar and a kitchen busy turning out brasserie-type meals like hamburgers and fries to-die-for, perfect steaks or grilled fish with fries, and huge salads filled with chicken, bacon, and more, keep this restaurant hopping. Their warm cobbler à la mode or chocolate cake and coffee make fine late-night snacks. Lunch and dinner daily. There's often a line on weekends, and reservations are not accepted. (Midtown)

INTERNATIONAL MARKET
(AND INTERNATIONAL HOUSE)
2010 Belmont Blvd.
Nashville
615/297-4453
$

The International Market is an Asian market that also serves a variety of Thai-inspired specialties from a steam table in the back. The tasty food, friendly atmosphere, and bargain prices make this one of Nashville's most popular spots for lunch or dinner. Insiders ask for specialties of the house, which the kitchen is happy to prepare if you have the time to wait.

Across the street is International House ($$–$$$, 615/297-4595), serving Thai haute cuisine—such as spicy red snapper or soft-shell crabs—that is well worth the elevated tab for exquisite service and outdoor seating among gardenia bushes and lime trees. Lunch Tue–Sat, dinner Tue–Sun. (Midtown)

IRELAND'S
204 21st Ave. S.
Nashville
615/327-2967
$$

An old favorite once stood on this same spot—home of the original "steak and biscuits"—baking powder biscuits stuffed with tenderloin bits and skerry fries (delicious crispy thin-fried potatoes). The original Ireland's, torn down nearly 20 years ago, has now reemerged as a spiffy new restaurant with a dark wood bar and a huge dining room. The owners are back in business, having never let the land go, even though several restaurants have come and gone since. The food tastes as good as ever, and lots of new specialties are sure to come. Save room for the fudge pie (a super-moist brownie with a crust). Lunch and dinner daily. & (Midtown)

MIDTOWN CAFÉ
102 19th Ave. S.
Nashville
615/320-7176
$$–$$$

Midtown Café is a favorite power-lunch spot near Music Row, located in what was once a house. Evenings are quieter, and the low lights are conducive to a romantic dinner. There's always a friendly bartender serving a nice selection of wines by the glass. The menu features American food with some interesting twists, such as Midtown pasta (linguini with marinara, pesto, and blue cheese) and Oriental chicken salad with citrus-soy dressing and crunchy chow mein noodles. Lunch weekdays, dinner daily. Reservations not accepted for lunch. & (Midtown—where else?)

MOSKO'S MUNCHEONETTE
2204 Elliston Place
Nashville
615/327-2658
$

Eat in or carry out from this newsstand, smoke shop, and lunch counter. Baked goods and special preparations like the toasted turkey munch sandwich—smoked turkey, sweet mustard, and fresh tomato on egg bread—or their exceptionally tasty chicken salad on croissants, keep customers coming in for more. It's a good place to grab some picnic fare, and the cold case in the back stocks import beers and bottled juices. Breakfast, lunch, and dinner daily. (Midtown)

PANCAKE PANTRY
1796 21st Ave. S.
Nashville
615/383-9333
$

A classic Nashville eatery, the fare is standard stuff—pancakes, sausage, bacon and eggs—but the quality is top notch and patrons don't mind sitting in very close quarters in order to enjoy their food. Kids will love "bears in the snow," chocolate pancakes with powdered sugar, and tiny "silver dollar" cakes. One version of the Music Row "power breakfast" can be observed (and often overheard) here.

The Pantry, long crowded into one large room has expanded into two

Be sure to sample the following Nashville-based food and drink (and you might want to take some home): Gerst Beer on tap (now bottled elsewhere); Market Street beer; Christie's Cookies (Christie Hauck's stroke of genius produces soft and luscious cookies that sell by the pound); Standard Candy Company's GooGoo Cluster.

big rooms in a nice brick building on its former site, anchoring the re "new" al of Hillsboro Village, much to the dismay of anti-gentrificationists. However, it's owned by the original family, and who's to say they can't have a new house if they want it? On weekends a line extends onto the sidewalk, and enterprising songwriters sometimes play for the crowd. Breakfast, lunch and dinner daily; closes early Mon. &. (Midtown)

PEACEFUL PLANET
1811 Division St.
Nashville
615/327-2033
$

Buffet-style service is all vegetarian—freshly prepared and always featuring vegan entrées and well labeled dishes for the picky eater and those with special diet needs. This place is airy and light-filled, a nice break any time of the day and always a friendly vibe. Breakfast, lunch, and dinner Mon–Fri 7–8:30, brunch Sun 9:30–2:30 &. (Midtown)

PROVENCE BREADS & CAFÉ
1705 21st Ave. S.
Nashville
615/386-0363
$

Provence is a country French–style bakery that makes perfect croissants, very thin baguettes, and an imaginative variety of breads, like buttermilk currant and flat Tuscan loaves, as well as succulent fruit tarts and fancy pastries. Diners can enjoy the breads along with coffee, homemade soups, a large variety of prepared salads displayed in a long case, and wonderful combination sandwiches in a cheerful salon facing the busy street outside. Open daily from seven in the morning. &. (Midtown)

ROTIER'S
2413 Elliston Pl.
Nashville
615/327-9892
$

Rotier's is Nashville's favorite college bar with booths, lots of import beers, and friendly service. Most people's hands-down favorite hamburger can be found here in the grilled cheeseburger on French bread. Rotier's also doubles as a diner, offering plate lunches. It is possible to snuggle into one of their old vinyl-covered booths and enjoy a totally healthy meal of steamed broccoli, baked potato, and squash casserole with a side order of fresh sliced tomatoes. As long as Mrs. Rotier is still on duty at the cash register, all will be well with the world. Lunch and dinner Mon–Sat. (Midtown)

SITAR
116 21st Ave. S.
Nashville
615/321-8889
$–$$
Sitar is a very small Indian restaurant

Midday Meal Favorites

Jocelyn Morneau, restaurant editor for *Nashville CitySearch* (*www.nashville.citysearch.com*), writes a regular column titled "Lunch Byte" in which she reviews lunch experiences. Below she lists some of her favorite places for midday meals, in order of how productive you can expect to be after paying the bill.

Where I go when I have to work after lunch:

1. **Corner Market** to taste the masterfully created Eclectic Salad. The combination of fresh strawberries, blue cheese, greens, and avocado in sesame vinaigrette justifies its signature spot on the menu.

2. **Food Company** for a sandwich of Thanksgiving-style turkey and you-just-can't-believe-it's-healthy low-fat artichoke spread. Meatless muffaletta packed with pesto is a close second.

3. **Koto** to meditate in the midst of a hectic day over the best bargain in town: soup, salad, cooked-to-order beef teriyaki, gyoza dumplings, and green tea—all for $5.

4. **Market Wraps** for any one of the trendy tortilla-wrapped sandwiches. Wrap it up, I'll take it.

5. **Provence** to ooh and ahh over the cheese and pastry cases, ultimately succumbing to any one of the tasty sandwiches, a side of roasted veggies, and—oh yes—dessert.

Where I go when I can nap after lunch:

6. **Bro's** for red beans and rice, cornbread, and lots of sweet tea to put out the fire.

7. **La Hacienda** for muchos chips, salsa, and real tacos on corn tortillas with fresh cilantro, lime, and avocado.

8. **Monell**'s on Fried Chicken Friday. Nothing compares to sharing bowls of good ol' fried chicken, country vegetables, and biscuits with strangers at someone else's family table.

9. **Séanachie Irish Pub** for a potato boxty and several spoonfuls of hot, homemade bread pudding.

serving fabulous, freshly-prepared cuisine. Their vegetarian dishes rival those of the best Indian restaurants, and the servers are genuinely helpful in accommodating diners' wishes.

Specialties include *karahai* dishes cooked in an Indian iron skillet. Aloo palak (spinach and potatoes) is especially good when done this way. They will also mix you a cocktail and Indian beers are available. Open daily for lunch and dinner. (Midtown)

SPORTSMAN'S GRILLE
1601 21st Ave. S.
Nashville
615/320-1633
$–$$

Sportman's Grille is a sports bar with TVs trained at the bar patrons, but there are several enclosed porch dining areas where you can choose to ignore the picture, if not all of the sound. Both locations serve up great burgers, a grilled chicken sandwich that's hard to beat, and fine smoked barbecue on delicious corn cakes. The West Nashville location is a favorite with families, particularly on Sunday nights. Lunch and dinner daily. Stays open late. Additional location: West Nashville. ਠ (Midtown)

SUNSET GRILL
2001 Belcourt Ave.
Nashville
615/386-3663
$$–$$$

Sunset Grill, a lovely quiet restaurant with dining rooms inside and out, is where Music Row and the rest of Nashville go for a serious lunch. The extensive menu, which could be characterized as "new American minimalist," offers "heart-healthy" selections (even for dessert) and draws on a wide variety of influences, especially the cooking of Louisiana and California. The fresh fish selections, which usually come grilled with appropriate herbs and paired with an unusual pasta, polenta, or potato preparation, are highly recommended. Salads and desserts are beautifully presented, there is an extensive wine list, and the service is always top notch. The dining room is open late—a great

time for people-watching at one of the in-crowd's favorite spots. Lunch weekdays, dinner daily. Reservations recommended. ਠ (Midtown)

SYLVAN PARK RESTAURANT
4502 Murphy Rd.
Nashville
615/292-9275
$

This one-room neighborhood restaurant is a Nashville phenomenon. The all-fresh-vegetable or "meat and three" plate lunches are consumed quickly here, and homemade pies must be ordered up front to save time. The lunchtime turnover is fast and furious, especially when it's "turkey (and dressing) day," and there is often a line. A good place for an early dinner without the crowds. The chocolate pie is an award winner. Lunch and dinner weekdays. Credit cards not accepted. ਠ (Midtown)

TIN ANGEL
3201 West End
Nashville
615/298-3444
$$

A handsome corner bar in an old brick building, Tin Angel also has a large, skylighted dining room. The menu here is eclectic and always interesting, with vegetarian selections in every category, and experimental daily specials. The Angel Louie pasta, Wilder Greens salad, and Parthenon Pita sandwich are some of the best simple veggie offerings in town, but Tin Angel also does a great meatloaf-and-fries catfish in a tortilla crust. The Salad Med—grilled shrimp, chickpeas, roasted eggplant, and feta over greens—was imported, along with a few other favorites, from the old Cakewalk menu by Rick and Vicki Bolsom, who have always owned Tin

Angel. Brunch Sun, lunch Mon–Fri, dinner Mon–Sat. & (Midtown)

VANDYLAND
2916 West End
Nashville
615/327-3868
$

This small lunchroom and soda fountain serves the kind of sandwiches that mom used to make—BLT, tuna salad, and grilled cheese—with a bowl of homemade chili or chicken noodle soup if you like. Sandwiches are made right before your eyes, and shakes and Coke are the beverages of choice. The front counter is filled with homemade chocolate candy. Lunch only Mon–Sat. Credit cards not accepted. & (Midtown)

NORTH NASHVILLE

MAD PLATTER
1236 Sixth Ave. N.
Nashville
615/242-2563
$$–$$$

Located in a historic storefront in Nashville's Germantown neighborhood, the Mad Platter has a cozy atmosphere enhanced by brick walls, white linens, and fresh flowers. Out of a tiny kitchen come beautifully arranged salads, unusual dinner specialties, and very rich desserts. The servers are knowledgeable, and a number of good wines, available by the glass, are suggested as pairings with entrées. Dishes such as roasted walleye pike with smoked tomato butter, or grilled ostrich (tastes like roast beef) with portabello mushrooms and sundried tomato Mornay sauce have earned this restaurant its favored standing among local food critics. The chef offers nightly three- and

five-course dinners, including wines for every course. Lunch weekdays, dinner Tue–Sat. Reservations recommended. & (North Nashville)

MONELL'S
1235 Sixth Ave. N.
Nashville
615/248-4747
$

Monell's is a family-style restaurant that serves "boarding house" fare in an old house in Germantown. Meat (like fried chicken) and three vegetables are the standard offerings, and desserts include banana pudding. Bowls of food are passed around the table and a full country breakfast is served on Saturday. For a truly southern experience, go to Monell's for Sunday "dinner" (the big hot lunch served at midday around these parts). Breakfast Sat, lunch Tue–Sun, dinner Tue–Sat. & (North Nashville)

THE SHACK SEAFOOD RESTAURANT
2420 Gallatin Pike
Madison

Market Street Brewery

Market Street Brewery and Public House

615/859-9777
$$

Diners waiting for a table at the Shack, located about 15 minutes up Gallatin Pike from downtown, can sip beer in a frosted mug, eat free roasted peanuts, and throw the shells on the floor. Kids will probably prefer the fried shrimp and oysters, but the menu contains oysters in all forms as well as a variety of broiled and steamed items for the health-conscious and both meat and vegetarian selections. Service is fast and friendly once you get to your table. The Shack takes reservations. Open nightly. ♿ (North Nashville)

SWETT'S RESTAURANT
2725 Clifton Ave.
Nashville
615/329-4418
$

In continuous operation by one family at several different locations since 1954, Swett's, formerly known as Swett's Dinette before it expanded into its spacious modern facility, has a well-deserved reputation for good food. Cafeteria-style service features a changing daily choice of meats, vegetables, and desserts. "Meat and two" (two vegetables) at Swett's comes with homemade corn bread. Lunch and dinner daily. ♿ (North Nashville)

EAST NASHVILLE

CHEROKEE RESORT & STEAKHOUSE
450 Cherokee Dock Rd.
Lebanon
615/452-1515
$$

The drive from Nashville—through Hendersonville or Hermitage—on Highway 109 is a beautiful one beside Old Hickory Lake. Just past

Reba McEntire's Starstruck Farm, you'll see the road to this place, a family-style steakhouse where they cook your food on the grill for you. It's BYOB, but rated top notch by friends in the know, and a good place to spot interesting folks stepping off their boats after an afternoon afloat. Open for dinner Tue–Sun. (East Nashville)

KELLEY'S KARRY OUT
400 Gallatin Pike
Nashville
615/868-9248
$

Green shamrocks on the side of the building give this place away. It's possibly the only drive-through "meat and three" in the world. Daily selections are featured on a marquee so passersby can read from their cars and wheel in for a plate lunch. Delicious homemade foods and friendly servers make this worth a little detour across the river. For those who prefer to dine in comfort, a small dining room has been added on in the back. Open Mon–Sat. Credit cards not accepted. ♿ (East Nashville)

RACHEL'S GARDEN
The Hermitage
4580 Rachel's Ln.
Nashville
615/885-5735
$

This pleasant cafeteria-style eatery is on the grounds of The Hermitage, but outside the admission gates so that visitors may dine whether or not they are visiting the former home of Andrew and Rachel Jackson. Daily "meat-and-three" plates are inexpensive, and desserts include lemon chess and fudge pies—both are very rich and delicious old-fashioned

GREATER NASHVILLE

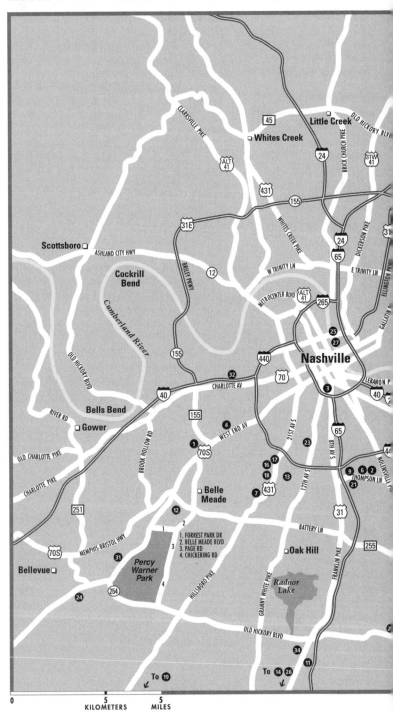

Little Creek
Whites Creek
Scottsboro
Cockrill Bend
Cumberland River
Bells Bend
Gower
Nashville
Belle Meade
Percy Warner Park
Bellevue
Oak Hill
Radnor Lake

CLARKSVILLE PIKE
OLD HICKORY BLVD
BRICK CHURCH PIKE
ASHLAND CITY HWY
BRILEY PKWY
WHITES CREEK PIKE
DICKERSON PIKE
ELLINGTON PKWY
W TRINITY LN
E TRINITY LN
METROCENTER BLVD
GALLATIN
OLD HICKORY BLVD
RIVER RD
CHARLOTTE AV
OLD CHARLOTTE PIKE
CHARLOTTE PIKE
BROOK HOLLOW RD
WEST END AV
21ST AV S
S 8TH AV
12TH AV S
THOMPSON LN
NOLENSVILLE
LEBANON P
BATTERY LN
MEMPHIS BRISTOL HWY
HILLSBORO PIKE
GRANNY WHITE PIKE
FRANKLIN PIKE
OLD HICKORY BLVD

1. FORREST PARK DR
2. BELLE MEADE BLVD
3. PAGE RD
4. CHICKERING RD

To 19
To 14 26

0   5   5
KILOMETERS   MILES

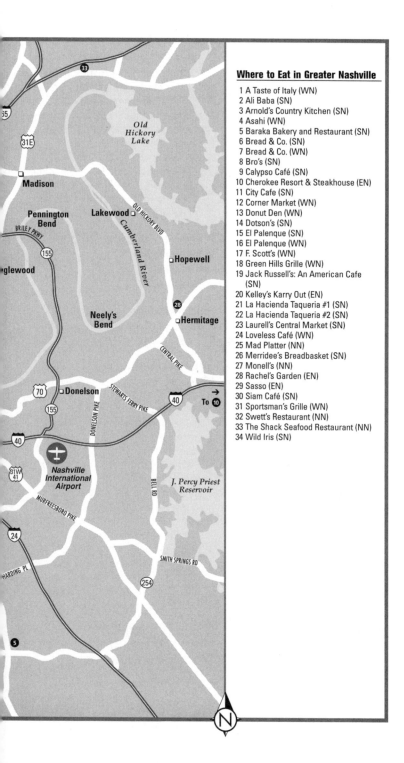

Where to Eat in Greater Nashville

1 A Taste of Italy (WN)
2 Ali Baba (SN)
3 Arnold's Country Kitchen (SN)
4 Asahi (WN)
5 Baraka Bakery and Restaurant (SN)
6 Bread & Co. (SN)
7 Bread & Co. (WN)
8 Bro's (SN)
9 Calypso Café (SN)
10 Cherokee Resort & Steakhouse (EN)
11 City Cafe (SN)
12 Corner Market (WN)
13 Donut Den (WN)
14 Dotson's (SN)
15 El Palenque (SN)
16 El Palenque (WN)
17 F. Scott's (WN)
18 Green Hills Grille (WN)
19 Jack Russell's: An American Cafe (SN)
20 Kelley's Karry Out (EN)
21 La Hacienda Taqueria #1 (SN)
22 La Hacienda Taqueria #2 (SN)
23 Laurell's Central Market (SN)
24 Loveless Café (WN)
25 Mad Platter (NN)
26 Merridee's Breadbasket (SN)
27 Monell's (NN)
28 Rachel's Garden (EN)
29 Sasso (EN)
30 Siam Café (SN)
31 Sportsman's Grille (WN)
32 Swett's Restaurant (NN)
33 The Shack Seafood Restaurant (NN)
34 Wild Iris (SN)

Tennessee specialties. Late breakfast and lunch daily. ♿ (East Nashville)

SASSO
1400 Woodland St.
Nashville
615/226-7942
$-$$

Chef-owners Anita Hartel and Corey Griffith, after time spent as lead chefs and sous-chefs at several of Nashville's best, have teamed with co-owner Nina Neal to create Nashville's most sophisticated new American cuisine restaurant. They have taken a two-story wooden storefront building and turned it into white-clothed, dark walled dining rooms, with a well-stocked wooden bar on the first floor. The lengthy menu thrives on pairing exotic, familiar and gourmet ingredients in thematic entrées such as Szechwan peanut-crusted salmon over crispy noodles with stir-fried bok choy, and pan-roasted chicken with mission figs, Yukon potatoes, apples, and lemon thyme. Vegetarian choices are enticingly original—vegetable tamales with papaya salsa, or Tuscan-style risotto with spinach aioli. The wine list is reasonable, descriptive, and well-chosen, and desserts usually include one or more kinds of creme brûlee and a homemade fruit tart of the day. This is one of the most exciting kitchens in Nashville, hidden on a side street in a historic residential neighborhood that is making a comeback among young Nashvillians. Lunch Mon–Fri, dinner Mon–Sat. ♿ (East Nashville)

SOUTH NASHVILLE

ALI BABA
216 Thompson Ln.
Nashville
615/333-3711
$

Persian specialties are featured in this tiny, charming restaurant with peach-colored tablecloths and exotic original art on the walls. All manner of authentic gyros are ready to slice, accompanied by fragrant basmati rice. Unusual spices flavor the Persian vegetable stew, and the daily soups, salads, dips, and spreads are freshly prepared and delicately seasoned. Lunch and dinner daily. ♿ (South Nashville)

ARNOLD'S COUNTRY KITCHEN
605 Eighth Ave. S.
Nashville
615/256-4455
$

Cafeteria-style breakfasts and lunches are presided over by Jack Arnold himself, who pours ice tea and takes money at the end of the line. Fresh vegetables, good hot breads (biscuits, rolls, corn bread, and corn cakes), and variety that includes a daily steamship round of roast beef and fried oysters on Friday, keep the customers coming back. Hot fruit cobblers are on the steam table occasionally, and there are almost always fried apples if the cream pies at the front of the line are too much for your sweet tooth. When Arnold's gets crowded, the patrons are willing to share tables, which makes for interesting company. Its location is close enough to Music Row for celebrity-spotting. Breakfast and lunch weekdays. Credit cards not accepted. ♿ (South Nashville)

BARAKA BAKERY
AND RESTAURANT
5596 Nolensville Rd.
Nashville

615/333-9285
$

Fresh pita from the oven and Middle
Eastern pastries are what qualifies
Baraka as a bakery, but it could just
as well be called a large restaurant
with a grocery store on the side.
Baraka, owned by two families from
Damascus, serves wonderful lamb
shawerma (marinated and sliced
from a skewer) and a roasted *baba
ganouj* that is out of this world. Their
fatayer—spinach, meat, cheese, or
herb pies—are inexpensive carry-
along meals in themselves. Eat in and
sample the fava bean salad on the
side, with Arab coffee for dessert and
a pistachio baklava to finish it off.
Late breakfast, lunch and dinner daily.
& (South Nashville)

BREAD & CO.
2607 Cruzen St.
Nashville

615/742-3522
$

For description, see listing in West
Nashville section. (South Nashville)

BRO'S
Nolensville Rd.
Nashville
615/350-8866
$

Bro's offers real Cajun food—red
beans and rice, gumbo, jambalaya,
boudin sausage. Eat in or take some
out for an instant gourmet picnic.
Beer only. Lunch Mon–Sun, dinner
weekdays. Credit cards not accepted.
& (South Nashville)

CALYPSO CAFÉ
722 Thompson Ln.
Nashville
615/297-6530
$

For description, see the Downtown

Mexican Madness

*Deann McCarty Bradford, manager of community relations for the
Nashville International Airport, is a Roswell, New Mexico, native who
has lived in Nashville since 1977. Every August she has a crate of
fresh green chiles shipped overnight so that she can make authentic rellenos.*

*"When I first moved here, the only 'Mexican' restaurants were
the franchises," says Bradford. "Fortunately, in the past five years
or so we have had an influx of real Mexican cuisine, and there are
places like El Palenque on Nolensville Road and Monterrey on
Murfreesboro Road where we love to go. We've even found Loco
Lupe's on Lebanon Road to use fresh green chiles and have very
good rellenos."*

La Hacienda Taqueria serves an authentic Mexican *barbacoa* on Saturday and Sunday. The lean crusty pork with red chile sauce on a soft taco makes a distinguished rival to Southern-style "Q."

Nashville section. Lunch daily, dinner weekdays. (South Nashville)

CITY CAFE
330 Franklin Rd.
Brentwood
615/373-5555
$

The legacy of Nashville's famous "meat-and-three" owner Hap Townes lives on in this little family restaurant. Erfie Williams, manager and cook for Hap Townes for 16 years, supervises the kitchen, which turns out homemade food worth a trip out of town to sample. Chicken and dumplings, turnip greens, and caramel pie keep the old-timers coming back—but it's the stewed raisins, a Hap Townes original, that make this place special. Lunch weekdays, dinner Mon–Thu. & (South Nashville)

DOTSON'S
99 E. Main St.
Franklin
615/794-2805
$

This is a well-loved Franklin home-cooking restaurant. Dotson's serves biscuits, bacon, eggs, sausage, and grits, as well as a full range of plate-lunch meals. Breakfast, lunch, and dinner daily. Credit cards not accepted. & (South Nashville)

EL PALENQUE
4407 Nolensville Pike
Nashville
615/832-9978
$

El Palenque is a nice two-room restaurant with booths all around and typical, brightly-colored hats and other decorations adorning the walls. Authentic dishes such as chile *rellenos*, chile Colorado, and *carne asada* are featured, along with the usual assortment of tacos, tostadas, and enchiladas. Opened in 1986, this is one of Nashville's first in a wave of real Mexican eateries and is still owned by its original owner. Lunch and dinner Mon–Sat. Additional location: West Nashville. & (South Nashville)

LA HACIENDA TAQUERIA
#1 AND #2
2615 Nolensville Rd.
and 15560 Old Hickory Blvd.
Nashville
615/256-6142 and 615/833-3716
$

This restaurant, which began as a tortilla factory, makes corn tortillas on the premises. A grocery store connected with it does a brisk business, but it excels as an authentic eatery and is always busy with Mexican patrons on Saturday and Sunday, when they prepare *menudo* (tripe stew) and *barbacoa*. No alcohol is served, but there are lots of Mexican soft drinks to try. Breakfast, lunch, and dinner daily. & (South Nashville)

JACK RUSSELL'S:
AN AMERICAN CAFE

2179 Hillsboro Rd.
Franklin
615/794-1444
$$

This is a true roadhouse, located next to the little CY grocery famous among Franklinites for carryout barbecue and morning sausage and biscuits. Jack Russell's, named, of course, for the owner's dog and every other dog whose snapshot is pinned up on the bulletin board, is decorated in barnwood siding. Part of the rough and cozy atmosphere is a wonderful aroma that wafts over from the meat and fish being smoked on the premises.

The lunch menu includes a pulled-pork BBQ sandwich and a smoked-chicken pizza, but it's the dinner specialties such as braised lamb shanks and marinated pork chop with sage pesto that cause folks to get back out on the road on Friday, Saturday, and Sunday nights. Beer is served, but patrons are invited to brown bag it if they like. Lunch and dinner Tue–Sun. & (South Nashville)

LAURELL'S CENTRAL MARKET
2317 12th Ave. S.
Nashville
615/292-1177
$

Take out or eat in from Laurell's Cajun-influenced counter, in a little up-and-coming neighborhood not too far from Music Row and the Belmont University campus. Crawfish Étouffée, fresh crab and crawfish cakes, jalapeño corn chowder, shrimp jambalaya, shrimp gumbo, red beans and rice all get the highest ratings. Prepared shrimp *remoulade* and Savannah chicken salads are ready in a cold case, as are spinach-basil lasagna and vegetarian gumbo for the non–meat eater. Get them to

make you a spectacular picnic, with some broccoli salad, Zapps chips, and a brownie to go. Lunch and dinner Mon–Sat. & (South Nashville)

MERRIDEE'S BREADBASKET
110 Fourth Ave. S.
Franklin
615/790-3755
$

Baked goods, homemade soups, yummy chicken-salad sandwiches on a choice of bread, and desserts to eat in or take home are the specialties of this lively establishment in downtown Franklin. There are enough tables for lingering over lunch or coffee and enough variety of healthful breads to try that patrons will want to take home more than one. Breakfast and lunch Mon–Sat. & (South Nashville)

SIAM CAFÉ
316 McCall St.
Nashville
615/834-3181
$

This nice little restaurant, one of Nashville's first Thai establishments, has excellent food, very polite service, and reasonable prices. The *sate* and *mee grob* appetizers and *tom kai* soup, shared by two or three patrons, can almost make a meal, but the whole snapper, cooked in a sweet hot sauce, is not to be missed. Lunch Mon–Sat, dinner nightly. & (South Nashville)

WILD IRIS
127 Franklin Rd.
Brentwood
615/370-0871
$$-$$$

A small dining room in a strip shopping center, Wild Iris has a nice bar along one side. Art on the walls and low lighting create a cozy feel. Servers here are knowledgeable

Coffeehouses

Nashville's coffeehouses—which in the true bohemian sense serve not only coffee but short-order food, live performances of music and poetry, and often a dollop of whatever's going around gossip-wise—are growing in number. Some even serve beer and stay up late. Check out any one of them for a jolt of more than just joe.

Bongo Java *(MN)*
> *2007 Belmont Blvd., 615/385-5282*
> *Hours: Breakfast, lunch, dinner weekdays;*
> *brunch Sat–Sun.*

Cafe Coco *(MN)*
> *210 Louise Ave., 615/329-2871*
> *Hours: Open 24 hours daily.*

Fido *(MN)*
> *1812 21st Ave. S., 615/777-3436*
> *Hours: Breakfast Mon–Sat.*

J&J's Market/Broadway Coffee and Tea *(MN)*
> *1912 Broadway, 615/327-9055*
> *Hours: Breakfast daily; lunch, dinner Mon–Fri.*

Kijiji *(NN)*
> *1413 Jefferson St., 615/321-0403*
> *Hours: Breakfast, lunch, dinner Mon–Sat.*

Radio Cafe *(EN)*
> *1313 Woodland St., 615/262-1766*
> *Hours: Breakfast, lunch, dinner Mon–Sat;*
> *mid-afternoon Sun.*

about the surprisingly artistic menu, which pairs each entrée with a suggested wine and displays a virtuosic command of ingredients. Salads are particularly nice, with special touches such as toasted nuts, citrus vinaigrettes, and spicy additions such as watercress, fennel leaves, and arugula to wake up the taste buds. Entrées range from coq *au vin* served in pastry to lobster Americaine, medallions of tender meat with caramelized vegetables in brandy cream. For dessert, try the refreshing European-style fruit and cheese platter. Lunch and dinner weekdays, dinner only Sat. ৬ (South Nashville)

WEST NASHVILLE

ASAHI
5215 Harding Rd.
Nashville
615/352-8877
$–$$
The sushi is beautiful at Asahi, and if you order carefully, you may get away for under $10. Service takes a while when they are busy, so it's best to order all the sushi you want the first time. Handrolls are particularly good at Asahi, as are some of the special appetizers. This is a tiny restaurant that can get quite full, but it's a comfortable place to go alone. The attentive servers will take good care of you, from the hot-towel greeting to recommendations of several kinds of cold sake. Lunch and dinner Mon–Fri, dinner only Sat. ৬ (West Nashville)

BREAD & CO.
4105 Hillsboro Pike/106 Page Rd. (two locations)
Nashville
615/292-7323 or 615/352-7323
$
Nashville's first European-style bakery offers a wide range of heavy country breads and a selection of delicate French pastries. Pastry, sandwiches, and coffees are available to carryout or eat on the premises, starting mornings at seven. Closed Sun. Additional location: South Nashville. ৬ (West Nashville)

CORNER MARKET
6051 Hwy. 100,

West End-Harding Rd. extended
Nashville
615/352-6772
$
Fresh produce racks greet customers who walk among rows of gourmet delicacies to the counter to place their order. Diners who pick up their delicious sandwiches, soups, and salads can eat in the store at tiny tables or out front at picnic tables. The only problem with stopping here for lunch or a wonderful continental breakfast is that it's hard to leave without an armload of fresh bread and cheese, a sushi-quality tuna steak, exotic salad greens, or Italian chocolates. Breakfast, lunch and dinner daily. ৬ (West Nashville)

DONUT DEN
3900 Hillsboro Pike
Nashville
615/385-1021
$
This cheery spot is open 24 hours, beckoning late-nighters after an evening of music, a formal party, or even a long night at the library. Homemade old-fashioned (unglazed) cake and yeast donuts are their specialty—try them chocolate-frosted or maple sugar–iced. They have milk. Open 24 hours daily. ৬ (West Nashville)

EL PALENQUE
2208 Crestmoor
Nashville
615/383-6142
$
For description, see listing in the South Nashville section. (West Nashville)

F. SCOTT'S
2210 Crestmoor Rd.
Nashville
615/269-5861
$$$

F. Scott's is a quiet, beautifully decorated restaurant with one of the nicest piano bars in town. Located outside of the city center in a suburban location, F. Scott's was chosen as the best restaurant in the *Nashville Scene*'s reader's poll in 1997 and 1998.

The menu, which changes four to five times yearly, features seasonal entrées ranging from salmon on a bed of red lentils and spinach to roasted and grilled meats like the braised lamb shank in rosemary broth. One or more vegetarian entrées are always included, and appetizers, such as pan-fried oysters with apple julienne and miso vinaigrette, soups like the lobster bisque with roasted corn relish, and desserts such as pear tart *tatin*, will make diners want to linger for a long time in the pleasant dining room.

Chef Margot McCormack, a graduate of the Culinary Institute of America, grew up in Tennessee. Nashvillians hope she is here to stay.

The nightly live jazz in the lounge is piped in to the restaurant, which adds a wonderful aliveness to the experience of dining here and might prompt you to request dessert and coffee be served in the bar. Dinner daily. Reservations recommended. &
(West Nashville)

GREEN HILLS GRILLE
2122 Hillsboro Dr.
Nashville
615/383-6444
$–$$
This is a new and improved kind of neighborhood bar and grill, with a bar in the center, two big dining rooms, two smaller windowside rooms, and a foyer too small for the number of people usually waiting in line. Green Hills Grille is a popular place, with enough panache to attract a wide range of customers, from music-business types to buttoned-down bankers. The menu has enough variety to satisfy a family of diverse eaters (they have a good children's menu). The basic hamburger is an event here, but so also

---

Nashville's Eclectic Cuisine

Anita Hartel, one of the first local chefs to grow her own kitchen garden for restaurant use, has cooked at F. Scott's, Cakewalk, and Tin Angel, and will soon be opening her own restaurant, Sasso, in East Nashville. She also worked a brief stint several years back as a private nutrition counselor to Wynonna Judd.

"The great thing about Nashville is that you can be working in a restaurant that's doing multiethnic cuisine, and just a mile or so down the road, be able to grab some wonderful home cooking at a 'meat and three,' like Arnold's, on your afternoon lunch break,"
remarks Hartel.

A hot dog stand on Music Row

are the rich but delicate tortilla soup, the Italian chop salad, and the crème brûlée. Lunch and dinner daily. Reservations not accepted. ♿ (West Nashville)

LOVELESS CAFÉ
8400 Hwy. 100
Nashville
615/646-9700
$

An old motel café, the Loveless has become famous around the country for its fabulous breakfasts of country ham, hot biscuits, and homemade peach and blackberry preserves. They even have a mail-order catalog. The fried chicken is excellent, and biscuits and gravy are also served at dinnertime. Reservations are a must; this place is packed to overflowing on weekends. They have expanded into a portion of the motel, with several rooms opened up to accommodate diners at a breakfast buffet. However, the original café dining rooms, with attentive service and foods prepared to order, are preferable. Breakfast, lunch and dinner daily. Reservations are

mandatory. Credit cards are not accepted. (West Nashville)

SPORTSMAN'S GRILLE
5405 Harding Rd.
Nashville
615/356-6206
$

For description, see listing in the Midtown Nashville section. ♿ (West Nashville)

A TASTE OF ITALY
73 White Bridge Rd.
Nashville
615/354-0124
$

A gourmet grocery and sandwich bar, this is a not-to-be-missed opportunity to munch a true *panini* (toasted sandwich with real *parma* ham and fresh mozzarella) or try a bruschetta (Tuscan bread with roasted peppers and olive oil) from which to gauge all others. Try them with San Pellegrino mineral water and a perfect espresso and you'll leave the café with a lighter step. Lunch Mon–Sat. ♿ (West Nashville)

Barbecue Joints

Barbecue joints in Music City aren't regular restaurants—they are stages set for one or two stars and a few sidemen. Smoked chicken or pork-shoulder sandwiches, whether pulled from the bone in feathery strips or chopped, are the main attraction. They should have almost no fat, and sauce should be added at the last moment before consuming. Add a side of slaw or beans and greens, and you have a filling meal for under $10. Here's a list of the best of the best and their specialties:

BAR-B-CUTIE, 501 Donelson Pike, Nashville
615/872-0207
In business since 1948, Bar-B-Cutie has recently opened several new restaurants around the area, including ones in Lebanon and Murfreesboro. Their pulled-pork barbecue has an excellent smoked flavor. Side orders include turnip greens; white, pinto, and baked beans; and corncakes instead of buns. Too bad their slaw is sub-par because they consistently serve the best barbecue sandwiches in town. Drive-through is an option at all restaurants. Lunch and dinner daily. (East Nashville)

CENTER POINT PIT BARBECUE, Gallatin Pike, Hendersonville
615/824-9330
Minced, chopped, and pulled pork with red slaw, white beans, or barbecue beans are the specialities of the house as are the "three little pigs" (three small sandwiches). A sign in the front window invites guests to "pig in or pig out." Breakfast, lunch, and dinner daily. (North Nashville)

CORKY'S BAR-B-Q, 100 Franklin Rd., Brentwood
615/373-1020
Memphis-based Corky's brought its famous ribs to Nashville several years ago (they do a major overnight air-mail business from the home location). Maybe I'm biased, but I don't think the sandwiches here are quite up to Middle Tennessee standards. Drive-through or eat in to taste Memphis-style chopped pork with a smoky sweet sauce. Lunch and dinner daily. (South Nashville)

HOG HEAVEN, 115 27th Ave. N., Nashville
615/329-1234
Hog Heaven is a barbecue stand right next to Centennial Park that has picnic tables under an awning out front. They not only have some of the best pulled pork pit barbecue in town, but they also serve vegetable plates, corncakes,

Zapp's potato chips, and smoked chicken and turkey. Fast and accommodating window service and free neighborhood delivery make this a great place to pack a picnic or to order room service to a West End-area hotel. Lunch and dinner Mon–Sat. (Midtown)

MARY'S KITCHEN AND CATERING, 1041 Jefferson St., Nashville
615/256-5509
With a pit out back and a counter opening directly onto Jefferson Street, Mary's Kitchen serves pulled-pork and rib sandwiches on white bread (the latter is not exactly a sandwich, since the bones are still in) with hot vinegar sauce until late at night. This place is a Nashville legend, and many stop by on the way home from the music clubs for a sandwich to go. Lunch and dinner Mon–Sat. (North Nashville)

RAY'S BAR-B-QUE, 610 N. Main, Goodlettsville
615/859-4288
Ray serves pulled pork and ribs smoked out front, granny's corncakes (Granny makes an appearance now and then behind the counter), homemade slaw, greens, and pinto beans. Ray says "hog in with us." Worth a stop on your way to the nearby Long Hollow Jamboree for a night of country dancing. Breakfast, lunch, and dinner daily. (North Nashville)

TENNESSEE'S BEST BBQ, 2014 West End Ave., Nashville
615/321-3800
Pulled-pork sandwiches with a choice of six different sauces created by a barbeque consultant—one in the style of each Southern state. A novel concept for a prototype franchise. Clean and friendly and the barbecue is moist and smoky. Drive through if you like. Lunch and dinner daily. (West Nashville)

TEX'S WORLD FAMOUS BBQ, 1013 Foster Ave., Nashville
615/254-8715
Tex prepares sliced-beef brisket with all the Texas-style fixings, pintos, potatoes, and slaw—and serves it with a sweet, dark sauce. Lyndon Johnson would be proud. Lots of ex-patriate Texans manage to find their way over from Music Row to lunch here. Lunch Mon–Sat. (South Nashville)

WHITT'S BARBECUE, 4601 Andrew Jackson Pkwy., Nashville
615/885-4146
Another Nashville original, Whitt's, with eight locations around town, is consistently voted "best barbecue in Nashville" in the *Nashville Scene* readers' polls. Whitt's offers good pork and beef sandwiches, and the vinegar-based sauce is tasty, but the barbecue tends toward the tender and mild, as opposed to the crusty and well-smoked taste that many afficionados prefer. Drive through at all locations. Lunch and dinner daily. (East Nashville)

5

SIGHTS AND ATTRACTIONS

Sightseeing in Nashville should, by rights, begin at the riverfront, since that's where the first settlers of "French Lick" built their stockade. Fort Nashborough stands near the spot where James Robertson, John Donelson, and about 200 other members of the "official" homestead party met their patron, Richard Henderson, to sign the Cumberland Compact in 1780, which requested a territorial charter from the state of North Carolina. A walking tour of the modern city will take you up Nashville's original Market Street (Second Avenue) to the quietly austere Davidson County Courthouse, built on the site of what was once the young town's teeming public market. Turning up Deaderick Street, a grand boulevard that leads one steadily towards the majestic War Memorial Building, this somber mood continues. At the top of the street, steps climb up to a large public plaza, with further steps leading into an open columned courtyard containing a large monument to the heroes of World War I. The height of the plaza, the graceful spaces, and the positioning of various pieces of monumental sculpture around it, all connote political power. The architectural plan of the War Memorial Auditorium, entered from the atrium-courtyard, refers to the idealized government of classical Greece. To the north, upon an ever higher hill, sits another Greek Revival building, the Tennessee State Capitol, designed by architect William Strickland. Clearly, this is a city whose ambitions have run high for almost all of its 200 years.

Leaving the "official" city center, a walk south will bring you to more pedestrian sights that have contributed to the making of Nashville's unique culture. The Hermitage Hotel, for example, was where both suffragists and anti-suffragists mustered support before the Tennessee legislature's decisive vote on the Nineteenth Amendment. Following Broadway, Nashville's original "main" street, west about five blocks, you come to another great civic gathering place, the Union Station Terminal, which sits on the edge of downtown above a wide gulch crisscrossed with railroad tracks. The significance of Nashville's role in the westward expansion of this country is symbolized in the short distance from the river to rail.

From its prominent heights, the city unfolds in fanning roadways toward the western horizon, past Vanderbilt University's solemn buildings arranged around grass quadrangles, to more leisurely spaces dedicated to a lifestyle of grace and ease, higher learning, and the pursuit of commerce, such as Centennial Park with its full-scale replica of the Parthenon (now a museum), its changing array of seasonal plantings, its band shell, and its perpetually lively duck pond; and Cheekwood, a Museum of Art and Botanical Gardens converted from the 1930s estate of one of America's barons of industry.

WALKING TOURS

The Metropolitan Nashville Historical Commission has designed a self-guided, two-mile walking tour of the city that begins at the reconstructed Fort Nashborough, the Cumberland Compact stockade overlooking the Cumberland River. The stop-and-read signposts are life-sized metal silhouettes of historic figures—you can't miss their greenish-blue presence—arranged along a line of the same color that runs down the middle of the sidewalk. An hour of moderate-paced walking and a quick scan of Nashville's historical sights provides a great orientation for visitors. For information and a printed copy of "City Walk," call the Historical Commission at 615/862-7970.

Historic Nashville offers a 1½-hour guided walking tour during the summer months that also begins at Fort Nashborough. The cost is $5 and tours are Saturday 10:30 a.m.– 2 p.m. year-round. A group of 10 or more can schedule a tour. For information, call 615/244-7835.

DOWNTOWN NASHVILLE

ACME FARM SUPPLY
101 Broadway
Nashville
615/255-5641
Acme Farm Supply's classic white building painted with Purina Chow's red-and-white checkerboard pattern is a friendly place to see Tennessee "farm culture" just like it always was, and a good place to purchase souvenirs the recipient might actually be able to use. For the locals, Acme is also the home of spring plant starts, bird feeders, and garden supplies. Mon–Sat 7:30–5. ♿ (Downtown)

THE ARCADE
Between Fourth and Fifth Aves.,
north of Church St.
Nashville
615/255-1034
The arcade is a two-story indoor shopping center with a glass-gabled roof dating from 1903. Stroll around the upper balcony, where the gold lettering on a frosted glass door may turn into "Sam Spade" before your very eyes. You can mail postcards from the charming U.S. Post Office branch here, get your old watch repaired by a master jeweler, buy antique buttons, ship fresh-roasted peanuts home, or grab a slice of great pizza fresh from the oven in a narrow restaurant called House of Pizza. Weekdays 6–6. Wheelchair accessible through lower level only. (Downtown)

DOWNTOWN NASHVILLE

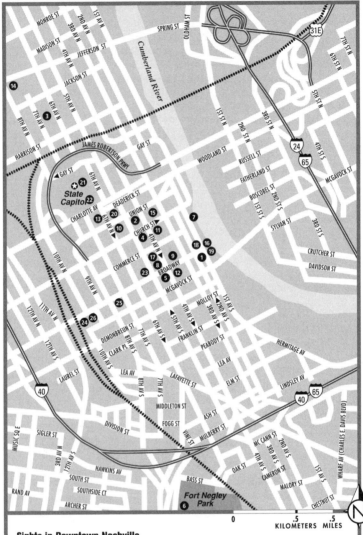

0   .5   .5
KILOMETERS   MILES

Sights in Downtown Nashville

1 Acme Farm Supply
2 The Arcade
3 Bicentennial Capitol Mall State Park
4 Downtown Presbyterian Church
5 Ernest Tubb's Record Shop No.1
6 Fort Negley
7 *General Jackson* Showboat/Music City Queen Opryland River Taxis

8 Gruhn Guitars, Inc.
9 Hatch Show Print
10 Hermitage Hotel
11 L & C Tower
12 Lawrence Brothers Records
13 Legislative Plaza and the War Memorial Auditorium
14 Nashville Farmers Market
15 Printer's Alley Historic District
16 Riverfront Park
17 The Ryman Auditorium

18 Silver Dollar Saloon
19 Tennessee Fox Trot Carousel
20 Tennessee Performing Arts Center
21 Tennessee State Capitol
22 Tennessee State Library and Archives
23 Tootsie's Orchid Lounge
24 Union Station
25 United States Customs House
26 United States Post Office

BICENTENNIAL CAPITOL MALL STATE PARK
Jefferson St., between Eighth and Sixth Aves. N.
Nashville
615/741-5280

On the site of the Great Salt (later known as French) Lick, where Indian hunting parties once followed deer and bison, where French trader Jacques-Timothe DeMontbrun came to trade with the Indians, where James Robertson had come on his exploratory visit into Cumberland country, stands the Tennessee Bicentennial Capitol Mall, dedicated in 1996 to commemorate 200 years of Tennessee history. The mall is based on a rectangular plan that leads the eye to the back of the capitol, which is on a hill just above the mall.

On one side of the mall is a garden of native limestone boulders and plantings arranged roughly to look like an outline of the state map, with medallions giving a brief description of each county carved into the walkways. Across a long, grassy, tree-lined plot is a timeline of Tennessee history, divided into 10-year segments, each marked by a granite pillar. Quotations from notable individuals concerning the events of each period, the founding of the state, the removal of the Indians, the slavery question, the Civil War, Reconstruction, Prohibition, and the Civil Rights movement are carved into low granite walls. ♿ (Downtown)

DOWNTOWN PRESBYTERIAN CHURCH
Church St. at Fifth Ave. N.
Nashville
615/254-7584

Built in 1851, this church is a rare example of the Egyptian Revival style. It was designed by American architect William Strickland, who also drew the plans for the Tennessee State Capitol. Stop in for a look at stained-glass windows with papyrus motifs and trompe l'oeil painted walls that simulate an Egyptian temple courtyard. The church, which has an active urban ministry, sponsors nondenominational lunchtime gatherings several times weekly for businesspeople and homeless people together, and opens its doors for occasional musical offerings inside its strange and magnificent sanctuary. Mid-Apr–Oct weekdays 8–4. Call above number to request a tour of the sanctuary. Wheelchair accessible (enter from lower level on side). (Downtown)

ERNEST TUBB'S RECORD SHOP NO. 1
417 Broadway
Nashville
615/255-7503

Visit the records, souvenirs, and memorabilia of the "Texas Troubadour" at Ernest Tubb's. Still a part of the Nashville music scene, Ernest Tubb's After-the-Opry Midnight Jamboree, which took place at the original Broadway location until fairly recently, has moved to where the action is: Shop No. 2 Music Valley, across from Opryland. (No slackers, the entrepreneurial folks running Ernest Tubb's have recently opened another store on Music Row, at 516 Demonbreun, as well as out-of-town branches in Pigeon Forge, Tennessee; Branson, Missouri; and Fort Worth, Texas.) Daily 9–6. During the summer the original downtown location stays open until at least 9 p.m. and sometimes midnight, with occasional live music shows. ♿ (Downtown)

FORT NEGLEY
St. Cloud Hill, off Chestnut St. above Greer Baseball Stadium,

**on the same street as the
Cumberland Science Museum
Nashville**

A Union Army fortification and muni-
tions storage bunker, Fort Negley was
constructed on a strategic hill overlooking downtown Nashville and the
Cumberland River during the occupation of Nashville. African American
laborers built the walls and earth-
works at Fort Negley with locally-
quarried limestone. The fort was not
finished until near the end of the war
and was rarely used. Restored by
the Works Progress Administration
in 1929, it is in disrepair once again
and is not currently open. The entrance gate is visible from the street.
(Downtown)

GENERAL JACKSON SHOWBOAT/
MUSIC CITY QUEEN/OPRYLAND
RIVER TAXIS
2808 Opryland Dr.
Nashville
615/889-6611

The *General Jackson* is a 300-foot,
four-deck, paddlewheel steamboat
that cruises morning, noon, and night

year-round, from Opryland to downtown Nashville and back. Daytime
cruises last two hours, and the three-
hour evening trips include a full stage
show in Opryland production style
(think Las Vegas crossed with the
Grand Ole Opry). Prices are $20–$60,
depending on whether cruise is day
or night. The 400-passenger *Music
City Queen* offers sightseeing cruises
that leave and return from Riverfront
Park in downtown Nashville during
the summer months. Round-trip fare
is $9–$12, with discounts for children.

The Opryland River Taxis run
from the Opry House parking lot (the
hotel runs a shuttle to the launch site)
to downtown Nashville's Riverfront
Park and back, Apr–Oct, $10–$13, discounts for children. ♿ (Downtown
and East Nashville)

GRUHN GUITARS, INC.
400 Broadway
Nashville
615/256-2033

This incredible guitar store is a pretty
famous place. Many of the instruments on display are museum pieces,

Gruhn Guitars, Inc.

Robin Hood

but musicians believe they deserve better—to be owned by a fine musician rather than laid to rest—so they are for sale, but at a pretty high ticket price. The knowledgeable staff cannot be matched anywhere, and Gruhn's mail-order catalogue represents a compendium of fascinating research. Mon–Sat 9:30–5:30. & (Downtown)

HATCH SHOW PRINT
316 Broadway
Nashville
615/256-2805

In business since 1879, Hatch is the oldest known show-poster print shop in the United States. The walls are covered with examples of historic vaudeville, minstrel, and country-music show bills, and the racks are filled with old wood and metal type, much of which is still in use. A fascinating stop on any tour, Hatch is also a great place to purchase Music Citiana. Weekdays 10–5, weekends during the summer months. & (Downtown)

HERMITAGE HOTEL
Sixth Ave. at Union St.
Nashville
615/244-3121

The Hermitage, a beautiful example of Beaux Arts architecture, was built in 1910 to rival the grand Maxwell House, which had been Nashville's premier hotel since its completion in 1869. The Hermitage was the scene of a major anti-suffrage meeting on the eve of the Tennessee legislature's vote in 1920. Photographs of the meeting and other photographs from the hotel's historical past can be found on the walls of the lobby and stairs leading to the bar and restaurant on the lower level. (Downtown)

L & C TOWER
Church St. at Fourth Ave.

Nashville

Nashville's first skyscraper, built for the Life and Casualty Insurance Company in 1957, was designed by local architect Edwin Keeble. The L&C tower has influenced succeeding Nashville buildings in two important ways. For many years the tower's 31-story height set the limit for any downtown building, and the cut limestone, black granite, and green-glass exterior set the tone for other important structures nearby such as the Third National Tower (1986) and the BellSouth Tower (1994). The L&C Tower is a private office building not currently open for tours. (Downtown)

LAWRENCE BROTHERS RECORDS
409 Broadway
Nashville
615/256-9240

The dusty racks at Lawrence Brothers hold the greatest hits of country music past and present. This is the tortoise of lower Broadway record shops, long ago outrun by the upstart hare, Ernest Tubb's Record Shop. Time spent here is a walk back in time to country music's age of innocence, when Opry fans from all over the state would come to Nashville and spend their hard-earned money on albums created in the mysterious studio surroundings of Music Row. Weekdays 8–6, Sat 8–7. & (Downtown)

LEGISLATIVE PLAZA AND THE WAR MEMORIAL AUDITORIUM
Sixth and Seventh Aves. N.,
between Union and Charlotte
Nashville
615/741-2692

You can't miss the majestic 1925 War Memorial Auditorium, which stands like a Greek temple looking down Deaderick Street toward the Cumberland River. Spread out before it is

An Insider's Guide to Nashville Sights

Robert Cheatham, director, Tennessee Humanities Council

"A place has never seemed a city to me unless you can visit it for a minimum of three days without an automobile and mainly on foot. By that definition, other than New Orleans, Savannah, and Charleston, suburbanization has destroyed most of the cities of the American South. But Nashville is struggling back.

For a carless visit to Nashville, your hotel choices are limited to downtown, unless you dock your yacht at Riverfront Park. Since I'm boatless, I'd opt for the Hermitage or the Crowne Plaza and ask for a view of the State Capitol and the War Memorial Plaza. This plaza is a grand public space—Nashville's living room—though many suburban Nashvillians would need good instructions to find it. To experience it in use, you might come during the Southern Festival of Books, a particularly good weekend to be carless in downtown Nashville.

Even when there are no festivities downtown, there is still plenty to do on foot or by means of pleasant public transportation. Most nights there will be something going at the Tennessee Performing Arts Center or the Ryman or the Arena. And day or night, you don't want to miss the *General Jackson* on the Cumberland passing by First Avenue or the view of downtown from the new Shelby Avenue pedestrian bridge.

But what makes a mainly walking visit to Nashville conceivable now, unlike just a few years ago, is what is called 'The District'—Second Avenue, lower Broadway, and Printer's Alley. It's easy to see 'The District' as too commercial, a bit trashy, and full of tourists who've come only for the myth, but that is true of Nashville itself and part of the spirit of the place. It's not only tourists that frequent this area. It's young people from the suburbs who come to see and be seen; families from throughout Middle Tennessee whose residents have long come to Nashville for their city needs; and a greater diversity of real Nashvillians brushing up against each other than you can see anywhere else within a space in which you can comfortably walk. It all feels like a city again."

Legislative Plaza, an expanse of granite blocks linking the State Capitol Building to Union Street. The plaza is site of the Southern Festival of Books held each October. War Memorial Auditorium, host to the Nashville Symphony until the Tennessee Performing Arts Center was built in the late 1970s, houses the Tennessee State Museum of Military History in its basement. Tue–Sat 10–5. Free. ♿ (Downtown)

NASHVILLE FARMERS MARKET
Eighth Ave. N. at Jefferson
Nashville

Enter the new, improved Nashville Farmers Market from either the Bicentennial Mall or Eighth Avenue. Distinctive architecture imitating an old-fashioned train shed houses the indoor portion of the market. Inside are carryout branches of several of Nashville's best local restaurants, a coffee bar, produce stands, and small, mostly food-related shops. Outside, under cover, are the vendors of garden plants and produce who have been the market's mainstay for many years. It is worth a visit if you are interested in the legend and lore of Tennessee's native fruits and vegetables. Open daily 9–6. ♿ (Downtown)

PRINTER'S ALLEY
HISTORIC DISTRICT
Between Church and Union and
Third and Fourth Aves. N.
Nashville

Printer's Alley was the center of Nashville's newspaper business ca. 1915, when printers, publishers, and newspaper offices lined one of downtown's back alleys. In the years to follow, the district became home to Prohibition-era speakeasies. From the 1950s on, Printer's Alley became

home to nightclubs and country-music dinner clubs, with stars such as Boots Randolph holding forth on a nightly basis. This faded but still fascinating entertainment corridor persists, with new clubs opening and closing every few years. It's worth a stroll through for local color, and maybe, just maybe, the chance to glimpse a star turn. ♿ (Downtown)

RIVERFRONT PARK
First Ave. at Broadway
Nashville

Soon to be home to a major piece of interactive public art, the Red Groom Carousel, Riverfront, located where Broadway dead-ends at the Cumberland River, contains a concrete-step amphitheater overlooking the docks where the *General Jackson*, *Music City Queen*, and other boats drop anchor. Riverfront Park, which contains well-used picnic tables and statues of some of the city's founding fathers, is also host to numerous music events, like the weekly "Dancin' in the District" summer concert series, the city's Fourth of July Fireworks Extravaganza with the Nashville Symphony, and a number of concerts and music festivals. At the northern end of the park is Fort Nashborough, which was rebuilt in 1930 on its original location facing First Avenue. Tue–Sun 9–5. Free. ♿ (Downtown)

RYMAN AUDITORIUM
116 Fifth Ave. N.
Nashville
615/254-1445 (tours),
615/889-3060 (tickets)

Built in 1892 by Captain Thomas Ryman, a riverboat captain who had lately been converted to the word of the gospel, the Union Gospel Tabernacle was first used for religious revivals. The original oak pews

TRIVIA

On August 9, 1920, the Tennessee state legislature became the 36th state to ratify the Nineteenth Amendment, giving the vote to women. The tally in the State House, deadlocked after a heated campaign, was tipped in favor of the amendment by only one vote, that of Harry T. Burn, a first-time representative from Niota, in McMinn County, whose mother had given him strict orders not to betray her cause.

are still intact, and even today the acoustics in the semicircular auditorium seem especially suited for gospel performances. When Ryman died in 1904 the name was changed to Ryman Auditorium and its programs were expanded to include visiting speakers and musical events. It soon became one of Nashville's premier music halls, accommodating traveling classical music productions, famous opera singers and stage personalities on promotional tours, and vaudeville shows.

In 1943 the Grand Ole Opry moved into the Ryman, and Nashville's oldest country-music stage show became almost synonymous with the name of its home stage. (The Opry moved out to the Opryland theme park in the mid-1970s; the park closed last year but the Grand Ole Opry is still held weekly at the "new" Opry House, and the Grand Ole Opry Museum remains open to the public right next door.) Now owned by Gaylord Entertainment, the Ryman was extensively remodeled in 1994 and features an impressive schedule of regular musical events, including rock and roll, progressive country and folk, bluegrass, gospel, and classical. The Ryman also produces an annual theatrical performance based on the life of one of the legends of country music, such as Hank Williams, Patsy Cline, and others,

and an annual classical series. Self-guided tours are available daily 8:30–4. $6 adults, $2.50 children ages 12 and under. & (Downtown)

SILVER DOLLAR SALOON
(now the Hard Rock Café gift shop)
Corner of Second and Broadway
Nashville
615/742-9900

Cheap food, drink, and lodging were available at this narrow corner bar during the late 1800s in the midst of Nashville's busy commercial district. This historic building is now the overwhelmingly popular Hard Rock Café gift shop, where the line to buy logo merchandise is often longer than the wait to get into the restaurant. Sun–Thu 11 a.m.–10:30 p.m., Fri–Sat 11 a.m.–midnight. (Downtown)

TENNESSEE FOX TROT CAROUSEL
Riverfront Park, Downtown

Artist Red Grooms, the creator of this brightly colored, cartoon-figured, working carnival carousel, intends for it to make a permanent impression on the Nashville arts scene. It will—in more ways than one! Not only is it hard-to-miss, located right at the focal point of lower Broadway and the Cumberland River, but it's loads of laughs to watch spin 'round, and the proceeds will benefit Nashville public art projects in the future. In his inimitable style, Grooms has made caricatures of famous Nashville figures like Andrew Jackson, Kitty Wells, Chet Atkins, and 33 others, that are both uproariously funny and good likenesses at the same time. Open 10 a.m.–sunset, Labor Day–Memorial Day, 10 a.m.–9 p.m. during the summer months. $1.50 per ride. (Downtown)

TENNESSEE PERFORMING ARTS CENTER
Fifth and Deaderick
Nashville
615/782-4000
TPAC, which takes up the lower levels of the James K. Polk State Office Building, houses three performing arts theaters: Andrew Jackson Hall, James K. Polk Theater, and Andrew Johnson Theater (see Chapter 12: Performing Arts). It also houses the Tennessee State Museum (see Chapter 8: Museums and Galleries). Works of art by contemporary Tennessee artists are displayed regularly in the TPAC lobby. Open daily. (Downtown)

TENNESSEE STATE CAPITOL
Charlotte Ave. between Sixth and Seventh Aves. N.
Nashville
Philadelphia Architect William Strickland, who worked as an assistant on the national Capitol, moved to Nashville in 1845 to supervise construction of Tennessee's state capitol building. Designed in Greek Revival style, it was not completed until 1859, five years after Strickland's death. The walls are covered with portraits of Tennessee governors and other notables, and the public rooms have been restored to their original nineteenth-century appearance. Tours can be arranged by calling the Tennessee State Museum at 615/741-2692. Mon–Fri 9–4. Free. (Downtown)

TENNESSEE STATE LIBRARY AND ARCHIVES
Seventh Ave. at Charlotte
Nashville
615/741-2764
This is the state's major repository of books, papers, microfilmed records, and clippings related to Tennessee's

Tootsie's Orchid Lounge, p. 96

Gary Layda

Downtown's Hidden Treasure

John Baeder, a Nashville artist and author of three wonderful books about American vernacular culture, Diners *(Abrams, 1978),* Gas, Food, and Lodging *(Abrams, 1982), and the latest,* Signs of Life *(Abrams, 1996), which is about hand-painted signs all over the South, has made a career of discovering hidden treasures right before our eyes.*

"There is an architectural treasure in Nashville that the majority of folk don't know about, don't care about, and, sadly, aren't interested in: the post office on Broadway. Maybe it's because the adjoining neighbor, Union Station, gets the attention. Yes, the post office says regally on its historical exterior what it is—a post office. However, take a peek inside and you will be welcomed to the finest art-deco transportation theme detailing to be found anywhere in the Southeast. From the details in the marble flooring to the tables used for posting and opening mail, the visual entertainment is stunning. If you like surprises and want to become aware of another form of lost artistry, go to the post office for a new course in art appreciation.

Behind the post office is a ghost. This ghost has been preserved in photos that I own, gifts from former district attorney Tom Shriver. It is the ghost of the original 'Pie Wagon,' a real honest-to-goodness manufactured diner. The photographs, which date the diner from the late '30s through the early '60s, show two incarnations. I have not done enough research to investigate when it was demolished. Perhaps one day I'll wander over to its namesake, a 'meat and three' on 12th Avenue, and ask some questions."

history and people, and is of special interest to genealogists, since copies of many Tennessee county records are available or can be borrowed for use in Nashville on microfilm. Visitors must secure a research pass and check belongings before working with archival collections. Mon–Sat 8–6. Free. (Downtown)

TOOTSIE'S ORCHID LOUNGE
422 Broadway

Nashville
615/726-0463

Legend has it that Grand Ole Opry performers used to slip across the alley between sets for a little nip at Tootsie's bar. Walls covered with autographed photos of stars and would-be stars, languid pickers and singers taking the stage one after the other, years of cigarette smoke oozing from every crack and crevice, the smell of stale beer, and a friendly bartender have provided solace from the storms of everyday life for working-class Nashvillians for decades. Classic Tootsie's now caters primarily to the tourist crowd, with occasional surprise celebrity appearances by Ryman performers. 10 a.m.–2 a.m. Live music starts at 10 a.m daily; Sun noon–2 a.m. No cover. ৬ (Downtown)

UNION STATION
1001 Broadway (at 10th Ave.)
Nashville
615/726-1001

Now a hotel, the Union Station Railway Terminal was dedicated on October 9, 1900. The Romanesque Revival–style structure, built of native limestone, was designed by Richard Montfort, chief engineer of the Louisville and Nashville Railroad. The terminal, whose main entrance was under large rough-cut stone arches facing Broadway, has a massive fireplace at the opposite end and skylights overhead that once illuminated the enormous waiting room, now the hotel lobby. The architectural detail-

ing, with its symbolic low-relief sculpture and finely carved patterns, is worth a look, and the hotel management is friendly to visitors wandering about in awe of Nashville's showplace of progress ushering in the twentieth century. (Downtown)

UNITED STATES
CUSTOMS HOUSE
Broadway at Eighth Ave.
Nashville

This immense Victorian-Gothic building, with its massive tower overlooking Broadway, was built in 1877 and was the first federal building constructed for Nashville during Reconstruction. It had been a campaign promise of Rutherford B. Hayes, and he came to lay its cornerstone in 1877. Its presence is a testimony to Nashville's past as a center of river commerce. After significant restoration in the mid-1980s, the Customs House today contains a variety of city, state, and private offices. (Downtown)

UNITED STATES POST OFFICE
901 Broadway
Nashville
615/255-9447

With its classic, blocky art-deco design, Nashville's old main post office, built in 1934, is still in use today, although the central sorting, shipping, and business operations have moved out to a modern facility on Royal Parkway near the airport. While the outside is relatively unremarkable but for the bands of decorative trim around the

TRIVIA

The saving of Union Station in the late 1970s was the first full-scale historic preservation effort in Nashville.

MIDTOWN NASHVILLE

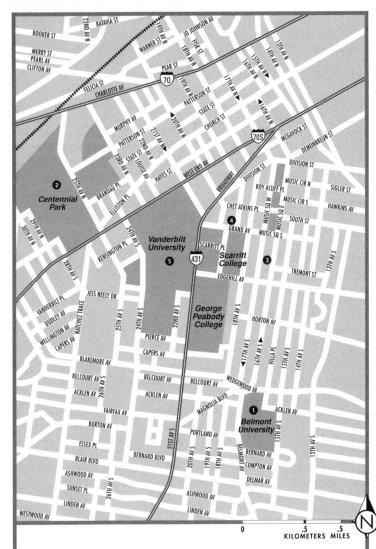

0   .5   .5
KILOMETERS MILES

N

Sights in Midtown Nashville

1 Belmont University
2 Centennial Park
3 Music Row
4 The Upper Room
5 Vanderbilt University

Future Plans

Planning is underway for Nashville's Frist Center for the Visual Arts, scheduled to open in 2000, which will fill all but the basement level of the historic downtown post office. A creative architectural rehabilitation will relocate the retail activities of the U.S. Postal Service (stamps and boxholder services) to the lower level and allow Nashville art lovers a magnificent new space that will function like a museum, but which will not house a permanent art collection. The center, slated to house an auditorium, restaurant, gift shop, and children's discovery gallery, will follow the model of the European kunsthalle, *a space for the display of traveling exhibits, regional artists, and local private and museum collections.*

doors, building base, and roof line, the interior, with its polished stainless-steel grille, shiny inlaid floors, and built-in counters and tables, is as sleek and businesslike as an ocean liner. By way of train, truck, and ship, the mail is carried to its destinations. Weekdays 7:30 a.m.–7 p.m., Sat 8–2. (Downtown)

MIDTOWN NASHVILLE

BELMONT UNIVERSITY
Wedgewood at the end of Music Row
Nashville
615/460-6000
Belmont University, a private coeducational institution affiliated with the Baptist Church, is on the grounds of what was once known as "Belle Monte," built in 1850 as a summer home for Adelicia Acklen, Nashville's wealthiest woman. For many years it was a famous girl's boarding school named Ward-Belmont. The white-columned facade facing down 16th

Avenue, built in 1895 and now the university's administration building, hides Adelicia's Italian villa–style house behind. The grounds and gardens of the original Belmont Mansion, which include a gazebo and garden statuary, have been restored and the house is open for tours (615/460-5459). June–Aug Mon–Sat 10–4, Sun 2–5; Sep–May Tue–Sat 10–4. $6 adults, $5.50 seniors, $2 children ages 6–12, children under age 6 free. & (Midtown)

CENTENNIAL PARK
West End Ave. and 25th Ave. N.
Nashville
615/862-8400
Built for the Tennessee Centennial Exposition of 1897, this well-used city park, neatly landscaped with seasonal plantings, includes a duck pond, a band shell, picnic tables, an arts activity center, the Centennial Sportsplex (see Chapter 10: Sports and Recreation), and the Parthenon (see Chapter 8: Museums and Galleries), a full scale concrete replica of

the Athenian original. Centennial Park is the site of many free annual events, such as the Tennessee Crafts Fairs (May and October), the American Artisan Craft Fair (June), the Nashville Shakespeare Festival (August), and concerts by the Nashville Symphony. ♿ (Midtown)

MUSIC ROW
16th and 17th Aves.
Nashville
The portions of these two parallel streets between Wedgewood and West End Avenues constitute the area of town known as Music Row, which includes the Country Music Hall of Fame and surrounding retail establishments, such as souvenir shops and for-profit "museums;" the headquarters of the Country and Gospel Music Associations (known as CMA and GMA) as well as BMI, ASCAP, and SESAC (copyright licensing agencies); offices for record labels and music-publishing companies; and a large number of recording studios. With the exception of the Country Music Hall of Fame and RCA's Studio B, which they operate as a museum as well as a working recording studio, most are not open to the public. Many visitors enjoy walking or driving along 16th and 17th

Avenues just to imagine what goes on behind closed doors of Nashville's music-industry hub. Sammy B's Restaurant, with a courtyard facing 16th, and the Idle Hour, a tiny tavern further down the same street, provide good people-watching on "the Row." During summer months there's a free Wednesday-evening country-music concert series called "Music on the Row," which sets up in a parking lot between Division and Demonbreun Streets, just across from the Country Music Hall of Fame, near Shoney's Inn. (Midtown)

THE UPPER ROOM
1908 Grand Ave.
Nashville
615/340-7207
An 8-by-17-foot carved replica of Leonardo da Vinci's *Last Supper* installed in a modern sanctuary is the highlight of the Upper Room museum's collection of religious art and artifacts, The museum, although modest in scale, is well researched and contains a variety of artifacts, including original manuscripts, early printed books, furniture, and decorative religious objects from around the world. Located in a complex of buildings affiliated with the Methodist denomination, the Upper Room, which publishes a devo-

Inside Belmont University's administration building lobby is the Heritage Project, a permanent exhibition about the history of Ward-Belmont that contains fascinating artifacts, including letters, photographs, and memorabilia. Ward-Belmont, an exclusive school for girls from 1913 to 1951, has many distinguished alumnae, including Clare Booth Luce, Lila Acheson Wallace, and Jean Faircloth (Mrs. Douglas) MacArthur. Probably the most well-known among them, however, was Sarah Ophelia Cannon, class of 1931, who became famous as Grand Ole Opry star Minnie Pearl. Open weekdays 8–5. Free.

tional magazine by the same name, its bookstore, and gift shop offer a short retreat for visitors to Nashville. On a quiet block near Music Row and Vanderbilt University, the Upper Room offers free tours on the hour and half hour by friendly guides. Mon–Fri 8–4:30. Free. (Midtown)

VANDERBILT UNIVERSITY
West End Ave. at 21st Ave.,
Hillsboro Rd.
Nashville
615/322-7311 (main operator)
Located at the end of Broadway, where it splits into West End Avenue and 21st Avenue South, is Vanderbilt University. Founded by railroad magnate Cornelius Vanderbilt in 1873 as a liberal arts college, it now includes an engineering school, a law school, a management school, and a medical school. George Peabody College, for many years a college of education, now houses Vanderbilt's departments of human development and educational psychology as an affiliate of Vanderbilt. Located just across 21st Avenue, Peabody was erected on the site of the former Roger Williams University, a private university for African Americans from 1876 to 1905. The well-tended grounds of Vanderbilt and its Peabody campus are a pleasant place for a stroll. Many of the most distinguished trees are labeled with species and common name and the brick pathways make for easy walking.

Both Sarratt Student Center, which includes a gallery, and the Vanderbilt Fine Arts Gallery (see Chapter 8: Museums and Galleries for listings) are open to the public free of charge. The main desk at Sarratt Student Center is a Ticketmaster outlet and can provide information about performing arts events both on the Vanderbilt campus and around town (see Chapter 12: Performing Arts). ♿ (Midtown)

NORTH NASHVILLE

FISK UNIVERSITY
1000 17th Ave. N.
Nashville
615/329-8500 (university operator)
Fisk University, named after Union General Clinton B. Fisk, opened in 1866 as one of the first historically black colleges. Its long and distinguished history will be partially revealed by a stroll onto its well-kept campus. Jubilee Hall, a brick-towered Victorian, houses an enormous portrait of the original Fisk Jubilee Singers (who traveled to raise money for the school in its early years) that was painted at the court of Queen Victoria. The Fisk University Chapel almost rings with a cappella spirituals even when today's Jubilee Singers are away on tour. The administration building, located at the center of the campus, is the former

Van Vechten Gallery on the Fisk University campus

Nashville Metro Historical Comm.

GREATER NASHVILLE

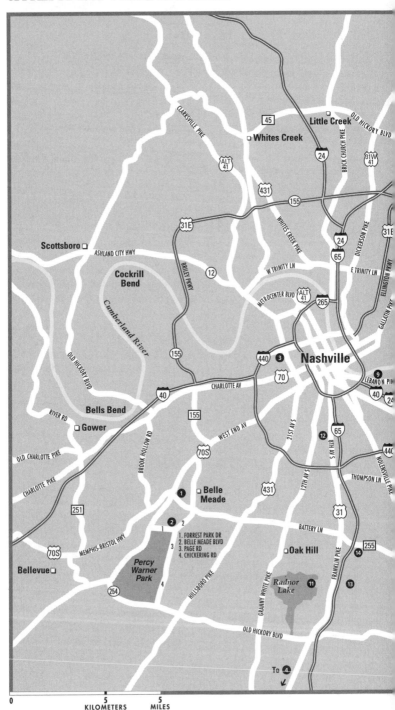

Little Creek
Whites Creek
45
24
CLARKSVILLE PIKE
ALT 41
431
155
OLD HICKORY BLVD
BRICK CHURCH PIKE
31W 41
WHITES CREEK PIKE
Scottsboro
ASHLAND CITY HWY
31E
BRILEY PKWY
12
W TRINITY LN
METROCENTER BLVD
ALT 41
265
E TRINITY LN
DICKERSON PIKE
ELLINGTON PKWY
GALLATIN PIKE
24
65
31E
Cockrill Bend
Cumberland River
OLD HICKORY BLVD
155
440
70
3
Nashville
9
LEBANON PIKE
40
24
RIVER RD
CHARLOTTE AV
40
155
21ST AV S
65
S AV H18
12
440
Bells Bend
Gower
BROOK HOLLOW RD
WEST END AV
70S
OLD CHARLOTTE PIKE
CHARLOTTE PIKE
251
431
12TH AV S
THOMPSON LN
NOLENSVILLE PIKE
1
Belle Meade
BATTERY LN
31
70S
MEMPHIS-BRISTOL HWY
2 2
1. FORREST PARK DR
2. BELLE MEADE BLVD
3. PAGE RD
4. CHICKERING RD
Oak Hill
FRANKLIN PIKE
255
14
Bellevue
Percy Warner Park
254
HILLSBORO PIKE
GRANNY WHITE PIKE
Radnor Lake
11
13
OLD HICKORY BLVD

To 4

0   5 KILOMETERS   5 MILES

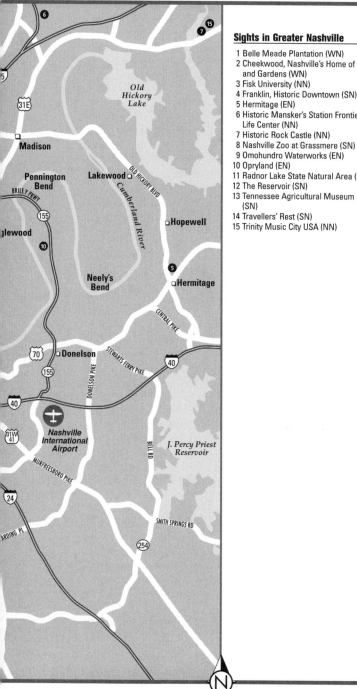

Sights in Greater Nashville

1 Belle Meade Plantation (WN)
2 Cheekwood, Nashville's Home of Art and Gardens (WN)
3 Fisk University (NN)
4 Franklin, Historic Downtown (SN)
5 Hermitage (EN)
6 Historic Mansker's Station Frontier Life Center (NN)
7 Historic Rock Castle (NN)
8 Nashville Zoo at Grassmere (SN)
9 Omohundro Waterworks (EN)
10 Opryland (EN)
11 Radnor Lake State Natural Area (SN)
12 The Reservoir (SN)
13 Tennessee Agricultural Museum (SN)
14 Travellers' Rest (SN)
15 Trinity Music City USA (NN)

library whose walls are covered with a mural program by famed Harlem Renaissance artist Aaron Douglas. The modern university library displays works of art by Douglas' mentor, Winold Reiss, and is home to the third-floor Aaron Douglas Gallery, which displays African art and has valuable archival holdings related to the Harlem Renaissance and after.

Directly across from the library is the Carl Van Vechten Gallery, which owns a portion of the Alfred Stieglitz collection of modern art and presents a schedule of changing exhibits (see Chapter 8: Museums and Galleries for listing). Fisk University Library hours Mon–Thu 7:45–5, Sat 9–5, Sun 2–10; 615/329-8733. (North Nashville)

HISTORIC MANSKER'S STATION FRONTIER LIFE CENTER
Moss-Wright Park, Caldwell Rd.
Goodlettsville
615/859-FORT
This is the area of first settlement around Nashville. Dutchman Kaspar Mansker built this fort or station in 1779, near the site of Mansker's Lick, where the long hunters (buckskin-clad frontiersmen who ranged far and wide in search of game they could sell for meat and skins, sometimes staying away from home for years at a time) had been finding animals attracted to the natural salt since they first arrived around 1768. The fort, which was reconstructed in 1986, includes a working blacksmith shop and offers "living history" demonstrations of frontier skills, many of which, like hide-tanning, were learned from the Indians. Many Tennesseans, like one of the men who works as a professional interpreter at Mansker's Station, are descended from marriages of European traders and the Cherokee, Chickasaw, or Creek Indi-

ans who occupied these hunting grounds in the early days of this country.

The site also includes the nearby Bowen House, the oldest brick structure in Middle Tennessee, which was begun in 1785 and finished in 1787. The house was restored in 1976. The gardens are filled with horsetail for making brooms and other things the early Tennesseans might have grown. Bowen House is now furnished with authentic period furnishings ca. 1790. Mar–Dec Tue–Sat 9–4:45. $5 adults, $3 students. ♿ (North Nashville)

HISTORIC ROCK CASTLE
Indian Lake Rd.
Hendersonville
615/824-0502
This house, two rooms of which date from the 1780s, was completed in 1796. Daniel Smith, who had the rock quarried locally and used some of Tennessee's virgin hardwoods for the structure and cabinetry, received the land on which Rock Castle stands as payment for the earliest surveys of the Tennessee territory, which he finished in 1784. Smith had trained professionally under Virginia physician/explorer Dr. Thomas Walker, who named the Cumberland Gap.

In 1793 Smith published a map of the lands west of the Cumberland Mountains. Daniel and Sarah Michie Smith's children both married into the John Donelson family, which made them cousins to Andrew and Rachel Jackson by marriage. Daniel Smith, who had served in the American Revolution, later served as a successor to Andrew Jackson in the U. S. Senate. Rock Castle is furnished in late-eighteenth-century style, with items typical to the region, but does contain two original pieces known to have belonged to the Smiths, as well as

Daniel Smith's over-200-volume library. Feb–Dec Wed–Sat 10–4, Sun 1–4. Last tour begins at 3:30. $5 adults, $4.50 seniors, $3 children ages 6–12. (North Nashville)

TRINITY MUSIC CITY USA
Music Village Blvd.
Hendersonville
615/826-9191

Located at what was once Twitty City, the estate of country star Conway Twitty, Trinity Music City encompasses the Trinity Broadcasting Network studios, the Conway Twitty Memorial Garden, the Auditorium, and a virtual-reality theater. The Christmas lights at Twitty City had become quite famous, so Trinity has continued the tradition, illuminating over 1 million lights during November and December each year. Tours of the WPGD-TV studios are offered twice daily, and live television broadcasts originate in the auditorium (the PTL Club is a regular visitor). The gift shop is named Gold, Frankincense and Myrrh, and the restaurant, the Solid Rock Bistro. Sun–Thu 10–6, Fri–Sat 10–9. Free. (North Nashville)

EAST NASHVILLE

HERMITAGE
4580 Rachel's Ln., just off Old Hickory Blvd.
Nashville
615/889-2941

The Hermitage, a beautiful white house with a columned porch, stands at the end of a graceful tree-lined driveway. With its various outbuildings, a period garden, an interpretive museum, guided house tours, and ongoing archeological excavations on the grounds, it is well worth a half-day visit.

This was the home of Andrew Jackson, seventh president of the United States (1828–1837), and his wife Rachel. They lived here together from 1804 until her death in 1828. After his Presidential term, Jackson returned to live at his beloved Hermitage until his death in 1845. When Jackson and his wife, the former Rachel Donelson (daughter of one of the founders of Nashville), bought this 425-acre farm, the "house" consisted of a complex of log cabins, of which two are still extant. By 1830 there was a brick two-story home and the farm had become a cotton plantation of 1,500 acres. Its 125 to 150 slaves raised enough foodstuffs, wool, and livestock to make it a self-sufficient working plantation.

Today the Hermitage is a white-brick, columned, Greek Revival–style house dating mostly from 1836, when it was extensively remodeled after a fire destroyed the upper floor and seriously damaged the lower story in 1834. The restoration of every detail of the 1836 decor is being carried

TRIVIA

Both Andrew and Rachel Jackson are buried in the Hermitage garden cemetery. Also buried in the cemetery are Jackson's favorite slave, Uncle Alfred, and a Creek Indian boy named Lincoya, whom Jackson had rescued at the Battle of 1812 and had hoped to send to West Point for his education.

out according to extensive surviving records of wallpaper, fabrics, and other furnishings. Some elements remaining from the plain, brick Federal-style house and the Palladian-style portico and flanking wings added in 1831 are still visible. Informed guides dressed in period clothing take visitors through the house. The short film shown in the Interpretive Center serves as a good introduction to the life of this complex, controversial figure—a hero to many, a brave soldier and leader, and a seemingly ruthless frontiersman.

Admission to the Hermitage includes a visit to Tulip Grove, an 1836 brick Greek Revival–style house built for Rachel's nephew, Andrew Jackson Donelson; and the Old Hermitage Church, which Jackson built in 1823 for his devout wife. Open daily 9–5, except holidays and the third week in Jan. $9.50 adults, $8.50 seniors and students, $4.50 children ages 6–12, $28 family (two adults and two or more children). Ground floor of the houses, grounds, and interpretive center are wheelchair accessible. (East Nashville)

OMOHUNDRO WATERWORKS
Hermitage Ave.
Nashville
615/862-7248
Still in use today and pumping as many as 90 million gallons daily, the original Omohundro Water Filtration Complex features a round tower in the Cumberland River for water intake and three brick buildings for storage and pumps. The 1889 George Reyer Pumping Station has a classic Victorian exterior featuring a diamond-patterned terrazzo floor, marble fittings, and wooden ceiling. The other two buildings were built in the 1920s; all are listed on the National Register of His-

toric Places. Tours may be arranged by calling the Metro Water Services Omohundro Drive Plant at the number above. Free admission and tour. (East Nashville)

OPRYLAND
2802 Opryland Dr.
Nashville
615/889-6611
This huge complex in northeast Nashville encompasses the Grand Ole Opry House, the Grand Ole Opry Museums, and the television studios of the Nashville Network (TNN). (Opryland Theme Park closed in 1998). Just adjacent to Opryland itself is the Opryland Hotel, a large convention hotel with as many wings and restaurants as a small city.

The Grand Ole Opry Museums can be visited free of charge (see Chapter 8: Museums and Galleries). The studios of the Nashville Network tape regular shows, with studio audiences, for widespread distribution. TNN is now an affiliate of CBS Televison (see Chapter 6: Country-Music Culture). Departing from the Opry-

The Bicentennial Mall, p. 89

land complex, the *General Jackson* paddlewheel steamer, the *Music City Queen* and the Opryland River Taxi service (east) all ferry visitors to downtown Nashville's Second Avenue. (East Nashville)

SOUTH NASHVILLE

FRANKLIN, HISTORIC DOWNTOWN
The Heritage Foundation Visitor Information Center
209 E. Main
Nashville
615/790-0378
Located approximately 20 miles south of Nashville, reachable by I-65 South, Hillsboro Pike, and Franklin Pike, this small town was voted a national favorite among small cities. Its entire 15-block downtown is listed on the National Register of Historic Places.

Any visit to Franklin should include tours of two prime historic sites, the Carter House (1830) and Carnton Plantation (1826). Apr–Oct Mon–Sat 9–5, Sun 1–5, Nov–Mar both sites close at 4 p.m. daily. (Carter House, 615/791-1861; Carnton, 615/794-0903) (South Nashville)

NASHVILLE ZOO AT GRASSMERE
3777 Nolensville Rd.
Nashville
615/833-1534
The Nashville Zoo at Grassmere, part of the Nashville Zoo, is an alternative zoo and interpretive nature center. American and indigenous Tennessee animals live as freely as possible in an authentic outdoor habitat. Seeing the Tennessee bison roam freely over the rolling hills of this former farm allows one to imagine how they might have looked at French Lick when Timothe DeMontbrun first visited the

area. The park also includes living exhibits of birds and wild plants and a changing exhibit gallery of wildlife art. Apr–Sep daily 9–6, Oct–Mar 10–5. $6 adults, $4 seniors and children ages 3–12, parking $2. ㄴ (South Nashville)

RADNOR LAKE STATE NATURAL AREA
Otter Creek Rd. between Hillsboro and Franklin Rds.
Nashville
615/373-3467
A north-woods experience hidden away in a fairly populated area of town, Radnor Lake State Natural Area was donated by the L&N Railroad. Wooded hills, from which one can catch a view of downtown on a clear day, surround a large, pristine lake. Ducks, geese, turtles, and deer are Radnor's most visible inhabitants, but occasional otter and mink appearances are recorded as well. Extensive hiking trails allow prime wildflower-viewing and bird-watching. Open dawn to dusk, with nature center and restroom facilities. Nature programs are often held at Radnor, as are outdoor excursions for children and adults. Free. One low-lying trail, from parking lot to dam to interpretive center, is wheelchair-accessible with assistance. (South Nashville)

THE RESERVOIR
8th Ave. S. at Argyle
Nashville
Part of the Omohundro Waterworks system, the reservoir was built between 1887 and 1889 on the site of what had been Fort Casino, a Union fortification constructed during Nashville's occupation and used during the 1864 Battle of Nashville. The elliptical reservoir, constructed of native limestone, holds 51 million gallons of

water and is still in use today. On November 5, 1912, the reservoir burst around midnight, flooding many nearby homes but causing no fatalities. Although the reservoir is not open for tours, visitors can admire it at close range. The repaired crack is visible on the southeast side of the structure. (South Nashville)

TENNESSEE AGRICULTURAL MUSEUM
Near Hogan Rd. between I-65 S. and Nolensville Rd.
Nashville
615/837-5197
The museum is located on the 200-acre grounds of the state's Ellington Agricultural Center, a research and administration facility supporting agronomy. A grand home, which was built in 1927 as a red-brick imitation of the Hermitage, and some of the outbuildings on the property once belonged to Rogers Caldwell, a Depression-era banker who made and lost a fortune. The Agricultural Museum contains farm artifacts from the nineteenth and twentieth centuries, along with the Agriculture Hall of Fame, which was established in 1937. Mon–Fri 9–4. Free. ♿ main floor (South Nashville)

TRAVELLERS' REST
636 Farrell Pkwy.
Nashville
615/832-8197
Travellers' Rest was home to John Overton, close associate of Andrew Jackson, founder of Memphis and Tennessee supreme court justice. Travellers' Rest, named after Jackson's horse Traveller, was erected in 1799. A simple white clapboard house, its quiet, well-kept grounds, including a smoke house, a weaving house, a formal garden, and magnolia trees

planted along the driveway (much as Overton must have directed) make this a good place to experience how Tennessee's well-to-do citizens lived in the early days of statehood. Original furnishings include furniture made in Middle Tennessee and important portraits of Andrew and Rachel Jackson. Tue–Sat 10–5, Sun 1–5. Free tours are provided; the last tour begins at 4 p.m. $6 adults, $3 children ages 6–11, children under age 6 free. (South Nashville)

WEST NASHVILLE

BELLE MEADE PLANTATION
5025 Harding Rd.
Nashville
615/356-0501 or 800/270-3991
One of West Nashville's largest landholders, William Giles Harding built his Greek-Revival mansion on a plantation of 5,300 acres that included a famous thoroughbred stud farm. Iroquois, from Harding's stable, was the first American-bred horse to win the English Derby in 1881. The Harding family continued to occupy Belle Meade for many generations, and today the house is furnished in Victorian style.

The present site, 30 acres of low rolling grounds, includes stables and a carriage house dating to 1890. Knowledgeable guides in period costume offer tours. A visitor's center, tearoom, and gift shop are scheduled to open during the summer of 1998. Mon–Sat 9–5, Sun 1–5. The last tour every day is at 4. $8 adults, $7.50 seniors, $3 children ages 6–12, children under age 6 free. (West Nashville)

CHEEKWOOD, NASHVILLE'S HOME OF ART AND GARDENS

1200 Forrest Park Dr.
Nashville
615/356-8000

A 55-acre expanse of gardens surrounds the Cheek Mansion, a Georgian-style English manor house built of Tennessee limestone in the early 1930s by Leslie and Mabel Cheek. Cheek, who was in the wholesale grocery business, made a fortune when Cheek-Neal Coffee company sold its Maxwell House brand (named after the famous Maxwell House Hotel downtown) to General Foods. The opulent Cheek house is now a museum of fine and decorative arts (see Chapter 8: Museums and Galleries), and the grounds house a botanical garden and a woodland sculpture trail that integrates contemporary art into the landscape setting.

Cheekwood's Botanic Hall is the location for flower and plant shows throughout the year. Three greenhouses are open to the public, and there are wildflower, herb, annual, and perennial gardens. An authentic Japanese garden is worthy of a meditative visit. The lovely setting provides a backdrop for jazz, blues, and symphonic music during the summer months. The Pineapple Room restaurant serves lunch and afternoon tea. Mon–Sat 9–5, Sun 11–5. Expanded hours during summer months allow visitors to linger longer while the light lasts: mid-Apr–Labor Day Mon–Thu 9–8. Closed holidays and the third Saturday in April. $8 adults, $7 seniors, $5 college students with ID, $3 children ages 6–17. Cheekwood on the Internet: *www.cheekwood.org* &
(West Nashville)

Meryl Truett

6

COUNTRY-MUSIC CULTURE

Because it is the international center for the production of country-music recordings in both audio and video formats, Nashville offers many opportunities to watch recordings or videos being made at close range and, on occasion, to rub elbows with up-and-coming stars. Tour buses can be seen parked all around town, and film and video support trucks often line the streets in front of clubs, historic buildings, or any scenic spot that can become a temporary backdrop for live music.

However, in Nashville, crossover music and other forms of culture feed into the mainstream of country music on a daily basis, so don't hesitate to partake of "unlabled" entertainment wherever you find it. (A general listing of music clubs can be found in Chapter 13: Nightlife.) By the same token, original country themes also move readily into the larger culture. Two notable examples in the past were Roger Miller's "Big River" on Broadway and Eddie Rabbit's stint as an opera singer; more recently, Johnny Cash made a recording with Seattle grunge bands on "American Songs." Don't miss the chance to brush up on your historical knowledge of all of the musical genres that have intertwined with country music by visiting the Country Music Hall of Fame (see Chapter 8: Museums and Galleries). The Hall of Fame now runs RCA's historic Studio B, once used by Elvis Presley and still booked today for professional recording dates, as a living museum.

As country music (and its offshoots) continues to spread, the appeal of old-time instruments, musical genres, clothing, food, and cultural customs that are intertwined with it also continues to spread. Explore pawn shops, second-hand stores, and small eateries all over town to expand your own taste of country, while also catching a glimpse of its still growing roots.

Before you make the rounds at the numerous country-music attractions, you'll want to check out the country-western clothing stores in Chapter 10: Shopping.

COUNTRY-MUSIC TV TAPINGS AND LIVE MUSIC SHOWS

GRAND OLE OPRY
2808 Opryland Dr.
Nashville 37214
615/889-6611 (information),
615/889-3060 (tickets)

The Grand Ole Opry started as a live radio program in 1925. The Opry is a not-to-be-missed experience, not so much for the music as for the ambience. If you are lucky enough to catch Brother Oswald or Charlie Louvin with Patty Loveless, Ricky Skaggs, or Alison Krauss on the same evening, you'll be able to see the unbroken links between new and traditional country. A casual atmosphere prevails, with fans wandering down the aisles to snap photos of their favorite stars or getting up during performances to grab a box of popcorn, a Coke, and a GooGoo Cluster. Radio announcers read commercials aloud during breaks in the music, just as they've been doing since the show's inception, as stage sets are rearranged behind the curtain. "Membership" in the Opry has always been a mark of acceptance for any country star. In the fast-changing, ever-more-trendy world of country-music, some members of today's Opry family may come as quite a surprise to dyed-in-the-wool country-music fans.

The Grand Ole Opry goes on-stage every Saturday evening of the year at 6:30 and 9:30. Friday-night shows are at 7:30. Tickets are $16–$18 and are sometimes available at showtime. Summer season can be overbooked, however, so it is best to call or write in advance for tickets. ♿ (East Nashville)

MIDNIGHT JAMBOREE AT ERNEST TUBB'S RECORD SHOP
(live radio broadcast on WSM-AM 650)
2414 Music Valley Dr.
Nashville
615/889-2474

Ernest Tubb's "After the Opry" radio show, which began in the original

Midnight Jamboree at Ernest Tubb's Record Shop

Meryl Truett

Carrying on the Tradition

Marty Stuart, Nashville's best-known mandolin player, first performed at the Opry in 1972 at the age of 13 as a member of Lester Flatt's band. Twenty years later, in 1992, he became a member in his own right. He has worked with most of the bluegrass greats, from Bill Monroe to Earl Scruggs. As a songwriter he idolizes Johnny Cash and Hank Williams Sr., among others, and as a performer he probably comes closest to Elvis Presley in sex appeal. Stuart considers himself a bridge between Nashville music's past and future.

"I was raised by the masters that invented the music around here. I'm one of their kids. I feel obligated to carry some of the pure things that they taught me into the twenty-first century. I mean hard-rockin' hillbilly music, that's what I feel. It flatters me that people that have never heard of Roy Acuff happen to like us, too! And that gives me a chance to tell 'em about Acuff."

(from liner notes on *Tempted*, MCA Records, 1991)

lower Broadway store (417 Broadway) when the Opry was performed in the Ryman, happens every Saturday night. Carol Lee Cooper is the current host, and admission is free. The Music Valley Drive store is adjacent to Tubb's Texas Troubadour Theater, which runs a theatrical performance based on the life of Patsy Cline every evening at 7 and Saturday at 2 p.m. Tickets are $15. For reservations, call 615/885-0028.

The "Nashville Cowboy Church," an interdenominational gospel service, is held at the theater every Sun morning at 10. Free. A gospel show is performed every Tue evening at 7 for $10. (East Nashville)

PRIME TIME COUNTRY
TNN (The Nashville Network)
Studios

Nashville
615/889-6611
This show tapes on a regular schedule, Mon–Thu 5–6:30 p.m., and includes the hottest new stars on the music scene. For a real tourist treat, join the studio audience. Tickets are free, but you must call ahead to reserve a seat. Call the Nashville Network information line at 615/883-7000. (East Nashville)

COUNTRY-MUSIC CONCERT VENUES

GRAND OLE OPRY HOUSE
2808 Opryland Dr.
Nashville
615/889-6611
The new Grand Ole Opry is a modern

There has been nothing like rockabilly before or since. It's an original form of music. And for me it takes me back to basics.

A Country Music Hall of Fame exhibit

hall with comfortable seats, wide aisles, and large second-floor balcony areas located approximately nine miles from downtown inside the Opryland theme park. The Grand Old Opry House replaced Ryman Auditorium as the home of the Grand Ole Opry when Opryland was built in the mid-1970s. In addition to the regular Friday- and Saturday-night performances, the Opry House is used for the annual Country Music Association Awards in October and for various concerts and events throughout the year. ♿ (East Nashville)

NASHVILLE ARENA
501 Broadway

Nashville
615/880-2850 (information),
615/255-9600 (tickets)
Opened in December 1996 with Amy Grant's Christmas Show, the glittering new Nashville Arena promises many more sold-out appearances by the largest-drawing entertainers in all musical genres. ♿ (Downtown)

RYMAN AUDITORIUM
116 Fifth Ave. N.
Nashville
615/254-1445 (information),
615/889-3060 (tickets)
This historic theater, which was built as a gospel tabernacle and later used for vaudeville shows before it became

"Music on the Row," a live country-music event, is set up every Wednesday night in June, July, and August in the large parking lot between Shoney's Inn and the Country Music Hall of Fame on Music Row. Since this free country-music series is co-sponsored by WSIX Radio (98), listen to the station for details of upcoming shows.

the original home of the Grand Ole Opry radio show, has great acoustics. Recently renovated, the Ryman has retained its wooden-bench seats and church-like orientation but has expanded its repertory to include the highest caliber of country, folk, and rock performances as well as occasional musical theater and classical works. Recent theater productions have included the life stories of Patsy Cline and Hank Williams Sr. The Ryman has been called the "high temple" of country music—an evening spent in this inspiring listening room will convince you why. Beer and soft drinks are available on the premises. ♿ (East Nashville)

STARWOOD AMPHITHEATER
3839 Murfreesboro Rd.
Antioch
615/641-5800
Outdoor shows and music festivals fill this outdoor venue's schedule during temperate months. Like a small version of the Wolf Trap Performing Arts Center outside Washington, D.C., Starwood has both covered seating and sloping lawn where concertgoers can sit or stand. A wide range of talent from Bob Dylan to Sting to James Taylor to Phish to the Lilith Fair has performed on Starwood's impressive bill over the past few years. Watch for country crossover artists as opening acts

Nashville's Recording Roots

Nashville recording studios serve the whole spectrum of the music industry, a fact that is not widely known. Performers like Ray Charles, Elvis Costello, Neil Diamond, the Pointer Sisters, Joan Baez, Bob Dylan, and scores of others have graced Music Row studios over the years. Many well-known pop stars of the 1960s, '70s, and '80s like Steve Winwood, Janis Ian, Kim Carnes, and John Hiatt are now floating in the Nashville orbit, contributing to the music being made here. This eclectic musical mix has gradually penetrated at least a portion of the country music consciousness and is contributing to the overall sophistication of the Nashville scene. MCA Records, which represents both country and R&B artists, put together an incredible 1994 album of duets between artists in both genres called "Rhythm, Country, and Blues." Hearing singers like B.B. King and George Jones bemoaning the fate of growing up poor in the South in "Patches" or Sam Moore and Conway Twitty drawing out the bluesy lyrics of "A Rainy Night in Georgia" will convince anyone that country and R&B share common blues roots.

for mainstream shows. & (South Nashville)

CLUBS FEATURING COUNTRY MUSIC

BARBARA'S
207 Printer's Alley
Nashville
615/259-2272
Barbara's features nightly entertainment in the club that used to belong to Boots Randolph. Located in Printer's Alley, Nashville's answer to Bourbon Street, Barbara's is a new entrant on the country music lounge scene. Open every night of the week. Sun is blues night, $3 cover charge. & (Downtown)

BLUEBIRD CAFÉ
4104 Hillsboro Rd.
Nashville
615/383-1461
The Bluebird is the place to be heard and seen in Nashville. A small and unprepossessing club in a strip shopping center, the Bluebird packs the crowds in for two shows on nights when a well-known artist is on the bill. The lineup usually leads off early, with two and sometimes three acts on most evenings, showcasing the kind of up-and-coming sincere song-

writers that Music Row publishers want to sign. Occasional big-name artists perform here when they are recording in town or want to try out some new material. It's often hard to get a table, so call for reservations in advance if possible. The Bluebird is for serious listeners only: You will be shushed if you talk during sets. Scan the standing-room-only bar for musicians who drop in regularly to hear their peers. Open daily. Writer's Night is held every Sun at 8 p.m., and "open mike" sessions are held every Mon at 6 p.m. & (West Nashville)

BLUEGRASS INN
418 Broadway
Nashville
615/726-2799
The Bluegrass Inn, long a famous name in several different Nashville locations, has been reborn on lower Broadway. Music featured is primarily bluegrass and country swing—the real thing for old-time-music lovers. Open daily 10 a.m.–2 a.m. & (Downtown)

CAFFE MILANO
176 Third Ave. N.
Nashville
615/255-0322 (concert line)
615/255-0073 (reservations)

This new entry on the live-music scene is a welcome one. A good sound system, good sightlines, and a fine restaurant backing up the varied list of national and local players in all genres make the slightly steep cover charge well worth the extra dollars. Nashville songwriters and acoustic musicians are sprinkled into the schedule alongside nationally known jazz, folk, and rock artists, and the occasional blues legend. Open daily. Cover charge $5–$20, depending on the talent booked. & (Downtown)

COURTYARD CAFE
867 Bell Rd.
Nashville
615/731-7228
Courtyard Cafe is a favorite songwriters' showcase bar in a suburban location near the giant Hickory Hollow shopping center complex. The pizza gets good reviews from friends who frequent this friendly bar. The café is set up as a music room with all tables facing the stage so its purpose is clear. It's a good spot to settle in with a cold one and hear current Nashville works. Lunch and dinner daily. No cover. & (East Nashville)

DOUGLAS CORNER CAFÉ
2106A Eighth Ave. S.
Nashville
615/298-1688
The Douglas Corner Café is the clos-

est thing Nashville has to a corner bar. The lineup in this fine listening room is local and often top quality. Take a chance on a "songwriters in the round" evening here. Acoustics and viewing are good, the service is friendly, there is a full bar, and the ambience is unpretentious. The only problems with Douglas Corner are that it is not open every night, and you must walk by the stage as you enter. Closed Sun. & (South Nashville)

GIBSON CAFE AND GUITAR GALLERY
318 Broadway
Nashville
615/742-6343
This lower Broadway venue has a friendly air, great sound system, and a professional stage for music. Owned by the Gibson Guitar Company, the café is open seven days a week and there is no cover charge for live music. A light menu is served at this nonsmoking, all-ages venue, and music is sometimes performed during lunch. Open daily 8 a.m.–1 a.m. & (Downtown)

JACK'S GUITAR BAR
2185 Nolensville Rd.
Nashville
615/726-3855
Jack's is a funky Friday night kind of beer bar located on one of Nashville's

most interestingly haphazard commercial strips. It is a friendly spot that occasionally books good local singer/songwriters. The bookings can vary from rising star to the first-time performer, so get a second opinion before you go. The bar provides the perfect setting for the country-music jukebox that plays between sets. Open Mon–Sat. (South Nashville)

RADIO CAFE
1313 Woodland St.
Nashville
615/262-1766
A regular schedule of local musicians makes this cozy corner a happening spot. There's always music on Wednesday, Saturday, and Sunday, and sometimes other days as well. A limited menu of daily specials, coffee, and beer are served. Good company and the intimacy of a neighborhood-supported establishment will make anyone feel welcome. The music is of surprisingly good quality, which just goes to show how many relatively unsung musical heroes are currently living in Nashville. Open daily. & (East Nashville)

ROBERT'S WESTERN WORLD
416 Broadway
Nashville
615/256-7937
Robert's, a former clothing store turned honky tonk that was the hip spot on lower Broadway for adventurous retro-country music, books music all day long during the tourist season. This is the place that made BR549 and Greg Garing semi-famous before they left Nashville. Bluegrass-emphasis shows begin daily at 9 a.m., with additional shows at 1, 5, and 9 p.m. There is no cover charge, but there is a one-drink minimum at this friendly place. & (Downtown)

SPRINGWATER
115 27th Ave. N.
Nashville
615/320-0345
You will not see any Music Row types at this divey neighborhood joint next to Centennial Park. The music is local

Elvis' Gold Cadillac

Robin Hood

Top Ten (plus two)
Nashville Musicians
By Michael McCall

Michael McCall, music critic for the *Nashville Scene* and
Nashville-based entertainment writer, offers a definitive list of
musicians who have had the most impact on Nashville music:

1. **Roy Acuff:** After Jimmie Rodgers, Roy Acuff was country music's
   second national star. His presence at the Grand Ole Opry is a primary reason why the Nashville-based live radio show—rather
   than the Big D Jamboree in Dallas, or the WLS Barn Dance in
   Chicago, or the Louisiana Hayride in Shreveport—became the
   place burgeoning country-music stars wanted to be invited to
   join. The Opry's all-star cast in the 1940s led to Nashville's
   becoming a recording center, eventually establishing it as the
   home base of country music.

2. **Hank Williams:** Although his recording career lasted barely three
   years, Hank Williams is the most universally revered country-
   music artist. His colorful, swinging honky tonk and lonesome bal-
   lads provided the music with a dose of honesty and energy. His
   legend looms large over country music more than four decades
   after his tragic death.

3. **Chet Atkins:** Outside of Nashville he's best known for his guitar
   innovations, an elemental, finger-picking style that proved
   incredibly influential in pop and country songs. In country music
   he has enjoyed an even bigger role as a music producer.

4. **The Everly Brothers:** The two young brothers from Kentucky created a brisk style of harmony-driven pop music that soared with
   youthful vigor.

5. **Patsy Cline:** Cline's sophisticated torch songs would reach fans
   far beyond the normal country-music audience, giving commercial Nashville recordings a broader-based respect than they had
   previously achieved.

6. **Loretta Lynn:** A prototypical country gal, Lynn climbed from the
   most remote section of Kentucky coal-mining country to become an
   international star. Her songs, country to the core, featured an out-
   spoken attitude and prideful honesty that, in highly personal terms,

chronicled the struggles of impoverished Southern women as they fought for more respect in their private and working lives. Along with Patsy Cline, Dolly Parton, and Tammy Wynette, Lynn opened up opportunities for women in country music, and she pushed the material toward realism instead of compliant romanticism.

7. **Kris Kristofferson:** A Rhodes Scholar with a love for Hank Williams, Kristofferson expanded the possibilities of a country song with his knack for blending poetic imagery into earthy phrases.

8. **Waylon Jennings:** Following a path forged by Willie Nelson in Texas, Jennings fought with the Nashville studio system in the early 1970s in an effort to wrestle more control over what songs he recorded and how they sounded. Until that point, record companies and session producers dictated the direction of artists, but Jennings' success gave some performers a stronger role in their recordings. In addition, his malevolent presence and long hair drew a younger, counter-culture audience to the music of Nashville.

9. **Jason & the Scorchers:** The best and brashest of the country-punk bands of the 1980s, Jason Ringenberg, Warner Hodges, Jeff Johnson, and Perry Baggs created a furious noise rooted in the most basic of country traditions. The band brought attention to a growing underground rock scene in Nashville while inspiring a national movement that came to be known as "cowpunk."

10. **Randy Travis:** After Kenny Rogers and Alabama steered Nashville toward a more middle-of-the-road sound, Travis came along to return a sense of Southern traditionalism to the music. With his drawling baritone and trad-country arrangements, Travis returned a sense of rural roots to the music. Fans responded by hungrily buying up this new version of an old sound, making Travis the first of the million-selling singers of the young country movement.

11. **Steve Earle:** Earle transformed the possibilities for the future of Nashville songwriting by penning gritty tales of blue-collar workers and dreamers set to a stripped-down, steel-belted rumble that blended the best aspects of country and rock.

12. **Garth Brooks:** Brooks brought a sense of dynamics and theatricality to country music in the 1990s, proving to be the right person to help the music reach a broader audience.

Annual Events in Music City

Browse the Music City Web site (www.nashville.musiccityusa.com) for exact dates and scheduled performers during the International Country Music Fan Fair (second week in June), the Nashville Entertainment Association's Extravaganza (January), the Nashville Songwriter's Association International's Tin Pan South (April), and Country Music Month (October). Citysearch (www.nashville.citysearch.com) also keeps abreast of musical happenings and upcoming major events, so you can check it out in advance and plan your trip to Nashville accordingly.

and sometimes hard to hear and see. The bar is casual in the extreme and everybody seems to know each other. You might happen upon a been-here-a-long-time-and-can't-get-a-break songwriter of surprising talent at Springwater—there are lots of them in Nashville. Open daily. A blues jam session is held every Monday evening beginning at 8. & (Midtown)

THE STATION INN
402 12th Ave. S.
Nashville
615/255-3307
This classic bluegrass and acoustic music club is a favorite with locals and visitors. Pitchers of beer, red-checked tablecloths, and posters from past bluegrass festivals surround music lovers at this friendly venue. The music is always good, the sound is excellent, the club is well-arranged so everyone can see, and you will have a good time no matter who you hear. Music begins around 9 p.m. and, because they do not take reservations, it's best to arrive early. Closed Sun. & (Downtown)

THE SUTLER
2608 Franklin Rd.
Nashville
615/297-9195
The Sutler is a friendly neighborhood bar that regularly books excellent local music and has outstanding national acts from time to time. Good sound, comfortably arranged tables, and a full bar make the Sutler a musician's hangout. Open daily. Sunday is Writer's Night. & (South Nashville)

TOOTSIE'S ORCHID LOUNGE
422 Broadway
Nashville
615/726-0463
Tootsie's is a classic beer tavern whose back door connects with the side entrance to the Ryman Auditorium through the alley. Pictures of country stars of the past adorn the walls. Go for the raucous decor and conversation, not for the music. Live music 10 a.m.–2 a.m. whether you wish it or not. No cover. & (Downtown)

12TH AND PORTER PLAYROOM
114 12th Ave. N.

Nashville
615/254-7236
One of Nashville's best listening rooms, the Playroom is often the choice for record label showcase concerts for new crossover country acts like the Mavericks. Call ahead to make sure you don't encounter alternative rockers by mistake, as this club books the full range of music. Closed Sun. & (Downtown)

WOLFY'S
425 Broadway
Nashville
615/251-1621
Wolfy's occasionally offers surprisingly good musical bookings, such as longtime Nashville session player Buddy Spicher and his band, in a German-influenced tavern where a honky tonk once stood. Next door to The Turf and across from Tootsie's Orchid Lounge (two of Nashville's true juke joints), Wolfy's offers a pleasant respite from the busy pace of Broadway. There is a full bar. Live music is featured nightly, usually

without cover charge. & (Downtown)

ZANIES COMEDY SHOWPLACE
2025 8th Ave. S.
Nashville
615/269-0221
Booked solid on Tuesday nights at Zanies is the Western Beat Roots Revival, a showcase of Texas and Oklahoma music by some of the finest practitioners in town. Zanies, located not too far from Music Row, also books occasional later-afternoon "showcase" appearances by musicians who need to be "seen" by Nashville's country power elite, so check newspaper listings when you get to town. Closed Mon; Wed–Sat are comedy nights. & (South Nashville)

DANCE CLUBS FEATURING COUNTRY MUSIC

LONG HOLLOW JAMBOREE
3600 Long Hollow Pike
Goodlettsville

Wildhorse Saloon, p.122

Donnie Beauchamp

615/824-4445

Long Hollow Jamboree features live music and country dancing that includes square dance, buck dance (traditional Appalachian clogging), and the two-step. Tue, Fri, Sat 5:30–11 p.m. The house band begins playing at 7:30 p.m. No alcohol is served and there's no smoking. Cover charge $2 Tue, $4 Fri and Sat. (North Nashville)

WILDHORSE SALOON
120 2nd Ave. N.
Nashville
615/251-1000 or 615/256-9453 (infor-
mation) or 615/251-1011 (tickets)

The Wildhorse features a 3,000-square-foot inlaid wooden dance floor, with state of the art sound, lights, and video. Dance lessons are free, and Wednesday is Buck Night, when beer costs $1. Wildhorse offers lunch specials and dinner is served until 10. There is a store selling Wildhorse logo merchandise and Friday nights are reserved for big-name concert acts, with ticket prices $8–$15. Open daily 11 a.m.–2 a.m. Cover charge $3–$6. ♿ (Downtown)

Cumberland Science Museum

7

KIDS' STUFF

There are many sides of Nashville for kids to enjoy. The entertainment industry side—with television tapings and glimpses of celebrities at the Hard Rock Café and Planet Hollywood—will provide excitement for kids. The historic side—which has a wealth of mansions that will be fun for kids to pretend they once lived in, and "living history" activities at other locations—will pique a child's curiosity. The great outdoors side—with guided nature programs and interpretive activities at several park locations year-round—will foster learning while you and the kids enjoy nature.

Nashville's urban- and suburban-culture side is the same as anywhere else— familiar fast-food restaurants, brand-name stores, shopping malls, public libraries, movie theaters, record stores, and skating rinks plentiful in and around the town—with familiar activities easily available. Perhaps most of all, being exposed to the hustle and bustle of a real city, with a "bat building" in the midst of its downtown, the rough and tumble ambience of lower Broadway's honky tonk row, shopping galore in the Second Avenue tourist district and at suburban malls, free musical events in the city parks, and the whispers of fame emanating from Music Row is bound to have a visceral effect on the fast-paced youngsters of today's world.

ANIMALS AND THE GREAT OUTDOORS

NASHVILLE ZOO AT GRASSMERE
3777 Nolensville Pike

Nashville
615/833-1534
A habitat for native animals and plants where kids can see bison roaming free. There's lots to do at Grassmere,

including indoor close-ups (viewing birds and other display creatures in temporary captivity) and outdoor "real life" encounters. This in-town branch location for the Nashville Zoo has lots of green space for running and walking off extra energy and an outdoor climb-upon structure built by parent volunteers (see Chapter 5: Sights and Attractions). As it makes its transition into a world-class zoo, Nashville Zoo will be adding new exhibits and animals in the upcoming months. ⅍ (South Nashville)

LONG HUNTER STATE PARK
2910 Hobson Pike
Hermitage
615/885-2422
Sunset canoe floats on Percy Priest Lake, accompanied by a park naturalist, or hikes around the lake at twilight are great opportunities to see nature in the wild. Activities are offered frequently during the summer. Call ahead to check schedule and reserve a space (see Chapter 9: Parks and Gardens). (East Nashville)

RADNOR LAKE STATE
NATURAL AREA
1160 Otter Creek Rd.
Nashville
615/377-1281
Family activities, like full-moon hikes and evening canoe paddling, often include sightings of deer, turtles, and baby geese. There's always some-

thing exciting enough to intrigue a child happening at Radnor, even if it's just the parade of dogs walking their owners. But those magical moments, when you spot a mother duck teaching her little ones to swim, a line of turtles sunning on a dead log, or a brigade of geese coming in for an aquatic landing, will transport both you and your child into a state of bliss.

Bathrooms are located in three different parts of the park, for the convenience of those with youngsters, and the nature center has a cool display of stuffed former Radnor dwellers on exhibit. Both the nature center and one short trail, marked with nature-watching signs, are wheelchair-accessible (see Chapter 9: Parks and Gardens). Open daily. Free. ⅍ (South Nashville)

WARNER PARK NATURE CENTER
7311 Hwy. 100
Nashville
615/352-6299
Warner Park naturalists and Friends of Warner Park offer a changing schedule of activities designed for specific age levels. The classes are free, and usually one day or evening only, so visitors to Nashville feel comfortable dropping in. These are exciting classes that kids love, like a nighttime walk with flashlights in hand entitled "Spying on Spiders;" or "Cold Hearted Friends," a hands-on class with snakes, lizards, and turtles. Chil-

---

T I P

The Nashville Wildlife Park at Grassmere has daily "critter encounters" at 11 a.m. and 2 p.m., and participatory feedings for children and adults on Saturday and Sunday at 11 a.m. and 3 p.m.

Top Ten Attractions for Kids

Barbara Moutenot, who met her husband, Roger, while running a New York recording studio, moved to Nashville four years ago. She is a freelance writer, education editor for *Nashville Parent* magazine, and the mother of two young boys.

"Many families I know move to Nashville because it is a great city in which to raise children. Here are a few of the attractions that stand out for my family."

1. **Cumberland Science Museum**—We may spend one hour or three there and always have fun. This museum appeals to all ages with its changing exhibits and permanent planetarium.

2. **Elliston Soda Shop**—Located in an interesting area to explore, the Soda Shop serves up thick milkshakes and authentic "meat and three" meals.

3. **The Sutler**—An old-time bar/restaurant where we can take our five-year-old to hear early-hour music—anything from rock to folk to country, it's the real thing.

4. **Dragon Park**—The nickname, of course, comes from the huge mosaic dragon built amid the sand and climbing gear.

5. **The Farmers Market**—The kids love talking to the farmers and picking out fruits and vegetables.

6. **The Nashville Zoo**—The zoo is well laid out for kids on foot and small enough to see in a few hours. Located 20 minutes outside of Nashville, it makes for a nice trip to the country.

7. **Davis-Kidd Bookstore**—A store with something for everybody: books, magazines, and a permanent toy train setup for children to enjoy. Lunch at the café is kid-friendly, with peanut butter and grilled cheese on the menu.

8. **Country Music Hall of Fame**—With a giant guitar, old cars, and Elvis music, this museum is fun even for those who don't like country music.

9. **Nashville Sounds' Games**—All the fun of a major league team for only $4 a head. Kids will love the organ music, the nachos, the Frisbee-catching dog, and the special giveaways at the Sounds' games.

10. **Nashville Zoo at Grassmere**—The Jungle Gym, an enormous wooden-beam structure with catwalks and rope nets, captivates almost any child immediately.

dren under age eight must be accompanied by an adult. (West Nashville)

STORY TIME

Local libraries, bookstores, and even shopping malls hold free story and activity hours for kids on a regular schedule. Here's a list, but call ahead to make sure the storyteller isn't on vacation the week you are in Nashville:

BARNES AND NOBLE
1701 Mallory Ln.
Brentwood
615/377-9979
This national bookstore chain hosts story hours on Monday and Saturday mornings at 11. (South Nashville)

BEN WEST DOWNTOWN PUBLIC LIBRARY
225 Polk Ave.
Nashville
615/862-5785
The Tom Tichenor Marionettes, famous among adults who grew up in Nashville, are named after their creator, a well-loved local puppeteer. Puppet shows are usually presented on Friday and the first and third Saturday of the month at 10:30 in the morning. Advance reservations required—visitors should call ahead on the chance that they might be performing during their Nashville stay. Regular storytimes are Wednesday mornings at 10:30. (Downtown)

BOOKSTAR
4301 Harding Rd.
Nashville
615/292-7895
Every Tuesday morning at 10 and every Sunday at 3, Bookstar holds a story hour for kids. (West Nashville)

BRENTWOOD PUBLIC LIBRARY
5055 Maryland Way
Brentwood
615/371-0090
Storytime is held every Tuesday and Wednesday morning at 10:30 and 11, but parents must call one day ahead to reserve a spot. (South Nashville)

DAVIS-KIDD BOOKSELLERS
4007 Hillsboro Rd.
Nashville
514/385-2645
A Saturday-morning Kidd's Corner, with different bookstore employees and guest readers holding forth before a young audience, is held at 11 at Nashville's hometown bookstore. (West Nashville)

HENDERSONVILLE PUBLIC LIBRARY
116 Dunn St.
Hendersonville
615/824-0656
Every Tuesday and Wednesday mornings at 10:30 is regular story hour for kids.

THE MALL AT GREEN HILLS
2126 Abbott Martin Rd.
Nashville
615/298-5478
The Kid's Club (Miss Tahra, Glenfreeda, the Good Witch, and other special guests) puts on a show for young kids every Saturday morning at 11. (West Nashville)

PUBLIC LIBRARY OF NASHVILLE AND DAVIDSON COUNTY
Green Hills Branch, 3801 Green Hills Village Dr.
Nashville
615/862-5863
This storytime, Tuesday morning at 10:30, gets high marks from the Nashville Scene. (West Nashville)

PUBLIC LIBRARY OF NASHVILLE AND DAVIDSON COUNTY
Southeast Branch, 2325 Hickory Highlands Dr.
Nashville
615/862-5871
This branch library offers a Spanish/English story hour. (South Nashville)

MUSEUMS

CHEEKWOOD, NASHVILLE'S HOME OF ART AND GARDENS
1200 Forrest Park Dr.
Nashville
615/356-8000
Special activities for kids are planned in conjunction with exhibits at Cheekwood, whose hidden gardens, beautifully landscaped grounds, and impressive limestone buildings and pools will excite any child. Hands-on art classes for children at different age levels are held throughout the year, most lasting four to six weeks. Check and see if there might be a seasonal event or one-day workshop happening while you are visiting Nashville. A brand-new education center completed in late 1998 will feature interactive galleries and hands-on exhibit-related activities aimed at young audiences. Mon–Sat 9–5, Sun 11–5. $8 adults, $7 seniors and college students, $5 children ages 6–17, children under age 6 free (see Chapter 8:

Museums and Galleries). & (West Nashville)

COUNTRY MUSIC HALL OF FAME AND MUSEUM
4 Music Square E.
Nashville
615/256-1639 or 800/816-7652
This lively museum has plenty of interactive exhibits to keep kids occupied. In addition to miniature dioramas depicting the history of country music that look like better-than-imaginable dollhouses, they'll like Elvis' gold cadillac and Burt Reynolds' *Smokey and the Bandit* race car. There is a short self-guided kids' tour through one portion of the museum. Kids will also enjoy riding the trolley (included in the price of admission) to the other sites. Studio B, a still-operating recording studio, offers a fascinating view into the process of recording, while Hatch Show Print, an operating print shop, gives constant demonstrations as they go about their business. Apr–mid-Sep 9–5, Memorial Day–Labor Day 8–6. $10.75 adults, $4.75 children ages 6–11, children under age 6 free (see Chapter 8: Museums and Galleries). & (Midtown)

CUMBERLAND SCIENCE MUSEUM
800 Fort Negley Blvd.
Nashville
615/862-5160
Originally the Nashville Children's

Nashville Parent, a free 60-page paper packed with original writing by local experts, is published monthly and can be found in grocery stores and kid-friendly spots all over town. Schedules of current events for kids are always included. Parents interested in planning ahead for a visit to Nashville can contact the publication by e-mail at *npinfo@nashvilleparent.com* to find out the cost of mailing a single issue. Annual subscriptions are $20.

Museum, the Cumberland Science Museum remains dedicated to children as an audience. Hands-on, high-tech exhibits and planetarium shows will keep kids of all ages fascinated. Apr–mid-Sep Tue–Sat 9:30–5, Sun 12:30–5:30; Memorial Day–Labor Day Mon–Sat 9:30–5, Sun 10:30–5:30. $6 adults, $4.50 children, children under age 3 free. All tickets are half-price on Tue noon–5. Planetarium shows 11 a.m., 1 p.m., and 3 p.m. for additional $1 (see Chapter 8: Museums and Galleries). (South Nashville)

HISTORIC MANSKER'S STATION FRONTIER LIFE CENTER
Moss-Wright Park, Caldwell Rd. Goodlettsville
615/859-3678
The hands-on demonstrations at one of the very first long-hunter forts in the area will thrill children of any age. The reconstructed fort has furnished living quarters and an operational blacksmith shop. Ongoing interpretive activities are given by museum educators dressed in period attire, like Johnny Menire, a Middle Tennessee descen-

dent of a French trader who married a Tennessee Cherokee, who had researched many of the Indian ways that were taught to the early settlers of the state. Mar–Dec Tue–Sat 9–4:45. $3 adults, $2 students. (North Nashville)

NASHVILLE TOY MUSEUM
2613 McGavock Pike, Music Valley/Opryland area
Nashville
615/883-8870
Constantly running trains make this crowded toy emporium come alive. Toys of all kinds, from dolls to soldiers to model boats and cars, fill the cases of this quirky amateur museum. Many of the antique toys are of historical interest and will fascinate adults, too. Apr–mid-Sep daily 9–5, Memorial Day–Labor Day daily 9–9. $3 ages 13 and over, $1.50 children ages 6–12, children under 6 free. (East Nashville)

ODDS AND ENDS

CREATIVE FITNESS CENTER
1207 Linden Ave.

Cumberland Science Museum

Nashville
615/383-9119
This low-key art school, for kids and adults, operates on a drop-in basis. There are classes and workshops that are divided into age groups, and each is a one-time event. Visitors are able to immediately enter into activities such as puppet-making, hand-building with clay, and beginning art explorations in a variety of media. Some projects have extra supply costs. Weeklong camps are planned during summer months. Call ahead or check out the Creative Fitness Center's Web site listing on CitySearch, *www .Nashville.citysearch.com*. (Midtown)

NASHVILLE CHILDREN'S THEATRE
724 Seventh Ave. S.
Nashville
615/254-9103 or 615/254-6020
This excellent theater company gears performances to curriculum-based learning and provides exemplary support materials for all plays, while incorporating humor and action into the entertainment. They produce a full season during the school year, and weekday mornings find their performance spaces just south of downtown filled with student audiences. Each production also has a weekend family series. NCT offers summer theater workshops for grades two through six and for junior high students. Call to see if there are any performances on the schedule during your planned stay in Nashville. (Downtown)

PLAYGROUNDS

ELMINGTON PARK
Between Elmington and Bowling Aves. at West End
Nashville

Elmington Park is a large park with playing fields, tennis courts, and a new playground furnished by Nashville's Junior League. Kids like being here because the other areas of the park are often lively with adult activities like softball, cricket, and even rehearsals of the medieval jousting events for the Tennessee Renaissance Festival. (West Nashville)

FANNIE MAE DEES' "DRAGON PARK"
Blakemore/Wedgewood at 22nd Ave. S.
Nashville
This park features a huge mosaic tile dragon that looks like the Loch Ness Monster emerging from the sea in several areas at once. The dragon incorporates benches, swings, and a water fountain, and it is great fun to climb on. It was designed by New York artist Pedro Silva and decorated by Silva and lots of neighborhood residents. The park has picnic tables, several play areas, and sidewalks that are good for skates. (Midtown)

PARMER PARK
Belle Meade, behind Belle Meade Plantation on Leake Ave.
Nashville
A favorite neighborhood park in a quiet spot, Parmer Park was built on the site of Parmer Elementary School, whose doorway arch still stands. The streets around this park are good places to skate, bike, or take a stroller because they are wide and not heavily traveled. (West Nashville)

KID-FRIENDLY RESTAURANTS

Chain restaurants such as Chuck E. Cheese, Cracker Barrel, Dalt's Grill,

Nashville Children's Theatre producing director Scot Copeland, p. 129

Darryl's 1827 Restaurant, and Shoney's offer special children's menus, as they do around the country. The Hard Rock Café and Planet Hollywood serve all-American food like hot dogs and burgers in exciting, media-blitzy atmospheres that provide distraction for kids, but parents should beware that there are long waits at these places during prime time that will try the patience of any child. Most Nashville restaurants work hard to accommodate family groups, but places that are already boisterous, like brew pubs or restaurants with major bar scenes, can be disastrous with children. The following local eating places will make kids feel especially welcome.

BENKAY JAPANESE RESTAURANT
White Bridge Rd.,
Lion's Head Shopping Center
Nashville
615/356-6600
Although this restaurant has a sushi bar, it lacks the formality of some Japanese restaurants, and kids will feel quite at home. The dining rooms fill up every day at lunchtime since the restaurant is in a busy shopping center near Belle Meade. For an introduction to Japanese custom, ask for a special, sit-on-the-floor booth. Picky eaters will love the "lunchbox" specials, where the fried shrimp and rice come in separate compartments, and there is a fresh peeled orange for dessert. ♿ (West Nashville)

BONGO JAVA
2007 Belmont Blvd.
Nashville
615/385-5282
This relaxed coffeehouse, in a bungalow on a neighborhood street, is a natural for kids. There are picnic tables out front, and they serve Fruit Loops, Pop Tarts, bagels, bologna and "pbj" sandwiches, and milk any time of day or night. Open 7 a.m. to midnight. ♿ (Midtown)

ELLISTON PLACE SODA SHOP
2111 Elliston Pl.
Nashville

615/327-1090

This one is a sure bet. Sit at the counter where they scoop the ice cream before your eyes, or in a booth with its very own mini-jukebox, and make sure to order a chocolate shake. Hamburgers, sandwiches, and plate lunches are all good, and the apple pie à la mode is superb. (Midtown)

FIDO CAFE AND COFFEE ROASTERS
1812 21st Ave. S.

Free Stuff

Kids love action. Get to know the town by driving around and looking at new construction sites, visiting some of Nashville's quirkiest architecture, strolling through the vegetable and flower stands at the farmers market, skating or biking around the adjacent Bicentennial Mall, finding some of the old fire stations, or watching planes take off.

__John C. Tune Airport__, Centennial Boulevard and Briley Parkway, 615/350-5000, is used primarily for small private and commuter planes. This airport is located just north of the city in the relatively isolated Cockrill Bend of the Cumberland River. __Nashville International Airport__, Donelson Pike at I-40, 615/275-1675, is another good bet for watching planes take off and land. The planes coming in to land pass right over I-40 or Murfreesboro Road, depending upon the wind direction. Look for a place to park off of Donelson Pike near the cargo area, just off Briley Parkway at Vultee Boulevard, or by the National Guard hangars on the south side of the airport.

Drive by and look at the architecture, and if they don't look too busy, ask if you can see the fire engines. During the month of December the folks at Nashville's downtown fire station put on a holiday light display that is worth seeing (it has moving parts). Both __Hillsboro Village__ and __East End__ are historic stations. General information: 615/862-8585. Other locations include downtown's Fourth Avenue S. and McGavock, Midtown's 21st Avenue S. (one block west of Blair Boulevard), and East Nashville's Holly Street.

Hillsboro Village
615/385-7959
Like its sister store, Bongo Java, Fido loves kids. The mascot, a cartoon puppy sign left over from former owner Jones Pet Store, serves as the theme for contests and promotions, and there are always drawing materials awaiting kids at the high counter. A super-fancy hot chocolate and a bagel sandwich or huge oatmeal cookie will win the mind of almost any youngster. It's a hip joint as well, with some of the friendliest and funniest servers in town. ♿ (Midtown)

MEDITERRANEAN CUISINE
400 21st Ave. S.
Nashville
615/321-8960
An inexpensive place across the street from Vanderbilt University and within walking distance of Music Row, Mediterranean Cuisine offers a mini-gyro for kids, along with several other special items. The hummus, tabouli, and baba ghanouj, to be eaten on pita strips, are fun, and

falafel is a healthy alternative to chicken nuggets. (Midtown)

WAY OUT WEST
3415 West End Ave.
Nashville
615/298-5562
Kids who come in dressed in Western wear get their pictures taken at this Western-theme restaurant. Breakfasts get rave reviews, so if you have some early risers, try something different to start the day off on a good foot. Opens daily at 7. ♿ (Midtown)

STORES KIDS LOVE

Whether shopping for kids or with kids, here are the *Nashville Scene* readers' poll favorites:

IMAGINATION CROSSROADS
3900 Hillsboro Rd.,
Green Hills Mall area
Nashville
615/297-0637
Early childhood learning and interac-

Nashville Toy Museum

Tennessee Tourist Development

tive toys are their specialties. This shop puts their merchandise to good use by offering preschool arts-and-crafts workshops on Tuesday and Wednesday mornings. There is an admission charge for the workshops. (West Nashville)

PHILLIPS TOY MART
5207 Harding Rd.
Nashville
615/352-5363
Phillips is an old-fashioned toy store with rows of boxed toys on shelves, hobby kits for model makers, and "name" dolls. In business for over 50 years, Phillips has recently expanded to twice its original size. They must be doing something right! &. (West Nashville)

Robin Hood

8

MUSEUMS AND GALLERIES

Situated as they are in locations as unlikely as a full-scale replica of the Athenian Parthenon, a reproduction English manor house, the basement of a performing-arts center, two Victorian brick gymnasiums, and a glass-front barn, Nashville's museums form an eclectic grouping. In a recent Nashville Scene *contest entitled "You Are So Nashville If ..." a reader bemoaned the fact that there is no major art museum in Nashville by quipping, "You are so Nashville if your art museum is at the airport." (The Nashville International Airport sponsors a year-round program of changing exhibits, but most of its "permanent collection" of Tennessee art resides in upper-level office spaces.) Happily, change is in the air. In 2000 the downtown post office will be substantially retrofitted so that it can reopen as a visual-arts center, a major downtown edifice that can fill the symbolic role of a city museum.*

Meanwhile, Cheekwood has incorporated site-specific contemporary sculpture and conceptual art into a wooded landscape and opened an education center for interactive learning. Perhaps most exciting is the news that the Country Music Hall of Fame is planning to move downtown. The three-story, state-of-the-art facility, with exhibits designed by the same prominent firm that created the U.S. Holocaust Museum, will provide an unforgettable experience for Nashville music fans.

ART MUSEUMS

CHEEKWOOD MUSEUM OF ART
1200 Forrest Park Dr.
Nashville

615/353-2140
The Cheek Mansion, built during the Great Depression by wholesale grocery magnate Leslie Cheek, now houses galleries containing Cheek-

wood's permanent collection of American art as well as a full series of temporary exhibits. Cheekwood is the legatee of the old Nashville Museum of Art, and thus has a number of pieces from the area's early art history in its holdings. One gallery is devoted to the limestone sculpture of Will Edmondson, a Nashville native who was the first African American artist to exhibit at the Museum of Modern Art (1937).

Other collections include English silver and Worcester porcelain. The Museum of Art proper will be closed 1998 through mid-1999 for renovation, but the Woodland Sculpture Trail, a union of nature and contemporary art, and the Learning Center, with its innovative display areas for contemporary art, are strong new attractions that will remain open. Visit the museum's interactive Web site: *www.cheekwood.org.* Mon–Sat 9–5, Sun 11–5. Extended hours Apr 15–Labor Day Mon–Thu 9–8. $8 adults, $7 seniors and students with ID, $5 ages 6–17. & (West Nashville)

FISK UNIVERSITY–AARON DOUGLAS GALLERY
Jackson St. and 17th Ave. N., Fisk University Library, Third Floor
Nashville
615/329-8720
Named after the most prominent visual artist of the Harlem Renaissance and the founder of Fisk University's Department of Art, the Aaron Douglas Gallery houses changing exhibits drawn from the university's permanent collections of African American and African art. Tue–Fri 11 a.m.–1 p.m. or by special appointment. Free. & (North Nashville)

FISK UNIVERSITY–CARL VAN VECHTEN GALLERY
D.B. Todd Blvd. and 17th Ave. N.
Nashville
615/329-8720
Housed in a red-brick Victorian building that was the university's first gymnasium, the Carl Van Vechten Gallery has a portion of the Alfred Stieglitz Estate on permanent display. This group of works includes pieces by Arthur Dove, Marsden Hartley, John Marin, Georgia O'Keeffe, and other American modernists, as well as an unusual Diego Rivera still life. The collection, which echoes the range of artists shown at Stieglitz' 291 Gallery in New York during the '10s and '20s, also includes an early painting by Picasso and prints by Cézanne, Renoir, and Toulouse-Lautrec, as well as some of the first African sculpture to be exhibited in the United States. O'Keeffe, who divided the Stieglitz estate into six parts (the other portions went to the Metropolitan Museum of Art, the Art Institute of Chicago, the Philadelphia Museum of Art, the Whitney Museum of American Art, and the National Gallery of Art), dedicated these works to Fisk in honor of Harlem Renaissance arts patron Carl Van Vechten, who was a close associate of Fisk's first African American president, Charles S. Johnson. The lower gallery features changing exhibits. Tue–Fri 9–5, Sat–Sun 1–5. Free. (North Nashville)

THE PARTHENON
Centennial Park, Metro Postal Service
Nashville
615/862-8431
A full-scale replica of the Athenian original, the *Parthenon* was first built in plaster as the art building for Tennessee's Centennial Celebration in 1897. It proved so popular that it

The Parthenon

was rebuilt in the 1920s to become a permanent art museum. Its holdings include the Cowan Collection of American paintings, copies of the Elgin Marbles, and a 42-foot sculpture of Athena Parthenos by contemporary artist Alan LeQuire. Tue–Sat 9–4:30, Sun 12:30–4:30. Closed Sun Oct–Mar. $2.50 adults, $1.25 seniors and students, children under age 4 free. ♿ (Midtown)

VANDERBILT UNIVERSITY FINE ARTS GALLERY
23rd and West End Aves.
Nashville
615/322-0605
Housed in a former gymnasium, the Fine Arts Gallery presents changing exhibits drawn from the university's permanent art collections, which range from classical antiquities to contemporary art, and small traveling exhibits. Located right off West End Avenue, the gallery reserves several parking spaces for visitors to this crowded campus. A quiet oasis, the gallery's recent emphasis has been on contemporary and modern works

tied to intellectual or literary movements. Mon–Fri 1–4, Sat–Sun 1–5. Closed during school breaks. Free. (Midtown)

SCIENCE AND HISTORY MUSEUMS

CUMBERLAND SCIENCE MUSEUM
800 Fort Negley Blvd.
Nashville
615/862-5160
Geared primarily to children, this science and nature museum located just to the south of downtown features hands-on permanent and traveling exhibits and daily planetarium shows. It is always filled with exuberant kids exploring how and why things work, and days during the school year can be packed with school field-trip groups. Changing thematic planetarium programs for teens and adults are shown on weekend evenings throughout the year. Apr–mid-Sep Tue–Sat 9:30–5, Sun 12:30–5:30; Labor Day–Memorial Day Mon–Sat 9:30–5, Sun 10:30–5:30. $6 adults, $4.50

seniors and children, children under age 3 free. Planetarium shows are $1 additional. Half price Tuesday afternoon. Web site: *www.csmisfun.org.* & (South Nashville)

NASHVILLE TOY MUSEUM
2613B McGavock Pike
Nashville
615/883-8870
This static and eccentric small museum, located in Music Valley across from the Opryland Hotel, will delight children and most adults with its wall-to-wall collections of historical toys. A train layout runs through the entire space. Apr–mid-Sep 9–5, Memorial Day–Labor Day 8:30 a.m.–9 p.m. $3 adults, $1.50 children, children under age 6 free. & (East Nashville)

SANKOFA AFRICAN HERITAGE MUSEUM

Self-Taught Artists

Dan Prince, founder of STAR (Self Taught Artists Resources, a nonprofit organization), has worked in the field of American self-taught art for more than 20 years. Documents from his field research can be found in the Special Collections at Vanderbilt University's Jean and Alexander Heard Library. He says the following about Nashville's self-taught artists:

"Like other parts of the rural South, the area surrounding Nashville has proven rich in inspiration for folk and self-taught artists. In recent years their work has become a respected part of the art scene, often supported first by artists (both visual and musical) who championed the creativity of these natural artists, and risk-taking art collectors. Due primarily to the encouragement they receive from this "grass roots" art market, these artists have been able to produce enough works to find their way into larger markets in southern cities like Atlanta, New Orleans, Birmingham, and Nashville—you'll find them here in Nashville in several galleries and museums around town. In recent years, the Tennessee State Museum has purchased contemporary folk art for their permanent collection of Tennessee art, as has the Nashville International Airport. Cheekwood Museum of Art has long held a notable collection of Nashville's best-known self-taught artist, William Edmondson, who was active in the 1930s and 1940s."

Memorabilia at the Country Music Hall of Fame

101 French Landing Dr.
Nashville
615/726-4894
This new museum, containing hundreds of pieces of African sculpture and utilitarian objects, opened in late 1997. The museum space is one large gallery filled with glass cases, each painstakingly labled with country of origin, tribe, and materials, but the effect is almost overwhelming because of the sheer number of objects. There is a book shop featuring publications related to African culture and African American heritage and religion, and a restaurant that serves lunch. Community outreach programs and innovative activities, such as a Pre Kwanzaa/Hanukkah celebration, have already made this museum an important part of the Nashville community. Mon–Fri 10–6, Sat 1–5, Sun 1–6. $10 adults, $5 seniors and students, children under age 12 free. (North Nashville)

TENNESSEE STATE MUSEUM
505 Deaderick St., in the James K.
Polk State Office Bldg., below the
Tennessee Performing Arts Center
Nashville
615/741-2692
The Tennessee State Museum's collections range from prehistoric artifacts to works of contemporary art. Particular strengths are permanent displays interpreting state history, politics, and personal accomplishments. Native American utilitarian and ceremonial objects, quilts, furniture, silver, and paintings made in Tennessee highlight the permanent collections. There is a regular schedule of temporary exhibits, which vary from art to decorative arts to all aspects of Tennessee-related history. The museum also holds educational and interpretive programs, free of charge, on a regular basis. Tue–Sat 10–5, Sun 1–5. Free. ♿ (Downtown)

SPECIALTY MUSEUMS

COUNTRY MUSIC HALL OF FAME
AND MUSEUM
4 Music Square E.
Nashville
615/256-1639 or 800/816-7652
The Hall of Fame is located in the heart of Music Row, on the corner of 16th Avenue South and Division Streets. This is the place to learn the origins of what we call "country" music—from its earliest legacies in the music of the British Isles and in African work songs, to its more recent manifestations as bluegrass, blues, gospel, Cajun, and rock 'n' roll. Exhibits range from musical instruments and historical dioramas and displays to costumes and interactive games. Elvis Presley's gold Cadillac is in the museum collection, along with brass plaques dedicated to music greats since the Hall of

Fame was founded in 1961. "Stars and Guitars," the Gibson Guitar centennial exhibit, curated by guitar great Chet Atkins, features a state-of-the-art interactive video presentation. A day pass to the Hall of Fame includes unlimited rides on the Nashville trolley, which runs the Music Row/Lower Broadway route every 25 minutes. The trolley stops at Hatch Show Print, a working nineteenth-century blockprint poster shop, and RCA's legendary Studio B Recording Studio, a much-sought-after recording venue.

Hatch Show Print sells the best print souvenirs in Nashville, and the Hall of Fame gift shop is a treasure trove of memorabilia, from the sublimely serious to the irreverent and ridiculous. Open daily year-round 9–5, Memorial Day–Labor Day daily 8–6. $10.75 adults, $4.75 children ages 6–11, children under age 6 free. Web site: *www. halloffame.org.* &
(Midtown)

GRAND OLE OPRY MUSEUM
2804 Opryland Dr.
Nashville

The Sources of Country Music

Nashville artist Marilyn Murphy, associate professor of art at Vanderbilt University, thinks that Thomas Hart Benton's The Sources of Country Music, *a mural commissioned with funds from the National Endowment for the Arts and the artist's final work, is one of the most exciting pieces of art in Nashville.*

"Thomas Hart Benton's rollicking 6-by-10-foot mural, displayed in a wonderful installation at the Country Music Hall of Fame that includes studies and a model, is the best permanent exhibit in town. An Appalachian woman with a dulcimer, an African American blues singer, and a cowboy with a guitar are among the many figures that swirl through the rhythmic composition. Full of life and sometimes surprising color (check out the curious green light behind the saddle!), this painting contains some of the major themes of country music as well as references to Benton's own rich body of work. The exhibit offers a fascinating look into the artist's mind and how the work of art was created, since many of the original sketches and preliminary paintings are on view, and two short videos document Benton's life and artistic process. A delight for anyone interested in music, art, history, or American life."

615/889-3060

Even though the Opryland Theme Park is closed, the Grand Ole Opry Museum remains open. Anyone coming to town for a performance of the Grand Ole Opry should allow time to see this small museum, which has separate Roy Acuff and Minnie Pearl collections, and focuses on such country-music notables as Patsy Cline and Marty Robbins, and on longtime Opry performers Hank Snow and Little Jimmie Dickens. A multiscreen video production highlights the museum exhibits. Mon–Thu 10:30–4:30, Fri 10:30–7:30, Sat 10:30–9:30, Sun 12:30–4:30. Free. ♿ (East Nashville)

HARTZLER-TOWNER MULTICULTURAL MUSEUM
Scarritt-Bennett Center
1008 19th Ave. S.
Nashville
615/340-7481

Housed on the second floor of the Wightman Library at Scarritt-Bennett Center, the Hartzler-Towner Multicultural Museum collection, containing artifacts from all over the world, was originally amassed by Methodist missionaries. The collections have been added to by generous donations from local and national collectors over the past few years, as its multicultural focus has become more clearly defined. Changing exhibits and educational outreach programs on such themes as storytelling and basketry are interpreted with a refreshingly objective, anthropological emphasis. Mon–Fri 8–8, Sat 9–5, Sun 1–6. Free. (Midtown)

GALLERIES

AMERICAN ARTISAN
4231 Harding Rd., Stanford Square
Nashville

The Frist Center for the Visual Arts

"For over 25 years I've been a merchant of fine American handcrafts as well as director of the annual Artisan Festival in Centennial Park. I have seen my share of visitors, tourists, and customers who grow more and more sophisticated and demand higher quality with each passing year. The Frist Center for the Visual Arts, soon to open in the downtown post office building, meets an aching need for these visitors—not to mention their children. I've often worried about young children who are brought to the Artisan as if it were a museum; now we will have a source to inspire and teach them. None too soon."
—Nancy Saturn, owner, American Artisan

615/298-4691
This gallery/shop, which has shown and sold fine crafts for over 25 years, has been a leader in a national trend toward recognition of artists who work in craft media. Nashville, home to many highly skilled craft artists, has become a ready and willing audience for the Artisans' annual outdoor show, held on Father's Day weekend, which features a changing cast of artists from all over the United States. This is Nashville's favorite place to find an artistic wedding gift or a piece of cutting-edge jewelry, or that special piece of handmade furniture, glass, or ceramic ware that will bring delight with every use. Open daily 10–6. (West Nashville)

THE ARTS COMPANY
215 Fifth Ave. N.
Nashville
615/254-2040
Local artists, both fine and folk, are well represented here. An eclectic mixture in a cheerful storefront space. Celebrity photographers such as Ed Clark (*Life Magazine*) and Marty Stewart are featured. Open Mon–Sat 10–5:30. Free. (Downtown)

ARTS IN THE AIRPORT
Nashville International Airport
Ticketing Level (three locations)
Nashville
615/275-1610
The airport features quarterly changing exhibits of paintings and photography by local and regional artists (with works often offered for sale), student art projects, and special exhibits ranging from quilts to interactive sculpture to stained glass. A current schedule of exhibits can be found on the Web site: *www.nash-intl.com* & (East Nashville)

BELMONT UNIVERSITY-LEU GALLERY
Belmont University Library
1900 Belmont Blvd.
Nashville
Belmont University's Leu Gallery features temporary exhibits and small traveling shows in such art media as graphic design, photography, ceramics, painting, drawing, printmaking, and sculpture in a beautiful two-gallery space adjacent to the art library reading room. The university's own students and faculty, working in all of the above areas of art, are often showcased, as are local collections. Mon–Fri 8–4, Sat 9–4:30, Sun 2–5. Free. & (Midtown)

BERDAHL'S GALLERY
2298 Metro Center Blvd. #101,
Fountain Square
Nashville
615/254-4547
The concentration on local contemporary African American artists makes Berdahl's unique. This storefront space has exciting works on view by a select group of mostly figurative painters, several of whom have been published nationally in poster and children's book form. Located in a busy movie theater complex, Berdahl's is open until 9 p.m. on weekends to accommodate leisure-time viewers. Tue–Thu 10–5, Fri–Sat 10–9. & (North Nashville)

CHROMATICS GALLERY
625 Fogg St., Chromatics
Photoimaging Services,
second floor,
Nashville
615/254-0063
Chromatics Gallery is Nashville's premier color lab, so it has historically been a crossroads of everyone in the business. Owner Ann Borum, long

active in the American Society of Magazine Photographers and editor of several books resulting from statewide photography projects, has opened an elegantly appointed second-floor gallery where she holds changing shows of outstanding national and local photography. Mon–Fri 8–6. Free. (Downtown)

CUMBERLAND GALLERY
4107 Hillsboro Circle
Nashville
615/297-0296

Cumberland Gallery, Nashville's top-drawer commercial fine art space, showcases regional and national contemporary artists of established reputation in monthly shows. This gallery, which has made an effort to recruit artists from the Southeast in its more than 15 years of existence, has broadened the reputation of Nashville as an art center by presenting some of the most outstanding artists at the annual Seattle International Art Fair. Tue–Sat 10–5. & (West Nashville)

FINER THINGS
1898 Nolensville Rd.
Nashville
615/244-3003

This impressive showroom of interior design displays both high-end manufactured wares and one-of-a-kind furniture, lots of cool lamps, and a wide range of mostly decorative artwork. Finer Things is located in a nondescript location near the Tennessee State Fairgrounds. It's worth a visit to see this imaginative renovation of a small industrial building, as well as to see works of art integrated into decor. Weekdays 9–5 and by appointment seven days a week. (South Nashville)

IN THE GALLERY
624A Jefferson St.
Nashville
615/255-0705

In the Gallery, a 10-year-old commercial art gallery in a historic building just north of the farmers market, was founded by photographer Carlton Wilkinson as a showcase for local artists, with an emphasis on African American art, photography, and African art—some of it surprisingly affordable. A variety of small gift items and posters are also available here, and visitors are always made to feel welcome. In the Gallery also serves as the semiofficial headquarters of N4Art, the Nashville African American Artists Association. Tue–Sat noon–5 and by appointment. (North Nashville)

SHELTON GALLERY & FRAME
4239 Harding Rd., Stanford Square
Nashville
615/298-9935

Folk art and works by twentieth-century artists with Nashville connections are featured at Shelton Gallery & Frame. Squeezed into a tiny space, this gallery sells an electic but fascinating mix of art by some names that might surprise visitors, such as Red Grooms and Chaim Gross. Mon–Sat 10–6. (West Nashville)

TENNESSEE ARTS COMMISSION GALLERY
401 Charlotte Ave.
Nashville
615/741-1701

Changing exhibits of Tennessee artists and annual visual art, craft, and photography fellowship recipients are featured at the Tennessee Arts Commission Gallery. This unassuming gallery located in a state office building on the corner of Fourth Avenue North and Charlotte, two blocks away from the Tennessee State Museum, is well worth a short walk for those who

Private Patronage/Public Art

"Public art is an important and missing piece of what makes a city unique and livable, and something Nashville has too little of. Realizing my new office building sat on such a public corner, I felt a responsibility to offer an expression that might help make the Hillsboro Village neighborhood that much more alive and vital. My good fortune was that my friend, Holton Rower, was at a moment in his work where he was attracted by the challenge and opportunity of creating a piece for this spot—where Magnolia Boulevard comes out of Music Row, and 21st Avenue comes from downtown. I am truly inspired as I drive in from Green Hills, past the massive signages of American-based global monoculture like Taco Bell, McDonald's, and Exxon, to come to the village and see this other symbol planted among the magnolia trees to stimulate feelings and thoughts of other dimensions."

—Joel Solomon, The Joel Solomon Company (Seed Capital and Real Estate Business), Nashville, San Francisco, Vancouver

---

want to see the best of Tennessee artists from across the state. Mon–Fri 8:30–4:30. ♿ (Downtown)

VANDERBILT UNIVERSITY– MARGARET CUNINGGIM WOMEN'S CENTER GALLERY
315 West Side Row, Franklin Bldg., Vanderbilt University
Nashville
615/322-4843
This tiny gallery features solo exhibits by area women artists, some of whom are highly accomplished, some just breaking into the world of showing art in public. If you are on campus, don't miss the chance to stop in. This is the best place in town to find out about women's creative support groups of all kinds, and it has

an outstanding resource library. Mon–Fri 8:30–5. No exhibits Jun–Aug. ♿ (Midtown)

VANDERBILT UNIVERSITY– SARRATT GALLERY
Sarratt Student Ctr.
Nashville
615/322-2471
Located in the lobby of Sarratt Student Center, just outside the Sarratt Cinema, this gallery features some of the finest contemporary art and craft exhibits around. Sarratt exhibits, often based on a theme, draw artists from all over the country. Installations and experimental works are sometimes featured, and the selection and presentation of artwork is always top-notch. Anyone

Twelve Nashville art galleries hold a Sunday Art Matinee on the third Sunday of each month from 1 to 5. It's free, and a portion of every gallery sale benefits the Tennessee State Museum Foundation.

interested in contemporary art (or film) will want to stop in during a stay in Nashville. Mon–Sat 9–9, Sun 11–9. & (Midtown)

WATKINS INSTITUTE
601 Church St.
Nashville
615/242-1851

Located in an institutional (concrete stairwells and linoleum floors) space in the heart of downtown, Watkins Institute was founded to be the city's adult education school. Over 100 years later, Watkins is still going strong, with exceptional art programs for children and a wide range of offerings for adults in traditional art media, as well as interior design and film-making. The bare-bones gallery/auditorium displays a regular schedule of exhibits by students in Watkins programs (adult and child) as well as occasional shows by individual contemporary artists and group shows organized by the local art community. Mon–Thu 9–8, Fri 9–2. Free. (Downtown)

ZEITGEIST GALLERY
Cummins Station, 209 10th Ave. S.,
Ste. 223
Nashville
615/256-4805

Zeitgeist, located adjacent to Manuel Zeitlin Architects, features contemporary art by fine local and regional artists. Housed in a high-ceilinged, glass-walled industrial space on the ground floor of the Cummins Station complex (a former warehouse space now home to offices, artist studios, restaurants, and shops), Zeitgeist mounts artful two- and three-person exhibits of paintings, drawings, sculpture, photography, and design. Don't be surprised to find artist-made lamps, tables, or even beds on display here. The opening receptions at Zeitgeist are the liveliest in town. Mon–Fri 9–5, Sat noon–3. (Downtown)

9

PARKS AND GARDENS

One of the things that makes Nashville a nice place to be is that green spaces to retreat to are always close at hand. There are 70 parks encompassing 7,000 acres of parkland in the city alone. In addition, Nashville is fortunate to have state natural areas and parks, such as Radnor Lake and Long Hunter State Park, located within in or on the fringes of the city limits.

When Nashville's flowering trees and plants come into bloom, a soft, warm magic settles over the town. As a result, Nashville is a gardener's town, with amateur practitioners at all levels, from the recreational weed-puller to those who have spent their lives developing some of the species that grow so well here, such as daylilies and irises. The season begins in February with annual gardening shows at the Convention Center and State Fair Grounds, where landscape designers show their talents and gardening suppliers show their products. A visit to Cheekwood in the spring will lure anyone out of the greenhouses and onto the grounds to follow a path from one luxuriantly blooming garden to another. Nashville has four fully distinct seasons, with accompanying foliage. Summer heat and humidity makes for an intense, almost tropical atmosphere that is conducive to the growth of brilliantly colored blooms as well as beautiful tomatoes, and fall colors rarely fail to give the city a month-long glow in October.

MUNICIPAL PARKS

CENTENNIAL PARK
West End and 25th Ave. N.
Nashville

615/862-8400
Centennial Park was the site of Tennessee's Centennial Exposition of 1897. At the time it was called the "white city," because the grassy fields

were populated with white plaster exhibition buildings, one of which, dedicated to the fine arts, was an exact replica of the Athenian Parthenon. The six-month event had over 1 million visitors, including President and Mrs. McKinley. When it closed, Nashvillians were reluctant to see the Parthenon destroyed. The building remained, and a year later the land was purchased to become a city park. It took four more years to create an official Park Board, but in 1902 Centennial became the second of Nashville's city parks.

Today the park is widely used by Nashvillians. It surrounds the Parthenon, rebuilt as a permanent structure in 1920 (see Chapter 8: Museums and Galleries). Centennial is a favorite place for picnicking, reading, playing Frisbee, and just hanging out with kids. It seems to have everything: a small lake with paddleboats and ducks, a band shell, an arts activities center, sports facilities (see Chapter 11: Sports and Recreation), commemorative statues,

and all manner of oddities, such as a steam engine, a concrete and metal ship's prow, and a fighter plane. Centennial's grounds are well-tended, and seasonal floral arrays—daffodils, tulips, hosta and cannas, mums—are always prominent in the front garden beds. Open 24 hours. Free. (Midtown)

RESERVOIR PARK
Eighth Ave. at Argyle St.
Nashville
Located just at the base of the massive round limestone reservoir, this little neighborhood park has tennis courts, a playground, picnic tables, and lots of trees—and it's very close to downtown. Even though the reservoir is not open to the public, it's a fascinating structure worthy of a walk. Built in 1889 on the site of a former Union fortification, the reservoir is still part of the city's waterworks system. A crack on the south side bears witness to the "day the dam broke," November 5, 1912, when 25 million gallons of

Green Space

Nashville is soon to have "greenways" connecting parks and recreation areas by walking and biking trails. A pathway running along the Cumberland River, a pedestrian bridge, and a corridor paralleling the I-440 loop are all part of the plans being formulated. The first manifestations of the new greenway can be seen in Shelby Walk, a pedestrian route leading from a small park and playground at Shelby and South Ninth Street to the park central, and Shelby Bottoms, a huge nature preserve in the same vicinity. For information about the Metro Nashville Greenways Commission, write to: Greenways for Nashville, Park Plaza at Oman Street, Nashville 37201, or call 615/862-8400.

Reservoir Park

water flooded homes in the neighborhoods below. (South Nashville)

SEVIER PARK
Clayton Ave. and Lealand Ln.
Nashville
615/862-8466

Sevier Park, located between Granny White (12th Avenue South) and Lealand Lane (10th Avenue South), and Kirkwood and Clayton Avenues, is a public neighborhood park with low limestone walls, playing fields, picnic shelters, a community center, and the Sunnyside Mansion, dating from the mid-nineteenth century. Two early log cabins stand near the house. This charming park is getting new attention as the adjacent street, 12th Avenue South, with several blocks of small businesses, gets a major facelift. The upcoming restoration of Sunnyside Mansion will soon create another draw for this interesting multiethnic neighborhood. Open 24 hours. Free. (South Nashville)

SHELBY PARK
Shelby St. at S. 20th St.
Nashville

615/862-8467

This 360-plus-acre public park, which was opened July 4, 1912, contains the first municipal golf course in Nashville (1924). The park stands on the site of a turn-of-the-century amusement park on property that was once part of a 640-acre parcel belonging to John Shelby, who served under Andrew Jackson during the War of 1812. Shelby Park has a 27-hole golf course (see Chapter 11: Sports and Recreation), playgrounds, and picnic areas. An additional 810 acres of Cumberland River flood plain, Shelby Bottoms, adjacent to Shelby Park, was purchased by a partnership of city and state to become the city's first major greenway. It includes a wetland preserve holding walking and biking paths, and will soon be linked across the Shelby Street Pedestrian Bridge to the greenway being developed along the Cumberland River as part of the new football stadium construction. Open 24 hours. Free. (East Nashville)

TWO RIVERS PARK
3150 McGavock Pike
Nashville

615/862-8400

Now a 12-acre site at the junction of the Cumberland and the Stone Rivers, Two Rivers Park, once an 1,100-acre estate owned by Andrew Jackson, includes a park, a municipal golf course (615/889-2675), and the home of Daniel McGavock, a 28-room mansion built in 1859. McGavock was married to the daughter of William Harding, who owned Belle Meade Plantation as well as this property at one time. The house is open for event rentals only (615/885-1112). (East Nashville)

WARNER PARKS
50 Vaughn Rd.
Nashville
615/370-8051

WARNER PARKS NATURE CENTER
7311 Hwy. 100
Nashville
615/352-6299

The parks, named after brothers Percy and Edwin Warner, total 2,664 acres, making them one of the largest city parks in the country. Percy Warner Park (approximately 2,060 acres) is entered through impressive double stone gates at the end of Belle Meade Boulevard. The entrance driveway system and tiered overlooks were designed by Bryant Fleming, the landscape architect for nearby Cheekwood. Percy Warner Park contains extensive hiking and horseback riding trails, stone picnic shelters, playing fields, and a steeplechase race course. Percy Warner, an industrialist who chaired Nashville's Park Board, Edwin Warner, and Luke Lea were instrumental in raising the money for preservation of the park lands, which were acquired from 1927 to 1930.

Edwin Warner Park, which adjoins Percy Warner at Old Hickory Boulevard, is entered from Highway 100, the park's northern boundary. It includes hiking trails, the Warner Parks Nature Center (see Chapter 7: Kids' Stuff), polo fields, and a Model Airplane Field, which is often the site of organized stargazing. The Works Progress Administration built many of

---

Warner Parks

"I continue to return to the Warner Parks for day-to-day recreation activities. This 2,600-acre wooded and hilly area has few equals in the country. I enjoy the hiking trails, jogging on the paved roads that are closed to traffic, and walking my dogs at the steeplechase course. The park loop road is the best bike workout in town—it is challenging and free of traffic congestion. Thanks are due to the WPA and the foresight of the city of Nashville for this wonderful area."

—Mark T. Fraley, attorney (former Director of Parks and Recreation for the state of Tennessee).

Cheekwood Botanical Gardens

the limestone structures in the Warner Parks, including seven entrance gates, two bridges, the picnic shelters, the steeplechase, and a number of retaining walls. Open daily year-round. (West Nashville)

GARDENS

CHEEKWOOD BOTANICAL GARDENS
1200 Forrest Park Dr.
Nashville
615/356-8000

Cheekwood, the grand manor house designed by architect Bryant Fleming for Leslie and Mabel Cheek in 1929 (see Chapter 8: Museums and Galleries), is surrounded by 55 acres of wooded and landscaped grounds including greenhouses and Botanic Hall, which contains botanic labs, meeting rooms, a library, and exhibition space.

The Cheekwood gardens, designed by Fleming at the time the house was built, contain extensive structural elements, such as the hollow "hill" on which the house sits, as well as artificial streams and pools. Fleming's landscape features are currently being restored to their past elegance, visible in the stonework walls and staircases, ironwork wisteria arbor, and a terraced vista. The gardens, as now planted, exhibit regional wildflowers, herbs, roses, native and exotic trees, and seasonal blooms such as daffodils, irises, tulips, and lilies. The greenhouses, which are open to the public year-round, maintain permanent collections of tropical rain-forest species, camellias and gardenias, and orchids. Botanic Hall maintains a schedule of programming that includes both art exhibits and flower and plant shows.

Outside, there is an authentic Japanese garden, built with materials brought over from Japan, complete with a ceremonial gate, a viewing platform, and a bamboo forest. Stepping stones are placed in order to create a measured cadence for walking, there is a lovely allée of gingko trees, and a raked gravel and boulder environment. It's a lovely place for quiet meditation,

The Greening of Nashville

"The city is beginning once again to acknowledge the Cumberland River, whose route includes downtown Nashville, as a vital force and important link through the city via a well-developed greenway system. In the past 10 to 15 years, Nashvillians have begun placing more importance on their green space and its role in improving quality of life, whether in their office development, neighborhood, or public park. We are a city growing toward a stronger green infra-structure that we can continue to build upon in years to come. The full benefit of what we are doing now will be realized by our children and grandchildren."

—Kim Hartley Hawkins, ASLA, Hawkins Partners, Inc.

where soft breezes through Cheek-wood's mature trees and birds calling across the meadows are bound to accompany. Cheekwood has just in-stalled an outdoor environment for works of contemporary art: a trail through the woods bordering the property that will bring viewers into contact with unusual pieces that play off and comment on the natural envi-ronment. (See Chapter 8: Museums and Galleries). Mon–Sat 9–5, Sun 12–5. $6 adults, $5 seniors and college students, $3 children ages 6–17, chil-dren under age 6 free. (West Nashville)

INTERNATIONAL GARDEN
Scarritt-Bennett Ctr., Grand Ave.
at 19th Ave.
Nashville
Just off Grand Avenue is a small, well-tended oval public garden with benches. This peaceful spot near Music Row features seasonal bloom-ing flowers planted to achieve bursts of brilliant color throughout the

spring and summer months. A quiet oasis, this lovely garden was given to Scarritt-Bennett in memory of Helen Baker Price. The dedicatory plaque reads "May Peace Prevail on Earth" in four languages and in Braille. A small parking lot adjacent to the gar-den makes this a convenient spot to stop and picnic or carry in bagels, coffee, and a Sunday paper. Free and accessible 24 hours a day. (Midtown)

NATURAL AREAS AND STATE PARKS

BLEDSOE CREEK STATE PARK
400 Ziegler's Fort Rd.
Gallatin
615/452-3706
This Tennessee state park is located within about a 20-minute drive of Nashville, on Old Hickory Lake, with 126 campsites, lake swimming, fish-ing, boat launch ramps, and hiking trails. It's a nice vacation spot, not too far from town, and is a fun place to

launch an exploration of the restored homesteads of some of the first settlers in the area. The park is named for Isaac Bledsoe, a "long hunter" who arrived in 1772. Free and open dawn to dusk. Registered campers pay a moderate fee per night. (North Nashville)

NASHVILLE WILDLIFE PARK AT GRASSMERE
3777 Nolensville Rd.
Nashville
615/833-1534

Grassmere encompasses 200 acres on a property donated in 1986 by the last descendants of Nashville's first sheriff, Michael Dunn, who built one of the area's first brick homes here in 1815. The site, which has been left a natural setting, was opened as a habitat for Tennessee's native animals in 1990 (see Chapter 5: Sights and Attractions). There is an interpretive center that includes an aviary and features changing wildlife exhibits. Memorial Day–Labor Day daily 9-6, Apr–mid-Sep daily 10–5. $6 adults, $4 seniors and children ages 3–12, children under age 3 free. Parking $2. (South Nashville)

LONG HUNTER STATE PARK
Hermitage
615/885-2422

Long Hunter State Park is a 2,400-acre day-use-only park located on the east bank of Percy Priest Lake. Percy Priest, formed by the massive Percy Priest Dam visible from I-40 as one enters Davidson County, is, at 14,200 acres, one of Tennessee's largest lakes. The visitor's center is open daily, and there is a paved and boardwalked nature trail that is wheelchair-accessible. Hiking, swimming, picnic areas, boat rental, ramp access, and fishing are all available. Open daily dawn to dusk. Free. (East Nashville)

THE NARROWS OF THE HARPETH STATE HISTORIC AREA
Hwy. 70 at Newsom's Station
near Pegram
615/797-9052

This 200-acre site along the Harpeth River includes Newsom's Mill, an 1862 turbine-powered limestone grist mill that was built by Joseph Newsom on the site of a mill destroyed by an 1808 flood. The Newsoms were settlers who came from Virginia. A limestone quarry bearing their name is located a mile to the south. This was once a thriving small community and a major rail stop. The narrows of the Harpeth State Historic Area includes some great swimming holes and there is also canoe access on the Harpeth

There's lots of wildlife to be found on even a casual walk at Radnor Lake. Here are some tips from the Tennessee Wildlife Resources Agency on how to spot them:
1. Wear natural-colored clothing.
2. Don't wear scents, such as perfume or lotion.
3. Take off sunglasses that may glint in the sun.
4. Move slowly and steadily, trying not to snap too many twigs.
5. Look for out-of-place shapes and motions—the more you get out in nature, the easier it will be to spot something unusual.

Favorite Dog Walks Around Town

Besides the city's numerous parks, Nashville's historic neighbor-hoods, most of which have sidewalks, make good places to walk a dog, and offer an architectural tour at the same time. If time per-mits, the hands-down choice among dog lovers is the steeplechase racecourse located on Old Hickory Boulevard in Percy Warner Park. Dogs are supposed to be on a lead, but this is a great place to let them run if they know their manners and won't chase or badger other dogs (or, on rare occasion, horses). Radnor Lake State Nat-ural Area only permits dogs along the lakeside road, but it is a lovely two-mile (round-trip) walk. Long Hunter State Park has a nice paved walk around the east side of Percy Priest Lake where dogs are allowed on leads. Around Percy Priest and Old Hickory Lakes, there are many unofficial "swimming holes" where people (and dogs) have been known to frolic in the water away from the ruckus of the boat launching sites.

River from the park (see Chapter 11: Sports and Recreation). Open year-round. Free. (West Nashville)

RADNOR LAKE STATE NATURAL AREA
1160 Otter Creek Rd.
Nashville
615/373-3467
Radnor Lake and its surrounding hills and woods occupy 953 acres of prime property that has resisted numerous recent encroachments. Its five hiking trails, interpretive woods walk, and organized program of nature activi-ties make this day-use park one of Nashville's most heavily utilized sites. Nashvillians of all stripes can be seen

walking, running, and biking here from dawn to dusk year-round.

The 85-acre lake, which at-tracts flocks of migrating birds and is home to ducks, geese, turtles, and even the occasional otter, was built in 1914 by the L&N Railroad as a water source for steam engines. In 1923 the railroad created a wildlife sanctuary and recreation area for use by the public, who eventually worked together with the Tennessee Department of Conservation to pur-chase the property in 1973. One of the trails at Radnor is accessible by wheelchair. Open daily dawn to dusk. Free. (South Nashville)

Gary Layda

10

SHOPPING

The range of shopping opportunities in Nashville probably spans as wide a variety of stores as anywhere in the country—from top-drawer clothiers like Brooks Brothers and Ann Taylor, to tucked away alcoves of collectibles and antiques, to country-music souvenir shops filled with cheaply made merchandise. Near the riverfront a multitude of stores along Second Avenue feature tourist souvenirs. A few blocks away on lower Broadway you'll find Hatch Show Print (a historic woodblock poster shop), Gruhn Guitar, two cool old record shops, and a last-remaining pawn shop where once there were many. Gruhn Guitar, a Nashville original, is considered by many to be the best guitar store in the United States. Musical instrument stores are worth a tour all their own if you want to put your finger on the life-pulse of this city. Sitting in the midst of a major craft-producing region, Nashville is a great place to acquire handcrafted items, either at a craft fair or at a gallery featuring fine crafts.

The Farmer's Market is home to several interesting Asian shops. Look for hard-to-find comestibles from the Middle East and Mexico at the Farmer's Market and at ethnic groceries all over town. Some of Nashville's best shopping is not in malls, so this chapter is divided into notable shopping areas, with some not-to-be-missed stores listed just below. Major department stores are located almost without exception in the malls, which are listed separately along with outlet stores.

SHOPPING DISTRICTS

Downtown

As in many cities across the country, Nashville's downtown department stores have closed, and most have moved to malls in outlying areas. Church Street, Nashville's traditional shopping street, strategically positioned between Legislative Plaza and Ryman Auditorium, is undergoing a revitalization, with a "pocket park" brightening the streetscape, a 30-story residential tower, and a major new public library soon to come. Cain-Sloan, once known as the "greatest store of the central South," is now the site of a parking lot at Fifth and Church. At Seventh and Church the former Castner Knott building will soon revert to residential use.

ACME FARM SUPPLY
101 Broadway
Nashville
615/255-5641
Everything from bags of feed and seed to basic hardware, dog beds, and plant starts can be found at Acme, which serves as a reminder that much of the land surrounding this city is pasture and farmland. Housed in a brick building painted white and emblazoned with Purina Chow's familiar red-and-blue checkerboard pattern, Acme, located at the intersection of Broadway and the Cumberland River, is one of Nashville's most visible landmarks. (Downtown)

THE ARCADE
Between Fourth and Fifth Aves. N.
Nashville
615/255-1034
The Arcade, a covered two-story walk-through shopping center in the central business district, houses small businesses, several restaurants open for lunch only, and a post office. Built in 1903, and located between Church and Union Streets, the Arcade has an old-timey atmosphere, housing stores that include Griffin Jewelry and Watch Repairing, Percy's (shoe) Shine, and the Peanut Shop, which fills the air with the tantalizing aroma of fresh, roasted nuts. (Downtown)

FRIEDMAN LOAN COMPANY
420 Broadway
Nashville
615/256-0909
The blocks of lower Broadway used to be filled with pawn shops where locals could shop for cameras, guns, and guitars. Friedman is the only one left. Check it out for a surprise bargain on one of those items. (Downtown)

GRUHN GUITARS, INC.
400 Broadway
Nashville
615/256-2033
This three-level store is practically a museum. Most Music City visitors will find no bargains, but musicians discover the guitars of their dreams here on a regular basis. George Gruhn has himself become a minor celebrity as word spreads of the authoritative body of guitar (and fiddle and mandolin) knowledge housed in his shop. Anyone who works at Gruhn becomes a de facto museum curator, so linger and learn as long as you can—you might just see a well-known musician wander in. (Downtown)

HATCH SHOW PRINT
316 Broadway
Nashville
615/256-2805
Hatch, a working print shop that specializes in hand-printed show posters, is a great place to pick up framable

souvenirs of Nashville. Wooden blocks and pieces of moveable type are stacked and displayed in every conceivable niche, with posters, on which one can almost read the history of the region's music, displayed on every inch of wall space. The shop is a historic site managed by the Country Music Foundation. (Downtown)

LAWRENCE BROTHERS RECORDS
409 Broadway
Nashville
615/256-9240
Were it not for a few relatively recent promotional posters taped to the counters, Lawrence Brothers would appear to be the shop time forgot. Take a deep breath of the grandma's-attic aroma and envision the days when the Grand Ole Opry was downtown and Lawrence Brothers carried the latest records of Patsy Cline and Hank Williams. Pick up an old album or even a 78 for a unique gift. (Downtown)

Shopping in Midtown

This area of town is a broad band that includes several pockets of commercial activity each with a distinctive identity, such as Elliston Place, Hillsboro Village, 12 South, and West End/Park Place.

COTTEN MUSIC CENTER
1815 21st Ave. S.
Nashville
615/383-8947 or 615/383-8911
You'll find friendly folks at this small guitar shop which has been in business since 1961. They also offer instruction on guitar and bass. (Midtown)

ELLISTON PLACE
Church St., between 21st and 23rd

Aves. N.
Nashville
This tiny strip of shops includes Elliston Soda Shop (see Chapter 4: Where to Eat), Elder's (used) Bookstore, and Mosko's (newsstand, smoke shop, and carryout counter), in addition to several restaurants and the famous Exit/In music club (see Chapter 13: Nightlife). (Midtown)

HILLSBORO VILLAGE
21st Ave. S. at
Wedgewood/Blakemore Aves.
Nashville
Hillsboro Village is one of Nashville's few remaining urban neighborhood shopping areas. Two blocks of shops including Carissa's Armoires, Davis Cookware and Cutlery, Davis Hardware (which always has a display of old radios playing out front), several small clothing stores, the Belcourt Theater, the Pancake Pantry (which always has a line on weekends), Provence (French bakery), Fido (coffee house), and Bosco's (brew pub) inhabit the main strip, with the very popular Sunset Grill and The Trace restaurants just behind (see Chapter 4: Where to Eat). (Midtown)

MOSKO'S AND THE MUNCHEONETTE
2204 Elliston Pl.
Nashville
615/327-2658
"Eat it, read it, smoke it" has been their motto for years. Hard-to-find magazines, cards for all occasions, out-of-town newspapers, a walk-in humidor, import beers, and a counter featuring sandwiches and baked goodies make this little shop a one-stop pleasure palace. Open daily. (Midtown)

PANGAEA
1721 21st Ave. S.

Nashville
615/269-9665
This store has imported clothing and handmade items, including folk art, mostly from Central and South America. This lovely shop is a good place to pick up a gift or an additional piece of clothing if the weather turns during your visit. (Midtown)

Shopping on 12th South

This spread-out strip of shops is undergoing a streetscaping that will give it uniform sidewalks, streetlights, and parking, as well as decorative touches like banners and public benches created by artists. New shops and businesses have opened recently to join old stand-bys Becker's Bakery and Corner Music.

BECKER'S BAKERY
2600 12th Ave. S.
Nashville
615/383-5554
This old-time bakery was around long before health-consciousness spelled out the evils of refined sugar and bleached flour. It's Nashville's traditional source for classic birthday cakes or fancy cupcakes for kids. Their small yeast rolls are a preferred holiday party favorite because they are perfect for sliced ham and turkey. (South Nashville)

CORNER MUSIC
2705 12th Ave. S.
Nashville
615/297-9559
Corner Music, a large establishment that caters to both individuals and recording studios, sells new and used instruments and recording and editing equipment and software. Check out their bulletin board if you want to do a little surreptitious "r & d" on the

world of Nashville's working musicians. (South Nashville)

FORK'S DRUM CLOSET
2707 12th Ave. S.
Nashville
615/383-8343
Right next door to Corner Music, Fork's Drum Closet has both new and vintage drums. They repair and refinish drum sets here, as well as offer drumming lessons. (South Nashville)

LAURELL'S CENTRAL MARKET
2317 12th Ave. S.
Nashville
615/292-1177
This gourmet carryout specializes in Cajun food. You can sit down and sample, or peruse shelves laden with brightly colored packages of popular New Orleans products such as Zapp's Potato Chips, Tabasco Sauce, and all the other Louisiana hot-pepper sauces (see Chapter 4: Where to Eat). (South Nashville)

MOTHER AFRICAN GIFTS
2407 12th Ave. S.
Nashville
615/269-9661
This friendly shop has sculpture, clothing, and decorative objects from Central and West Africa. Mr. Osei's lilting voice will keep you asking questions about the varied works of art he has on display. African batik cloths and palm-fiber handbags can be found among the wearable items. (South Nashville)

Shopping on Nolensville Road

Shops run by members of Nashville's ethnic communities keep opening up and down this long street of non-descript shopping centers. Partaking of culinary culture is a reward in itself, but many of these foreign shops also stock their shelves with interesting domestic products that offer novel solutions to ordinary household needs.

BARAKA BAKERY
5596 Nolensville Rd., South Plaza Shopping Ctr.
Nashville
615/333-9285
Fresh baked pita and Middle Eastern pastries qualify this restaurant/grocery store as a bakery, but their shelves are stocked with hard-to-find products from both the Middle East and Central Asia—bins of rice and grains, spice mixtures, canned goods (see Chapter 4: Where to Eat for additional listings). (South Nashville)

LA HACIENDA TAQUERIA
2615 Nolensville Rd.
Nashville
615/256-6142
A tortilla factory and Mexican grocery store with a fabulous lunch counter, La Hacienda makes flour tortillas on site, stocks lots of Hispanic staples, and serves traditional menudo (tripe stew) on Sundays. (South Nashville)

PHONOLUXE
(See listing under New and Used Books and Records.)

Shopping at West End/ Park Place

Just up the street from the Vanderbilt campus is a shopping area on both sides of the street that contains such restaurants as Cakewalk/Zola and Houston's (see Chapter 4: Where to Eat), a day spa, a grocery store, and lots of small specialty shops.

CUMBERLAND TRANSIT
(See Chapter 11: Sports and Recreation.)

MADE IN FRANCE
3001 West End Ave.
Nashville
615/329-9300
Imported antiques and contemporary

France Comes To Nashville

Karin Eaton, a Nashvillian who lived in Paris as a fashion model, is the founder of Ironware International, a company that imports original designs in French hand-forged iron. She says the following:

"Since I first started going years ago, I have always found fun and eclectic things at Nashville's monthly flea market. These can add a humorous note to the more serious antiques I found at the flea markets in France. Combining funky touches with elegant furniture creates a comfortable informal setting and provides great conversation pieces."

home furnishings designed by French artisans are for sale at Made in France, one of the primary retail locations for Nashville-based Ironware International (contemporary designs in furniture, lamps, sconces). (West Nashville)

SCARLETT BEGONIA
2805 West End Ave.
Nashville
615/329-1272

South American imports make this women's clothing store a great place to find colorful, all-cotton, and fashionably simple clothing at surprisingly good prices. This direct import store has been in business for over 20 years, and the owners work with the makers in South America to ensure production of clothes that are always in style. A large assortment of decorative items, jewelry, woven goods, and small works of art fill the store, so

Shopping Hot Spots

Recent transplant from Washington, D.C., Cindy Wall lists her favorite places to shop, and stop, in Nashville:

1. ***Mosko's***—*For big-city news (i.e.* The New York Times*) on a Sunday morning.*

2. ***Johnson's Meat Market***—*For nitrate-free bacon, sausage without preservatives, meat the way it was meant to be.*

3. ***Souvenir shops near the Country Music Hall of Fame***—*Of course they're tacky, but that's the point—buy early and in bulk for the Christmas season.*

4. ***Cumberland Transit***—*Fly fishermen head to the back of the store. They'll tell you where the fish are biting and what they're biting on (and then sell it to you).*

5. ***Nolensville Pike***—*If you can't get it somewhere on this long stretch of road, you don't need it. You name it, Nolensville Pike has it—pawn shops, junk shops, ethnic markets. It is the last stand against the "malling" of America.*

6. ***Rotier's***—*Milkshakes and grilled cheese sandwiches, perfect with kids (or with a hangover).*

7. ***Radio Café***—*To sample home-town hip in East Nashville—if only every neighborhood had one*

8. ***Bongo Java***—*A must-visit for anyone who only equates Nashville with country music.*

it's always a pleasure to browse here.
(West Nashville)

TEAM NASHVILLE
Park Place Shopping Ctr.
Nashville
615/321-5257
A small shop crammed with running
shoes and clothes, swimwear, and
other sporting goods. The helpful
staff will almost always give you a 10-
percent discount on purchases. (West
Nashville)

WEST END DISCOUNT
LIQUORS AND WINES
2818 West End Ave.
Nashville
615/320-1446
Helpful and knowledgeable employees at this midtown store can steer
you to a good choice of pre-chilled
wine or champagne before an outing
or special occasion. They have a selection of wines from around the
world. (West Nashville)

Belle Meade Plaza and
White Bridge Road

*This area includes Belle Meade
Plaza, a strip shopping center, which
runs under the White Bridge Road
via-duct. Merchants include Office
Depot, H. G. Hill Grocery Store (local,
highly thought of), the nicest Kroger
store in the city, Belle Meade Drugs,
Goldie's Deli, Nashville Wine & Spir-
its, and Crystal's For Fine Gifts and
Jewelry (a shop belonging to country-
music star Crystal Gayle). (West
Nashville)*

AMERICAN ARTISAN
4231 Harding Rd., Stanford Square
Nashville
615/298-4691
High-end crafts by nationally known

artists and lots of useful handmade
things are for sale at the American
Artisan. A favorite place to buy wedding gifts, the American Artisan
wraps theirs in distinctive silver
boxes with brightly colored ribbons
that signal exciting treasures within.
Their annual craft fair, held in mid-
June, is regarded by many as the best
in town. (See Chapter 8: Museums
and Galleries for additional listing.)
(West Nashville)

CRYSTAL'S FOR FINE GIFTS AND
JEWELRY
Belle Meade Plaza Shopping Ctr.
Nashville
615/292-4300
This opulent shop was started by
singer Crystal Gayle, sister of Loretta
Lynn, to provide the perfect choice of
wedding gifts and fancy collectible
glassware. (West Nashville)

NASHVILLE WINE AND SPIRITS
4556 Harding Rd., Belle Meade
Plaza, under Crystal's
Nashville
615/292-2676
This good-sized store has a wide and
unusual selection of wines because
they import some wines directly. As
a result they can offer sound advice
on your choices. A favorite among
Nashville wine connoisseurs. (West
Nashville)

A TASTE OF ITALY
ITALIAN MARKET
73 White Bridge Rd., Paddock
Place Shopping Ctr.,
Nashville
615/354-0124
She's French, he's Italian, and together they have brought top-quality
ingredients to the Nashville retail
market. Several kinds of prosciutto,
many cheeses, and all manner of

hard-to-find bottled, canned, and dried goods are available. Have an espresso while you shop. Coming soon: Nashville's first gelato! (West Nashville)

WESTGATE PLAZA
Harding Rd. at the Hwy. 70/ 100 split
Nashville

This Belle Meade–area strip shopping center includes antique stores, dress shops, Bella Linea (fine linens), Auld Alliance Gallery, and McClure's (local department store considered by many to be Nashville's best clothing store for men and women). (West Nashville)

BREAD & COMPANY
106 Page Rd.
Nashville
615/352-7323

This fine bakery features wholegrain and European breads made without preservatives, as well as a coffee bar, European pastries, and sandwiches for carryout. (West Nashville)

CORNER MARKET
6051 Hwy. 100
Nashville
615/352-6772

This is a gourmet grocery with exotic as well as fresh local produce, fresh fish, and lunch and breakfast items prepared on premises. The Corner Market could be named an honorary branch of Dean and DeLuca, with fresh produce, fresh fish, carryout foods, and prices to match. (West Nashville)

McCLURE'S
6000 Hwy. 100
Nashville
615/356-8822

(See Major Department Stores below.) (West Nashville)

Shopping in Green Hills

Green Hills is located on Hillsboro Pike between Crestmoor and Hobbs Roads. Several small shopping areas ring the Mall at Green Hills. Locally owned stores such as K & T: The Lamp Store, Tanner & Co., Great Harvest Bakery, and Service Merchandise (yes, it started in Nashville) can be found here.

BOTANICA
2211 Bandywood Dr.
Nashville
615/386-3839

Stop by Botanica for gardening inspiration. This store is always brimming with unusual plant starts and seeds, fine garden tools, and accessories, and its front yard is an exhibit of garden ornamentia. Helpful staff, good sales, and an unusual approach to design set Botanica apart from ordinary nursery stores. (West Nashville)

BREAD & COMPANY
4105 Hillsboro Pike
Nashville
615/292-7323

See listing above. (West Nashville)

K & T: THE LAMP STORE
2213 Bandywood Dr.
Nashville
615/292-6590

A great selection of lamps, antiques, and handmade objects, including handpainted lampshades by local artists, can be found at K & T. (West Nashville)

THE MALL AT GREEN HILLS
(See listing under Shopping Malls below.)

UPTOWN'S SMOKE SHOP
3900 Hillsboro Rd.
Nashville
615/292-6866   (West Nashville)

1745 Galleria Blvd.,
CoolSprings Mall
Nashville
615/771-7027   (South Nashville)
Open every day, Uptown's carries
cigars, pipes, coffee, and imported
beers. They were in Nashville, with a
walk-in humidor, before the cigar
craze hit. Uptown's is a fun hang.
They'll give you free coffee while you
wait for your companion to browse
the serious smokes.

Shopping on Jefferson Street

*This is the historic African American
shopping street of Nashville. Where
once there were theaters and cafés,
coffeehouses and galleries are coming in one by one. Near both Fisk and
Tennessee State Universities, the arrival of students each fall lends the
street a lively atmosphere.*

ALKEBU-LAN IMAGES
2721 Jefferson St.
Nashville
615/321-4111
African American books, prints,
posters, and wearable items can be
found at Alkebu-Lan Images. (North
Nashville)

**OLD NEGRO LEAGUE
SPORTS SHOP**
1213 Jefferson St.
Nashville
615/321-3186
The Old Negro League Sports Shop
features African American sports
memorabilia, particularly that drawn
from the history of segregated baseball teams. (North Nashville)

WOODCUTS FRAME SHOP
1613 Jefferson St.
Nashville
615/321-5357
Woodcuts Frame Shop specializes in
African American prints and posters.
They also offer custom picture fram-
ing. (North Nashville)

OTHER NOTABLE STORES

Country Western Clothing

BOOT FACTORY
(Genesco boot outlet)
1415 Murfreesboro Rd.
Nashville
615/367-7660
Genesco is a Nashville-based shoe-
maker of Johnson & Murphy, Bass,
Rockport, and other shoes. The Boot
Factory offers up to 60-percent
discounts on boot prices. (East
Nashville)

GILL & ARNOLD
214 E. Main St.
Franklin
615/791-1207

Old Negro League Sports Shop

Meryl Truett

The always very fashionable "Sweet-hearts of the Rodeo" (Janis Gill and Christine Arnold, who are sisters) have opened a women's clothing and accessory store in historic Franklin. (South Nashville)

KATY K'S RANCH DRESSING
113 17th Ave. S.
Nashville
615/259-4163
Katy K's offers hip country show clothing for women. (Midtown)

MANUEL EXCLUSIVE CLOTHIER
1922 Broadway
Nashville
615/321-5444
Fine-quality, hand-tailored Western wear is for sale at Manuel Exclusive Clothier, which is a favorite of country-music performers. (Midtown)

SHEPLER'S WESTERN WEAR
1615 Gallatin Pike
Nashville
615/865-2043
Real cowboy clothes—rugged, durable and classic. (North Nashville)

TRAIL WEST WESTERN STORE
615/264-2955
Hendersonville
Six locations, including Second Avenue, Music Valley, and Hendersonville.

FOOD AND DRINK

FRUGAL MACDOOGAL'S LIQUOR WAREHOUSE
701 Division St.
Nashville
615/242-3863
Best prices in town, and always good advice on a large selection of wines and beers. (Downtown)

Hatch Show Print

Hatch Show Print

GLOBAL MARKET
1513 Church St.
Nashville
615/327-3682
The Global Market is a small, friendly grocery featuring Asian, Italian, Middle Eastern, Spanish, British, and Central American foods. There is usually exotic fresh produce, such as cilantro, mangos, lemon grass, and fresh ginger. Prices are always good. (Midtown)

JOHNSON'S MEAT MARKET
343 53rd Ave. N.
Nashville
615/298-5742
Johnson's features hand-cut, aged, and nonpreserved meats in their long-time shop located one block off Charlotte Avenue. (West Nashville)

LA HACIENDA TAQUERIA
2615 Nolensville Rd.
Nashville
615/256-6142
See listing above under Shopping on Nolensville Road. (South Nashville)

THE PRODUCE PLACE
4000 Murphy Rd.
Nashville
615/383-2664   (Midtown)
or
7107 Hwy. 70S
Bellevue
615/662-1184   (West Nashville)
The Produce Place offers the most beautiful fresh produce and a limited selection of gourmet grocery items, including coffee beans and breads from local bakeries.

SUNSHINE GROCERY
3201 Belmont Blvd.
Nashville
615/297-5100
Nashville's oldest organic grocery, Sunshine (now owned by the Wild Oats chain of health food stores) has everything for the environmentally conscious, from fresh produce to bulk flours and grain, to pet foods, to toilet paper. They have filtered water processing equipment and a food counter preparing daily specials for take-out and eat-in at the brand-new dining area. (Midtown)

NEW AND USED BOOKS AND RECORDS

Nashville, which once had as many as three locally owned bookstores, is down to one homegrown establishment, Davis-Kidd Booksellers, which retains its name and character even though it too was purchased by a small independent bookstore chain last year. Barnes & Noble, and its affiliates Bookstar and Walden Books, are here in force. Tower, with a major store on West End Avenue just across from the Vanderbilt campus, has driven nearly all the other record stores out of business.

For used goods, there are lots of possibilities. Hanging around Nashville's used book and record stores is probably one of the best ways to absorb local culture and learn something of Nashville's history—both literary and musical. The excellent Antiquarian Book Fair, held in conjunction with the Tennessee Humanities Council's Southern Festival of Books, will introduce collectors to a number of the private dealers in the area and will be of great interest to anyone interested in American history or rare books.

BOOKSTAR
4301 Harding Rd.
Nashville
615/292-7895
Located in the former Belle Meade Theater, Bookstar has one of the largest inventories in Nashville, which is offered at slightly discounted prices. The theater marquee announces author signings. They have a newsstand and a large children's department, and they feature books of local interest in a front lobby display. Open daily. (West Nashville)

DAD'S OLD BOOK STORE AND AUTOGRAPH GALLERY
4004 Hillsboro Rd.
Nashville
615/298-5880
Dad's, hidden away in Bavarian Village (across from Davis-Kidd Booksellers in Green Hills) was voted best used bookstore in the 1996 *Nashville Scene* reader's poll. Collectible books are featured, with an emphasis on famous people, first editions, and fine book sets. (West Nashville)

DAVIS-KIDD BOOKSELLERS
4007 Hillsboro Pike
Nashville

615/385-2645

Nashville's best bookstore, hands-down. This store is almost as well organized as a library, the selection is extensive, the staff is knowledgeable, and special book orders can often be obtained within a day. *The New York Times* best-seller list books are displayed at the front of the store; all books on the list are discounted 25 percent. Books by regional authors are featured, Davis-Kidd sponsors regular book signings in the store, and they keep an inventory of autographed copies. The complete newsstand, including foreign magazines and nationwide newspapers, is next to a section selling cards, gifts, and stationery. The extensive children's area hosts well-attended Saturday story hours, and the audio section includes both music and books on tape.

Started in Nashville by Karen Davis and Thelma Kidd, the Davis-Kidd chain, which includes stores in Knoxville, Jackson, and Memphis, now belongs to Joseph Beth, an independent bookstore chain located in Lexington, KY. Open daily, with a café upstairs featuring delicious snacks, light meals, and local songwriter nights. (West Nashville)

ELDER'S BOOK STORE
2115 Ellison Pl.
Nashville
615/327-1867
For many years, the elder Mr. Elder was the authority on Tennesseana, and the store, a delightful jumble, reflects his interests. Antique maps are a specialty here. Mon–Fri and Sat until 2 p.m. (Midtown)

GREAT ESCAPE
1925 Broadway
Nashville,
615/327-0646
This funky store buys and sells comic books, records, tapes, CDs, movies, and more. You never know who you'll meet and you may find some promo CDs (brand new) on sale. (Midtown)

PHONOLUXE
2609 Nolensville Rd.
Nashville

Davis-Kidd Booksellers, p. 163

Davis-Kidd Booksellers

Shopping for Souvenirs

Whoa, buddy! Have we got some tacky souvenirs here in Nashville. If you are in search of country-music kitsch, you will not be disappointed. The Country Music Hall of Fame has endeavored to take the high road by providing a variety of educational and useful items in their gift store, but they still have a good sampling of the rest of it.

Likewise, the Parthenon has served as the inspiration for some truly cool souvenirs that are on sale in their Centennial Park museum shop. You can hardly miss the screaming billboards with huge faces of the stars in front of the shops on Music Row, in the Music Valley area near the Opry House and Opryland Hotel, and lately on Second Avenue's commercial strip. Both the Hard Rock Café and the Nashville Country Club Restaurant have their own shops, with mostly wearable items. New to lower Broadway is Planet Hollywood and the NASCAR Cafe, adding a whole new level of celeb/merchandise to the shopping bags parading down Nashville streets.

615/259-3500
Used records and CDs are bought and sold here. Eyeing the bins carefully will often yield new CDs for used prices, as turn over in Nashville's music world is fast and furious. Well-organized, with a helpful staff, Phonoluxe is *the* place to find recordings from the 1950s to the present. The prices, for both buying and selling, are slightly better than those at Great Escape. (South Nashville)

TOWER RECORDS-VIDEO-BOOKS
2404 West End Avenue
Nashville
615/327-8085
Tower has the widest selection of records in town, with genres and displays divided into jazz, world music, rock, country, gospel, showtunes and soundtracks, and more. Listening stations scattered throughout the store are a nice way to sample new music and promotional prices usually coincide with shows by the same artists in Nashville. Tower does good in-store events, and their staff is usually helpful when one is in search of music that defies their categories. The video selection includes more foreign and "art" films than Blockbuster, while the bookstore offerings are mainstream. (West Nashville)

MAJOR DEPARTMENT STORES

PROFFITS NASHVILLE
General Offices,
CoolSprings Galleria

615/771-2100

A Nashville original, formerly known as Castner-Knott (bought out in mid-1998) is a full-service department store that has extensive women's and men's clothing departments, shoes, housewares and home furnishings, cosmetic counters, a bridal registry, a ticket and travel service, a beauty shop, and gift wrap. The downtown store closed in 1996, but there are five suburban locations (these are all in malls): Bellevue, CoolSprings, Green Hills, Hickory Hollow, and Rivergate. (South Nashville)

Nashville's Publishing Past

Nashville, a publishing center, has a literary tradition that stretches back many years. Both the Fugitives (pre WWI poets) and the Agrarians (depression-era essayists) were associated with Vanderbilt University, and both James Weldon Johnson and Langston Hughes were writers-in-residence at Fisk University. For a long time the vast majority of printed matter emerging from Nashville presses was religious in nature—the Baptist Sunday School Publishing Board, United Methodist Communications, and numerous bible publishers are located here.

Over the years, the industry, already serving an educational market, has diversified to include secular publishers like The Southwestern Company. Nashville's Rutledge Hill Press, after striking it rich with H. Jackson Brown's Life's Little Instruction Book, *has emerged as a strong local independent publisher specializing in history, decorative arts, and culture of the South. Ingram, one of the country's largest book and periodical distribution companies, is headquartered in Nashville, and all manner of books and magazines are printed here. Because of Ingram's presence, a wide selection of the latest magazines is always available on local newsstands. The vaunted Southern literary heritage, of which this region is justly proud, surfaces yearly in early October at the Southern Festival of Books: A Celebration of the Written Word, which is sponsored by the Tennessee Humanities Council and includes writers from all over the country. As they do during the three-day festival, authors also journey to Nashville to read from and sign their latest works at Davis-Kidd, Bookstar, and Barnes & Noble on a regular basis.*

Music Row souvenir shops

DILLARD'S DEPARTMENT STORES
CoolSprings Store
615/771-1701

Dillard's, also a full-service department store, took over what many considered to be Nashville's best, the locally owned Cain-Sloan stores, several years ago. Dillard's has locations at Bellevue, CoolSprings, Donelson Plaza, Harding, Hermitage, Green Hills, Hickory Hollow, and Rivergate. (South Nashville)

J.C. PENNEY COMPANY
CoolSprings Store
615/771-7743 or 800/222-6161 (catalogue telephone shopping)

Tried and true J.C. Penney is still in both the full-service department store and the catalogue order businesses. All stores include beauty parlors and portrait studios. Penney's has stores at CoolSprings, Hickory Hollow, and Rivergate. (South Nashville)

McCLURE'S STORES
Belle Meade Store
615/356-8822   (West Nashville)

Brentwood Store
615/377-3769   (South Nashville)

Primarily a clothing store, hometown favorite McClure's features top-of-the-line merchandise for men and women, including shoes and accessories. In order to keep their clothing selections up-to-the-minute, McClure's regularly has great sales. It is where Nashville's fashion-conscious shop.

PARISIAN
Cool Springs Galleria
615/771-3200

This Birmingham-based upscale department store is one of the area's nicest.

SHOPPING MALLS

BELLEVUE CENTER
7620 Hwy. 70S
Nashville
615/646-8690

West of the city about 10 miles, just off I-40, is one of the area's newest and nicest malls. Abercrombie and Fitch, Banana Republic, Eddie Bauer,

Antiques/Flea Markets

The Nashville Flea Market, a huge, wide-ranging affair that usually occupies at least four buildings, three outdoor sheds, and a good portion of the parking lot at the State Fair Grounds, is a great place to find almost anything—from piles of brand-new cotton socks to railroad memorabilia to baby ducks. It occurs on the fourth weekend of the month, all day Saturday and Sunday. What is considered antique shopping in Nashville can range from stores offering English furniture with extremely high price tags, to cute shops that offer reproduction furniture and potpourri, to a "real-thing" establishment selling a wide variety of used items that are over 50 years old (an American "antique"). Nashville has an antique district located along Eighth Avenue South, not far from the Fairgrounds.

Other clusters of antique stores can be found with a short drive out of town to the main street of Goodlettsville, the town square in Lebanon, and on the side streets of Franklin. Stopping at antique/junk shops located in old gas stations, barns, or storefronts along the highways leading out of town or in the little towns around Nashville is highly recommended. In these little-visited spots there are untold treasures still awaiting the knowledgeable buyer. Here is a listing of some of the more notable antique shops in town:

BELMONT ANTIQUES, 3112 Belmont Blvd., Nashville
615/383-5994
Only open Thursday through Saturday, this quiet, uncrowded shop features furniture and odds and ends. (Midtown)

DOWNTOWN ANTIQUE MALL, 612 8th Ave. S., Nashville
615/256-6616
Next to the railroad tracks and close to downtown, this mall has rooms and rooms of amazing things, including lots of furniture. (Downtown)

EIGHTH AVENUE ANTIQUE DISTRICT

This strip includes a number of shops with different emphasis on period and style, such as the **Art Deco Shoppe** at 2110 Eighth Avenue S., 615/386-9373, and **E.H. Sadler** at 2108 Eighth Avenue S., 615/298-5002, which features Edwardian-era dark oak furnishings and men's clothing and gifts. Several, including **Dealer's Choice** at 2109 Eighth S., 615/383-7030, hold regular Friday-night auctions.

A hip combination of old and new can be found at **Fusion** located at 2108 Eighth Avenue S., 615/297-7977, a shop sharing space with E.H. Sadler but featuring a far different atmosphere—treasures of the recent past combined with lots of current handmade works by local artists.

GREEN HILLS ANTIQUE MALL, 4108 Hillsboro Rd., Nashville 615/383-9851 or 615/383-4999

This large, well-run establishment has lots of different vendors. (West Nashville)

RED WAGON ANTIQUES, 6234 Nolensville Rd., Nashville 615/832-6005

More junk than antiques, but fun nonetheless, and the drive is worth it. Nolensville Road is lined with salvage places, quasi–antique shops, commercial businesses of all kinds, and some of Nashville's best ethnic restaurants. (South Nashville)

TENNESSEE ANTIQUE MALL, 654 Wedgewood Ave., Nashville 615/259-4077
WEDGEWOOD STATION, 657 Wedgewood Ave., Nashville 615/259-0939

These long, low buildings house lots of enticing booths that look as if they contain the contents of long-abandoned attics. Even though you'll meet lots of strolling shoppers on Friday and Saturday, there are bargains to be found in housewares, clothing, jewelry, and memorabilia any given day of the week. (South Nashville)

WHITE WAY ANTIQUE MALL, 1200 Villa Pl., Nashville 615/327-1098

Just off Music Row, this is a favorite place to take out-of-towners. You'll find attractively presented antiques and lots of good vendors, and the owner is a knowledgeable collector. (Midtown)

the Disney Store, and Godiva Chocolates are here, as well as the Tennessee Museum Store, which is operated by the Tennessee State Museum. (West Nashville)

COOLSPRINGS GALLERIA
I-65 S. at Moore's Ln.
Nashville
615/771-2128
Located about 15 miles directly south of Nashville, CoolSprings Mall (Nashville's newest) includes Dillard's and Castner-Knott, as well as Parisian, Ann Taylor, the Gap, Uptown's Smoke Shop (a local favorite), and a 10-screen multiplex theater. (South Nashville)

HARDING MALL
Harding Place and Nolensville Pike
Nashville
615/833-6327
Castner-Knott and Marshall's department stores are at the center of this older mall, not too far from the airport, which includes 60 stores and restaurants and a movie theater. (South Nashville)

HICKORY HOLLOW MALL
I-24 E. at Bell Rd.
Nashville
615/731-6255
This huge mall, located about 10 miles southeast of the city, includes Castner-Knott, Dillard's, J.C. Penney, and Sears, as well as two theater complexes and 15 restaurants. Strollers and wheelchairs are provided free of charge. (South Nashville)

THE MALL AT GREEN HILLS
Hillsboro Pike and
Abbott-Martin Rd.
Nashville
615/298-5478
It's hard to believe from present appearances that this is one of Nashville's oldest neighborhood shopping malls. Completely redone in the last several years, the Mall at Green Hills has incorporated Dillard's and Castner-Knott into a fancy two-level structure featuring Laura Ashley, Bachrach's (fine menswear), Eddie Bauer, Brooks Brothers, Brookstone, Crabtree & Evelyn, the Limited, the Nature Company, Ann Taylor, and Williams-Sonoma. (West Nashville)

RIVERGATE MALL
1000 Two Mile Pkwy. at I-65
Nashville
615/859-3456
Once the largest mall in the region, Rivergate still draws shoppers from nearby Kentucky towns like Bowling Green and Hopkinsville. About 12 miles north of town, not far from Goodlettsville, it includes the same anchor stores as Hickory Hollow, although it is a somewhat older mall and slightly smaller. Nearby are several multiple-screen movie theaters, lots of restaurants, and most of the major car dealerships in Nashville. (North Nashville)

OUTLET STORES

GENESCO OUTLET
1415 Murfreesboro Rd.
Nashville
615/367-7660
Genesco is a long-time Nashville-based shoemaker of Johnson & Murphy, Bass, Rockport, and other shoes. (East Nashville)

OUTLET VILLAGE OF LEBANON
I-40 at exit 238
New in 1998, featuring such attractions as a Nike factory store and

a Coach Leather outlet, this multi-colored village of shops is located about 20 miles east of Nashville. Visible from the highway, it looks like fantasy land. (East Nashville)

ONE HUNDRED OAKS MALL
719 Thompson Ln.
Nashville
615/383-8350
One of the area's first shopping malls, One Hundred Oaks is now a discount shopper's mecca. Close to I-440 and I-65 south, near the Hillsboro/Green Hills area, this shopping center has a Burlington Coat Factory and OFF Fifth (Saks Fifth Avenue out-let), as well as PetSmart and Media Play. There is even a Bible Factory Outlet —is nothing sacred anymore? (South Nashville)

STEINMART
Brentwood Store
615/370-3735
This Mississippi-based fashion discount store features a good selection of men's, women's, and children's clothing, gifts, and home furnishings, all at great prices. Stores are located on Franklin Road (Brentwood), Gallatin Pike (Madison/Rivergate area), and White Bridge Road (Belle Meade). (South Nashville)

Nashville Conv. & Visitors Bureau

11

SPORTS AND RECREATION

A wide variety of sports, for both active and passive participants, are available in and around the city. Nashvillians head to nearby lakes, pools, and rivers to ward off the summer doldrums and to the abundance of city and nearby state parks during the crisply energizing days of spring and fall. The rolling hills of Middle Tennessee lend themselves to challenging golf courses as well as to horseback riding and bicycling.

Sports-car racing and pro wrestling are popular spectator sports in this region, along with football and baseball. Nashville's new downtown arena will make it possible for the city to recruit a pro basketball team someday. Meanwhile, Nashville Kats arena football, the Nashville Predators ice hockey team, and concerts by country music's huge moneymakers will dominate its schedule. Vanderbilt University's Lady Commodores (basketball) have an avid local following, and every few years the men's team, once a regional powerhouse, does exceptionally well. Although tailgating is seen before Vanderbilt football games all around the perimeter of the campus, it is mostly carried on by the "away" fans. True Nashvillians are more likely to park in Centennial Park on a crisp fall evening, grab a bite to eat nearby, and walk to Vanderbilt's Memorial Gym for a rousing night of roundball. Just over the horizon is a football stadium for the east bank of the Cumberland River, which will become a reality in 1999 as the new home for the Tennessee Oilers.

Since Nashville is located in a large geographic basin surrounded by a ring of lower hills, you have to drive about 90 minutes outside of town in any direction to find canoeable waters or rock-climbing routes. Boat racks are common on Nashville cars, however, and sporting-goods stores are well stocked with climbing gear and fly-fishing equipment. Nashvillians are not averse to making the trek for the sports they love.

PROFESSIONAL SPORTS

Auto Racing

HIGHLAND RIM SPEEDWAY
6801 Kelly Willis Rd.
Greenbrier
615/643-8725
Highland Rim Speedway, a quarter-mile oval track, is supposed to be the fastest in Tennessee. It's located about 20 miles north of Nashville. (Races are held every Saturday, March–October, beginning at 7 p.m. (gates open at 4). $8 adults, children ages 11 and under free with paid adult. Directions: Take I-65 N. to exit 104 at Ridgetop, then Hwy. 257 W. (North Nashville)

NASHVILLE SPEEDWAY USA
P.O. Box 40307
625 Smith Ave.'
Tennessee State Fairgrounds
Wedgewood Ave. between
Nolensville Rd. and I-65 S.
Nashville
615/726-1818
Many country-music stars are involved in this sport, either as drivers or as team sponsors, so watch the pits for famous faces. A NASCAR course, the Nashville Speedway USA features racing every Saturday at 6:30 p.m. April through September. Gates open at 4. $10–$20 adults (depending on the type and length of race events), free children ages 11 and under. NASCAR special events include the Busch Grand National Series (all seats $47 reserved/$32 general admission) on April 3 at 1 p.m.; a Craftsman Truck Series (all seats $42 reserved/$30 general admission) on July 10 at 2:30 p.m.; a Slim Jim All Pro Series (all seats $25 adult general admission and $10 children ages 11 and under) on October 2 at 6 p.m.; and a Mark Collie Charity Celebrity race featuring Country Music and NASCAR Stars (all seats general admission $10) on October 27 at 7 p.m. (South Nashville)

Baseball

NASHVILLE SOUNDS
Greer Stadium
534 Chestnut St.
Nashville
615/242-4371

Nashville's Racing Scene

Country music and race cars seem to be favored by the same audience, at least in this area. Just as local bluegrass festivals crop up at volunteer fire departments, city parks, and high school stadiums, and country stars headline the events at annual county fairs, so most small cities in Tennessee seem to have dirt and drag-strip tracks located somewhere on the outskirts of town. Many country stars either drive race cars or support drivers with their own race-car teams. Be sure to check out the infield for celebrity action.

The Sounds are a Triple A farm team for the Pittsburgh Pirates. Greer Stadium, with its guitar-shaped scoreboard, is located close to downtown, and parking can usually be found at the nearby Cumberland Science Museum, on the other side of Fort Negley (see Chapter 5: Sights and Attractions) from the stadium. Check out the stone gates of this Civil War fortification as you head to the stadium. Nashville's temperate weather means there are many comfortable nights during the 72-game season, which runs from mid-April through mid-September. Tickets are cheap, the fans are friendly, seats are nearly always available, and special fireworks shows are regular occurrences. $8 box seats, $4 general admission, $1 off tickets for seniors and children under age 12, except for exhibition games and special events. Parking is free, and there are always giveaway promotions for kids. (South Nashville)

Football

**NASHVILLE KATS
(ARENA FOOTBALL)
Nashville Arena
501 Broadway
Nashville
615/254-KATS (information and
season tickets)**

615/255-9600 (Ticketmaster for individual tickets)

Indoor football season runs April through August, with eight home and eight away games. Games are on Friday evenings at 7:35 (televised games are sometimes held on Monday nights). Tickets are $9. (Downtown)

TENNESSEE TITANS

**(Stadium scheduled to be completed in 1999, season begins in Fall 1998 at Vanderbilt Stadium)
615/733-3000 (administrative offices)
Ticketmaster, 615/255-9600 or
Ticket office, 615/341-7627**

The Houston Oilers, now renamed Tennessee Titans, have occasioned the construction of a grand new downtown stadium. (Downtown)

Ice Hockey

**NASHVILLE PREDATORS
Nashville Arena
501 Broadway
Nashville
615/770-2300 (information),
615/770-PUCK (tickets)**

Nashville's new NHL team arrived just in time for the 1998 season. Games are held Mon–Sat evenings at 7:30, Sun at 7. $10–$60 tickets, all reserved seats. (Downtown)

CMT/ABATE, 519 Donelson Pike, a statewide organization for motorcyclists, schedules local rides and events (615/883-5024). They can furnish information on area happenings such as the two all Harley-Davidson events that are held annually by the American Motorcycle Racing Association in Bowling Green, Kentucky (65 minutes north of Nashville on I-65). The events are the All Harley Drag, a sprint race in late July; and the AHD National Finals, a quarter-mile race in early October.

At one time, horse racing was one of Tennessee's most popular spectator sports. It was Andrew Jackson's great love, and in the 1830s and '40s, Nashville was known as one of the country's primary racing cities. The Nashville Race Track, located just north of the river where Metro Center is today, had four tracks. The 1843 Peyton Stakes had the largest purse of any race in the country. Belle Meade Plantation was a well-known thoroughbred nursery. Horse racing, no longer legal in Tennessee, has fallen victim to antigambling factions. These factions have also managed to squelch proposals for a state lottery and do away with church bingo in the process.

Soccer

NASHVILLE METROS
615/771-8200

Games are played at Columbia Stadium on Donelson Pike in Mill Creek. This pro team also sponsors a youth soccer league. (East Nashville)

RECREATION

Bicycling

The rolling hills around Nashville make great bicycling territory in every direction. The Tennessee Department of Transportation has mapped five state tours, some of which include state roads on the outskirts of the city. Tour maps are available from: TDOT, Bicycle Coordinator, James K. Polk State Office Building, 505 Deaderick, Suite 700, Nashville 37243; 615/741-2848. The Nashville Bicycle Club schedules weekly rides for all skill levels (615/269-6683). The Hendersonville Fire Department (North Nashville), sponsor of the annual Bike Ride Across Scenic Sumner (BRASS) road race, will send you a race map

of a beautiful 30-mile course on country roads (615/822-1119).

Motorcycling

There are a growing number of "closet bikers" in Nashville—musicians, Music Row executives, high-powered lawyers—who own vintage bikes and find the country roads around the city very much to their liking. There's always a nice array of machinery parked curbside next to the Hard Rock Café, which has "biker nights" on occasional Wednesdays. The more visible biker crowd can also be found at blues bars such as the Boardwalk and Third and Lindsley. The Gold Rush on Elliston Place has always been a favored hangout for bikers, as are any of the brew pubs in town.

To find out more about the scene, check with the local motorcycle dealerships, who have up-to-the-minute information on races, road rallies, and motorcycle events. Here is a list of outfitters that offer outreach to afficionados, as well as the curious public:

BOSWELL'S
401 Fessler's Ln.
Nashville

615/256-0737
A Harley-Davidson dealership with a grill. Open for lunch Mon–Sat. (East Nashville)

C&S
I-40 W. at 46th Ave.
Nashville
615/297-7500
A Harley-Davidson dealership that serves free Harley-Davidson-brand coffee and popcorn. (West Nashville)

CUSTOM CYCLE WORKS
435 Donelson Pike
Nashville
615/885-3377
Custom Cycle, located near the Airport, is a longtime favorite in Nashville that sells clothing as well as customized Harleys and used bikes. No gimmicks here, just bike business. (East Nashville)

R&B
939 Fourth Ave. S.
Nashville
615/244-6643
R&B is a high-performance shop and the "home" of several champion H-D racing bikes that make stopping in "just to look" OK. (Downtown)

Boating

Percy Priest and Old Hickory Lake, the two big lakes nearest to Nashville, are heavily used for pleasure craft of all kinds, from sailboats to ski boats to houseboats and Jet Skis. The U.S. Corps of Engineers manages the recreation lands, and private concessionaires run the marinas. Boat rentals can often be arranged through the marina operators. Boat ramp access is available at many marked locations around both lakes.

For information about the seven lakes in the Cumberland River watershed, contact the Natural Resource Management Branch of the Corps of Engineers, P.O. Box 1070, Nashville, Tennessee 37202; 615/736-5115.

Public Marinas
Both Percy Priest Lake and Old Hick-

Sailboarding on Percy Priest Lake

Tennessee Tourist Development

ory Lakes also have private marinas where sailboats are moored and boats of all kinds can be launched.

**ELM HILL MARINA
(PERCY PRIEST LAKE)
3361 Bell Rd.
Antioch
615/889-5363   (East Nashville)**

**OLD HICKORY MARINA
(OLD HICKORY LAKE)
2001 Riverside Rd.
Nashville
615/847-4022   (North Nashville)**

Bowling

**INGLEWOOD BOWLING CENTER
3401 Gallatin Rd.
Gallatin
615/262-1472**
This 1950s classic won the 1996 *Nashville Scene* "Best Bowling Alley" award. A church-league hangout, Inglewood has a no-beer policy, but the snack-bar burgers and shakes get good reviews. (North Nashville)

**MELROSE LANES
2600 Franklin Pike
Nashville
615/297-7142**
Melrose is friendly to league and nonleague bowlers alike. It's an old-fashioned alley where you can drink beer while you bowl. Open

Mon–Sat 8:30 a.m., Sun 1 p.m. (South Nashville)

Camping/Backpacking

While no public camping is permitted in city parks, and all of the state facilities in metro Nashville are day-use sites, there are a number of Tennessee state parks in the counties immediately surrounding Nashville that do offer sites for tent camping and short hiking trails. The closest major backpacking opportunities are located an hour or so to the east and south of Nashville, in the Cumberland Mountains. State park sites are available on a first-come, first-served basis.

For a list of Tennessee State Park facilities or more information, call 615/532-0001 or 800/421-6683. Listed below are sports stores/outfitters that sell and rent camping equipment. They are usually good sources for locations of other prime camping areas.

Outfitters

**CUMBERLAND TRANSIT
2807 West End Ave.
Nashville
615/321-4069**
Camping, backpacking, climbing and fly-fishing equipment are for sale at Cumberland Transit, which also rents equipment for many activities. The bulletin board is a good source of

used goods as well as outdoor happenings. (Midtown)

BLUE RIDGE MOUNTAIN SPORTS
108 Page Rd.
Nashville
615/356-2300
7090 Bakers Bridge Ave.
Cool Springs Galleria
615/771-5650
Blue Ridge Mountain Sports sells camping, backpacking, and climbing equipment and rents camping gear. They have the best hiking and walking boot selection in town and staff are friendly and knowledgeable. (West Nashville, South Nashville)

WILDERNESS SPORTS
73 White Bridge Rd.
Nashville
615/356-5230
Wilderness Sports sells camping, backpacking, boating, and climbing gear and also offers rentals, instruction, and organized trips, with a special emphasis on white-water kayaking. (West Nashville)

Camping Areas

BLEDSOE CREEK STATE PARK
400 Ziegler's Fort Rd.
Gallatin
615/452-3706
This small state park, open year-round, has 126 campsites on Old Hickory Lake. Reservations are not taken for campsites, but this out-of-the-way park is a good one to try when others are booked. (North Nashville)

CEDARS OF LEBANON STATE PARK
328 Cedar Forest Rd.
Lebanon
615/443-2769
Offering hiking trails through what they claim is the largest red cedar forest in the country, this nice park has 117 campsites, a nature center, swimming pool, horseback riding, and a recreation lodge that is often the site of local square dancing. (East Nashville)

EDGAR EVINS STATE PARK
I-40 E.
Silver Point
615/858-2446
Located on Center Hill Lake, about an hour east of Nashville, this park has 60 campsites, lake swimming, and hiking trails in a hilly, wooded area. (East Nashville)

LONG HUNTER STATE PARK
I-40 E.
Hermitage
615/885-2422
Even though Long Hunter is a day-use park, overnight backpacking is allowed with reservations. Many of the trails at this beautiful park follow Percy Priest Lake. (East Nashville)

MONTGOMERY BELL STATE PARK
Rte. 1, Box 39
Burns
615/797-9052
This park is popular with groups because of its lodges and large resort-type inn. Located about an hour west of Nashville, off I-40 near Dickson, the park facilities include hiking trails and primitive camping shelters. (West Nashville)

OLD STONE FORT STATE PARK
I-24 S.
Manchester
615/723-5073

Just over an hour south of Nashville is a Mississippian Indian site that is now preserved within state park boundaries. The park has 51 campsites and hiking trails leading to the beautiful bend in the Duck River, on which the fort was sited. Old Stone Fort State Park provides a rare opportunity to camp within what may have been a ceremonial compound. (South Nashville)

Canoeing

Canoeing is one of the nicest ways to experience the Tennessee country-

Biking in Nashville

For the best biking in town, try one of the following three routes:

1. BELLE MEADE BOULEVARD (and contiguous neighborhood streets)
"The boulevard," as it is often called, is lined with huge homes set well back from this divided street with a grass median strip. Locals run, walk, and bike along this road daily. The streets leading into Belle Meade Boulevard are relatively flat and well-maintained, making this an ideal spot for riding with family groups. (West Nashville)

2. RADNOR LAKE
Otter Creek Road, which passes by the lake, extends from Hillsboro Pike to Franklin Pike and makes a nice ride, although it can be busy at certain times of the day. If you ride out Granny White Pike (12th Avenue), which extends from Woodmont Boulevard to Old Hickory Boulevard (avoid morning and afternoon rush hours), Radnor makes a nice destination. (South Nashville)

3. WARNER PARKS
There are several entrances to Percy and Edwin Warner Parks: one at the end of Belle Meade Boulevard, one at Highway 100, one at Old Hickory Boulevard, and one at Chickering Road. Any of these will lead to a series of paved roads that wind through the hilly, wooded parks. A moderately difficult hour-long ride starts and ends at the Belle Meade Boulevard gates. (West Nashville)

side. Pack a picnic and head out for a day of pastoral scenery. The Harpeth is the closest canoeable river to Nashville. However, it's best to go after spring rains, because this river tends to go shallow in spots. The canoe-rental places listed for the Harpeth are roughly 15 miles west of Nashville via Highway 70 or I-40 West to Kingston Springs. Just outside of Gallatin, about 20 miles north of town, is Station Camp Creek, a tributary of the Cumberland. The Buffalo River is both wider and deeper than the Harpeth, so the 1¼-hour trip each direction is worth making in the summer months. Take I-40 west to the Linden/Waverly exit 13 (65 miles). The Caney Fork River, wide and gentle, crosses under I-40 East six times as the road heads toward the Cumberland Mountains, about 40 minutes out of town.

Canoeing on the Harpeth River

Tennessee Tourist Development

BUFFALO RIVER CANOE RENTAL
Nine miles south of I-40
Lobelville
615/589-2755
Canoes, kayaks, rafts, and primitive camping are available at Buffalo River Canoe Rental. Open mid-Mar–Oct. (West Nashville)

CANEY FORK CANOE TRIPS & SHUTTLES
Rte. 1, Box 106
Silver Point
615/858-4585
In addition to canoe rentals, Caney offers fishing guide services. Open Mar–Oct. (East Nashville)

CUMBERLAND TRANSIT (CANOE AND KAYAK RENTAL)
2807 West End Ave.
Nashville
615/321-4069
Cumberland Transit is one of Nashville's most helpful and well-equipped outdoor outfitters. They also carry backpacking, climbing, fly-fishing, and biking gear. (Midtown)

FLATWOODS CANOE BASE (BUFFALO RIVER)
Hwy. 13
Flatwoods
615/589-5661
In addition to canoe rental, Flatwoods offers some primitive camping sites. Open Mar–Oct. (West Nashville)

FOGGY BOTTOM CANOE RENTAL (HARPETH RIVER)
1270 Hwy. 70
Kingston Springs
615/952-4062
In addition to canoes, Foggy Bottom also rents small metal fishing boats known as "john boats." (West Nashville)

HARTLAND CANOE RENTAL, INC. (BUFFALO RIVER)
473 Barren Hollow Rd.,
½ mile east of Hwy. 13,

at Buffalo KOA campground
Waverly
615/296-1306
Hartland is open year-round. This outfitter offers rentals for excursions on the Buffalo River. (West Nashville)

NUMBER ONE CANOE RENTAL
(STATION CAMP CREEK)
2040 Nashville Pike
Gallatin
615/452-5789 or 615/452-4135
Judge for yourself whether or not Number One Canoe Rental really is #1. Open Apr–Sep Sat–Sun. (North Nashville)

TIP A CANOE (BUFFALO RIVER)
Hwy. 13
Flatwoods
615/254-0836 or 800/550-5810
This is the oldest canoe rental company in Tennessee. Open Memorial Day–Labor Day. (West Nashville)

TIP A CANOE (HARPETH RIVER)
1279 Hwy. 70
Kingston Springs
615/254-0836 or 800/550-5810
Offering canoe rentals and primitive camping. Open Mar–Oct. (West Nashville)

WILDERNESS SPORTS
73 White Bridge Rd.
Nashville
615/356-5230
Canoe and kayak rental as well as car racks are available at Wilderness Sports. (West Nashville)

Climbing

Climbing and rappelling are practiced around the Middle Tennessee area, usually in the hilly north and east on rock bluffs overlooking the Caney Fork, Red, and Cumberland Rivers. More extensive rock-climbing areas are located 90 minutes or more to the east and south in the Cumberland Mountains, around the Obed River and the South Cumberland State Recreation Area. Ask about climbing gyms and charted routes around the area at the outfitters who carry climbing equipment listed in this chapter under Camping/ Backpacking.

Fishing

Tennessee requires a fishing license for residents and nonresidents over 12 years old. These may be obtained, for 3- to 10-day periods, at marinas, sporting-goods stores, and convenience stores near lakes and rivers. The second Saturday in June is "no permit" day on public waters in Tennessee.

For more information about fishing in and around Nashville, contact the Tennessee Wildlife Resources Agency, P.O. Box 40747, Ellington Agricultural Center, Nashville 37204 (615/781-6500).

Steve White, architect with Bullock, Smith & Partners, fondly recalls white-water kayaking on the challenging waters of East Tennessee before he became a dad. Now he and seven-year-old son, Jesse, drive west for a day of satisfying canoeing on the beautiful, not-too-swiftly flowing Buffalo River.

Outfitters

CUMBERLAND TRANSIT
2807 West End Ave.
Nashville
615/321-4069
Fly-fishing equipment, books, and advice are available at Cumberland. Check their busy bulletin board for guide services and used equipment. (West Nashville)

GAME FAIR LTD.
99 White Bridge Rd.
Nashville
615/353-0602
Fly-tying and fly-fishing equipment and antique bamboo rods and reels are available here. (West Nashville)

SOUTH HARPETH OUTFITTERS AND FLY FISHING SCHOOL
P.O. Box 218226
1116 Kingston Springs Rd.
Nashville
615/952-4186 or 615/320-5660
Ernie Pacquette and colleagues offer private on-stream lessons, fly and light-tackle fishing, and guide services. (West Nashville)

Fitness Clubs

ARMO'S BODY SHOPPE
1907 Division, just off Music Row
Nashville
615/321-0714
Armo's is a weight room located in the Music Row area and a good spot to watch for celebrities. (Midtown)

DOWNTOWN ATHLETIC CLUB
520 Commerce St., across from Convention Center
Nashville
615/271-2616
The Downtown Athletic Club offers daily rates, indoor parking, a track, aerobics, a weight room, racquetball, volleyball, basketball, and a whirlpool, sauna, and steam room. (Downtown)

STEPS
2207 21st Ave. S.
Nashville
615/269-8844
No membership is required. This facility is a training gym run by professional sports medicine practitioners Dr. Irv Rubinstein and Dr. Kathy Alexander. (Midtown)

THOMAS FRIST CENTENNIAL SPORTSPLEX
25th Ave. N. at Brandau
Nashville
615/862-8480
The city's sports complex is located right next to Centennial Park. It

includes indoor swimming, an outdoor tennis center, and indoor ice-skating. (Midtown)

Golf

Metro Parks and Recreation Public Courses

The many Nashville public courses are usually located near neighborhoods. The courses offer moderately challenging play at nominal fees. Here's a list of metro Nashville courses in all parts of town:

HARPETH HILLS
2424 Old Hickory Blvd., next to
Warner Park Steeplechase
Nashville
615/862-8493   (West Nashville)

McCABE GOLF COURSE
100 46th Ave. N., off Murphy Rd.
Nashville
615/862-8491   (Midtown)

PERCY WARNER GOLF COURSE
Forrest Park Dr.
Nashville
615/352-9958   (West Nashville)

SHELBY GOLF COURSE
2021 Fatherland St.
Nashville

615/862-8474   (East Nashville)
TED RHODES GOLF COURSE
1901 Ed Temple Blvd.
Nashville
615/862-8463   (North Nashville)

TWO RIVERS GOLF COURSE
3150 McGavock Pike
Nashville
615/889-2675   (East Nashville)

Resort Courses

HERMITAGE GOLF COURSE
3939 Old Hickory Blvd.
Nashville
615/847-4001
Host of the Sara Lee LPGA Classic, Hermitage was voted best golf course by *Nashville Scene* readers. (East Nashville)

LEGENDS CLUB OF TENNESSEE
off Franklin Rd. and
Mack Hatcher Pkwy.
Franklin
615/791-8100
This course was designed by pro Tom Kite. Guests of some area hotels will receive a coupon for $5 off. Hotel guests can use their confirmation number to reserve a tee time up to 30 days in advance. (South Nashville)

Day Hikes in Nashville

The state parks contiguous to the Nashville area (see listing under camping/backpacking) all have trails suitable for day hikes. Radnor Lake and Warner Parks, both listed in this chapter under Bicycling, are the best in-town locales for extended hiking.

SPRINGHOUSE GOLF CLUB AT OPRYLAND HOTEL
off Briley Pkwy. at
Music Valley Dr.
Nashville
615/871-7759
This 18-hole course is home of the PGA Senior Tour Bell South Classic. (East Nashville)

Horseback Riding

There is lots of horse culture in Williamson County, southwest of Nashville. Driving down Old Hillsboro Road, Franklin Pike, or Highway 96 will take one past working horse farms with extensive barns. Watch the newspapers for notices of polo matches and the annual Iroquois Steeplechase event in May. Several stables in the area offer trail rides.

BIOTA RANCH
5220 Ridge Hill Dr.
Joelton
615/876-6062
Open year-round, Biota Ranch has more than 20 miles of bridle trails on a 750-acre preserve. Riding lessons are also offered. (North Nashville)

CEDARS OF LEBANON STATE PARK
328 Cedar Forest Rd.
Lebanon
615/443-2769
(See their listing under Camping Areas.)

JU-RO STABLES
7149 Cairo Bend Rd.
Lebanon
615/449-6621
Ride through open fields or woodland trails at Ju-Ro Stables. Primitive camping, Western and English tack, and lessons are available. (East Nashville)

MUSIC CITY RIDING ACADEMY
7455 Hwy. 100
Nashville
615/353-4790
A full-service boarding facility which offers riding lessons and summer camp for children in a family atmosphere. (West Nashville)

Steeplechase

Mary Entrekin

Running

Nashville's relatively flat terrain makes it an ideal city for running, especially through the historic neighborhoods, which tend to have sidewalks and wide streets. (Check the listings in this chapter under Biking for good places for a long-distance run.) The Nashville Striders offer regular weekly group running events (informal) every Wednesday at 5:30 p.m. behind the Arts Activity Center in Centennial Park and on Saturday morning at eight at the main entrance to Percy Warner Park. Call them at 615/353-0822 or 615/327-5356 for more information. The Tennessee State Parks sponsor an Annual Running Tour, which takes place during the fall and winter months at different parks around the area.

Both Long Hunter State Park (East Nashville) and Montgomery Bell State Park (West Nashville) are race sites. Call the Tennessee Department of Environment and Conservation, 615/532-0103, or the individual parks for more information and route maps. The Vanderbilt University track on Natchez Trace at Blakemore Avenue is open to the public when not being used for official track functions.

Ice-Skating

ICE CENTENNIAL
(See Thomas Frist Centennial Sportsplex under Fitness Clubs.)

Swimming

Metro Parks and Recreation Public Indoor and Outdoor Pools

In the hot Nashville summertime, open swim (outdoors) is free of charge at Metro pools. Metro pools offer basic facilities—pools and concrete patios enclosed by tall fences. Call 615/862-8480 for hours.

GLENCLIFF
Antioch Pike
Nashville
615/862-8470   (South Nashville)

PEARL-COHN
904 26th Ave. N.
Nashville
615/862-8471   (North Nashville)

WAVE COUNTRY
Two Rivers Pkwy.
Nashville
615/885-1052
Wave Country has a "wave pool" that exercises while you stand still. Kids scream and shout at this one! Operated by Metro Nashville Parks and Recreation, this is the only outdoor summer pool that charges admission. Memorial Day–Labor Day. (East Nashville)

WHITES CREEK
7277 Old Hickory Blvd.
Nashville
615/876-4300   (North Nashville)

THOMAS FRIST CENTENNIAL SPORTSPLEX
25th Ave. at Brandau
Nashville
615/862-8480
Features an indoor lap and wading pool. The pools are open Mon–Thu 6 a.m.–9 p.m., Fri 6 a.m.–7 p.m., Sat 8:30–6, Sun 1–5. $6 adults, $5 children. (Midtown)

Tennis

There are free Metro Parks and Recreation outdoor tennis courts located all over town.

THOMAS FRIST CENTENNIAL SPORTSPLEX
25th Ave. at Brandau
Nashville
615/864-8490

This Metro Parks and Recreation facility has both indoor and outdoor courts. (Rates: Outdoor courts are $4/hr. for adults, $3/hr. for seniors and children ages 18 and under. Mon–Fri 8–5; after 5 p.m. and all day Sat and Sun rates are $5/hr. Indoor-court rates are $10/hr. Mon–Fri noon–4, $12/hr. after 4 p.m. and all day Sat and Sun. (Midtown)

MUSIC CITY SHERATON
This hotel has outdoor tennis courts for guests. (See listing in Chapter 3: Where to Stay).

Yoga

YOGA SOURCE
209 10th Ave. S.
Nashville
615/254-9642

Walk in classes, in different types of yoga and at all skill levels, are offered several times a day Mon–Sat for about $10 a class. (Downtown)

Nashville Conv. & Visitors Bureau

12

PERFORMING ARTS

Although it is affectionately known worldwide as Music City, USA, Nashville has a broad range of cultural events going on year-round, from classical music, opera, and Broadway theater to community-based folk music, innovative original dance, and dramatic performances ranging from poetry readings to Shakespeare.

Over the past few years Nashville music lovers have witnessed more and more interplay between musical genres in a city that is truly becoming a nexus for creative innovation. There are many classically trained musicians in Nashville who move easily between two different worlds: day on Music Row, night on the Symphony stage. And there is a community spirit here—of cooperation and striving to make Nashville the kind of place their children will want to stay—that stems from that same creative community. Many Nashville jazz players support the efforts of the W.O. Smith Community Music School, where they give lessons to deserving young musicians who pay according to need. And a growing number of Nashville club and coffeehouse owners are featuring noncommercial artistic performances, such as one-person theater and poetry, art exhibits, independent film, even visiting tourist musicians, so that Nashville's avant garde can keep the blade of its artistic edge sharp.

THEATER

**AMERICAN NEGRO
PLAYWRIGHT THEATER
Various venues**

615/871-4283
Outstanding dramatic productions, sometimes incorporating music and dance, based on African American history and cultural heritage are

presented on a quasi-regular basis by the American Negro Playwright Theater. Actor Barry Scott, who also acts in Tennessee Repertory Theatre productions, founded the American Negro Playwright Theater with a specific purpose in mind—to expose young people to the distinguished history of African Americans. His original plays *Harlem Voices* and *A Joyful Noise* capture the stories and songs of the Harlem Renaissance and Fisk University's Jubilee Singers.

CHAFFIN'S BARN
DINNER THEATER
8204 Hwy. 100
Nashville
615/646-9977
Chaffin's was the first dinner theater in the country to perform Shakespeare. Dinner and a show at this institution near the city limits can be a fun first-time theater outing for parents traveling with teenagers. Although some of the country-music tourist attractions feature Vegas-style shows accompanied by dinner, this is the only true dinner theater in town (See Chapter 13: Nightlife.) (West Nashville)

CIRCLE PLAYERS
Johnson Theater (TPAC)
P.O. Box 121462
Nashville
615/383-7469 (information)
Presenting a varied repertory, the Circle Players, Nashville's oldest local company, performs at the Tennessee Performing Arts Center several times yearly. Plays range from modern classics to contemporary drama and comedy, with actors drawn from the local acting community—Nashvillians might even recognize their lawyer in the cast. &
(Downtown)

LAKEWOOD THEATER COMPANY
2211 Hadley Blvd.
Old Hickory
615/847-2585
Lakewood Theater Company offers a varied repertory of local interest productions. Performances are Friday and Saturday, with a matinee on Sunday. This up-and-coming company has a steadily building audience among those living in the Hendersonville/Old Hickory Lake area. (North Nashville)

MOCKINGBIRD PUBLIC THEATRE
Various venues
615/255-5518
In this new company, some of Nashville's finest actors perform old and new regional works as well as classics such as *The Importance of Being Earnest* and *Night of the Iguana* and more contemporary dramatic plays. It's the most groundbreaking theater troupe in town—watch for a production being mounted during your stay for cutting-edge direction, impressive professional acting, and creative staging.

NASHVILLE CHILDREN'S THEATRE
724 Second Ave. S.
Nashville
615/254-9103
Many of this company's marvelous productions are designed to create socially responsible learning about the history of other peoples and cultures, and they are always well performed, interactive, and non-didactic. Performances are generally on weekday mornings with two shows for the convenience of school groups, but the public is welcome. Inquire about weekend family series and sign-interpreted shows. & (Downtown)

NASHVILLE SHAKESPEARE
FESTIVAL

A performance at the Blair
School of Music

Musicals and classic works of the American theater dominate the schedule of Nashville's most successful theater company, which performs *A Christmas Carol* yearly along with at least one terrific original production per season. Tennessee Rep, as the company is affectionately known, has brought professional-level theater to Nashville, and its fully staged productions are lively and entertaining. Tickets are $8–$30. (Downtown)

CLASSICAL MUSIC AND OPERA

BELMONT UNIVERSITY SCHOOL OF MUSIC
1900 Belmont Blvd.
Massey Auditorium
615/460-5636
Belmont University's excellent music department spawns a number of performing musical groups, including the Belmont Camerata, the University Orchestra, a jazz ensemble, and a concert band. Watch for listings of their free performances on campus and elsewhere. (Midtown)

BLAIR SCHOOL OF MUSIC
2400 Blakemore Blvd.
Nashville
615/322-7651
Vanderbilt's Blair School of Music, home to some incredible musicians who are performers as well as teachers, has a lovely small music auditorium with fine acoustics. If you can attend a performance at Blair while you're in town, do so. Tickets are reasonably priced, and concerts and recitals are often held on Friday and Saturday evenings at 8 p.m. The Blair String Quartet has gained a national reputation, and the Blair Brass Quintet, the Blair Collegium Musicum, and

2814 12th Ave. S.
Nashville
615/292-7703
One of Nashville's top companies, this group mounts free Shakespeare performances during the month of August in Centennial Park. During the school year they provide educational programs in the public schools while performing occasional imaginative and well-acted productions of their own. (South Nashville)

TENNESSEE PERFORMING-ARTS CENTER
505 Deaderick St.
Nashville
615/791-7985
(See listing under Performing Arts Venues, below.)

TENNESSEE REPERTORY THEATER
Polk Theater (TPAC)
427 Chestnut (administrative office)
Nashville
615/244-4878

other ensembles composed of Blair faculty lead the city in innovative classical performance. ♿ (Midtown)

NASHVILLE CHAMBER ORCHESTRA
Paul Gambill, Conductor
Various venues including Blair Recital Hall
615/292-7815

NCO has made a name for itself by performing original commissioned works by Nashville composers that sometimes cross classical with traditional music. One recent piece was written for mountain dulcimer and chamber orchestra—a first. NCO also performs in the communities surrounding Nashville, and works with senior citizens and other groups to bring the experience of classical music into the public realm. Their concert repertoire is varied and accomplished. See them if you can while in Nashville.

NASHVILLE OPERA
Polk Theater (TPAC)
Fifth and Deaderick
Nashville
615/292-5710

The Nashville Opera usually performs one major production a year on two contiguous weekends in the spring, often with visiting soloists. This professional company has been building a reputation over the past 10 years or so for fine shows with talented local casts. The recent performance of an original opera based on *The Turn of the Screw* was well conceived and innovative and totally captured the imagination of a large audience. ♿ (Downtown)

NASHVILLE SYMPHONY
Jackson Hall (TPAC)
Fifth and Deaderick
Nashville

615/329-3033

The fine Nashville Symphony, conducted by Maestro Kenneth Schermerhorn and assistant conductor Karen Lynne Deal, has over the past 10 years achieved full-time status, attracting professional musicians from around the country to join the outstanding classical players already here. Many classically trained Nashville Symphony players also double as session musicians for all types of recording.

Seats can usually be found on the day of performance from subscribers who notify the symphony that day. The varied music schedule includes at least one local-interest program per year and many outstanding guest soloists. During the summer months the symphony performs free concerts at the Centennial Park Band Shell and on the lawn at Cheekwood for about the price of a regular symphony ticket. ♿ (Downtown)

RYMAN AUDITORIUM

The Ryman's popular classical series, only two years old, has featured groups such as the Vienna Boys Choir and the Orchestra of the Academy of St. Martin in the Fields (see Performing-Arts Venues, below). ♿ (Downtown)

SCARRITT-BENNETT CENTER SERIES
Wightman Chapel
1008 19th Ave. S.
Nashville
615/340-7485

This series offers free performances by notable local classical musicians in a beautiful stone church auditorium on this well-kept campus located between Vanderbilt University and Music Row. Stroll around the

Sidewalk of country and western stars' imprints

campus and peek your head in if you hear strains of organ music emanating from the chapel. ♿ (Midtown)

DANCE

NASHVILLE BALLET
Polk Theater and Jackson Hall (TPAC)
Fifth and Deaderick
Nashville
615/244-7233

A highly skilled classical company celebrating its 10th anniversary in Nashville, the Nashville Ballet offers a seasonal subscription series including at least one company premiere piece yearly and occasional world premieres. Over the past few years the company has been swept into an exciting realm by artistic director Paul Vasterling, who has recruited new dancers and challenged the troupe with his own cutting-edge choreography. They are making waves here with innovative works such as a production of *Firebird* that includes a modern-dance scene in which the performers

dress in hip streetwear. Fri and Sat evening performances, Sat and Sun matinees. (Downtown)

TENNESSEE DANCE THEATER
Polk Theater (TPAC) and other venues
615/248-3262

This modern-dance company is immersed in regional vernacular, performing original works based on anything from quilts to the Mississippi fife and drum music of Otha Turner. Children will enjoy the comedic edge to performers' styles, but the pieces often carry strong adult messages. Highly unusual and worth seeing, this company received raves in New York and has toured Europe. (Downtown)

TENNESSEE PERFORMING ARTS CENTER AND VANDERBILT UNIVERSITY
New Directions Series
Jackson Hall (TPAC)
505 Deaderick St.
Nashville
615/741-7975

The New Directions Series works

to bring major companies like the Alvin Ailey American Dance Theater (full company) to Nashville. Performances are held either at TPAC or Vanderbilt's Langford Auditorium, depending on the size of the prospective audience and production needs of the performers. It's an innovative way to bring exciting cultural events to Nashville. (Downtown)

PERFORMING-ARTS VENUES

BLAIR RECITAL HALL
Blair School of Music

2400 Blakemore Ave.
Nashville
615-322-7651
This hall, which has wonderful acoustics, is the performance auditorium for the Blair School of Music, on the Vanderbilt Campus. The Blair School of Music's regular recitals are worth going out of your way for if you are a classical music aficionado. &
(Midtown)

DARK HORSE THEATRE
4610 Charlotte Ave.
Nashville
615/297-7113
This former church is a charming

Seasonal Venues

Several of Nashville's historic houses, museums, and parks hold summertime music events on their grounds, where you can bring a picnic and spread a blanket for a relaxing early evening of jazz, blues, classical music, theater, or dance. Here's a listing:

*   **Belle Meade Plantation**, 5025 Harding Road, Nashville, 615/356-0501, and **The Hermitage**, 4580 Rachel's Lane, Donelson, 615/889-2941, feature the Tennessee Jazz and Blues Society series on alternate Sundays during the summer months. Tickets may be obtained from Ticketmaster or by calling TJBS at 615/386-7500.*

*   At the **Centennial Park Bandshell**, the Metro Parks and Recreation program hosts free concerts by the Nashville Symphony in summer. Call the symphony at 615/255-5600 for more information or contact Metro Parks at 615/862-8400 for a schedule of events.*

*   **Cheekwood**, 1200 Forrest Park Drive, 615/356-8000, hosts several concerts by the Nashville Symphony each summer. Spread a picnic out on the beautifully landscaped grounds and listen to classical music wafting through the air for an unparalleled experience. Ticketmaster has tickets, or call Cheekwood for details.*

Dan Brewer

Nashville Children's Theatre, p. 188

small theater with nicely slanted rows of seats so that every one has good sightlines. The ambience is informal, but the performances by local companies are top-notch. Coffee and cookies in the tiny lobby at intermission make this the closest thing Nashville has to an off-Broadway theater. (West Nashville)

GRAND OLE OPRY HOUSE
The Grand Ole Opry House sometimes books mainstream pop and rock acts. See Chapter 6: Country-Music Culture for a detailed description. & (East Nashville)

LANGFORD AUDITORIUM, VANDERBILT UNIVERSITY
615/322-3471
This 1,200-seat auditorium of Vanderbilt Medical Center is used for small chamber concerts, jazz, dance performances, and theater. It is home to Vanderbilt's Great Performances series, an annual subscription series that includes at least two important modern-dance companies yearly. & (Midtown)

Z. ALEXANDER LOOBY THEATER
2301 Metro Center Blvd.,
off Eighth Ave. N.
Nashville
615-862-8456
Metro Parks and Recreation runs this very nice auditorium located in the same building as a branch of the public library. Many local theater groups perform at Looby. & (North Nashville)

NASHVILLE ARENA
Broadway at Fifth Ave. S.
Nashville
615/880-2850
The Nashville Arena can seat around 18,000 concertgoers, hockey fans, and event audiences. In Nashville's dreams, the Grammy Awards will one day be broadcast from this innovative piece of architecture, which includes a radio tower and is oriented catty-corner to the Ryman Auditorium. & (Downtown)

NASHVILLE MUNICIPAL AUDITORIUM
417 Fourth Ave. N.
Nashville

615/862-6390

Nashville's oldest concert venue, this 1960s-style round structure has, for most music and large-scale production events such as the International Figure Skating Championships, been replaced by the new Nashville Arena on Broadway. Over the years, however, its 9,000-plus seats have accommodated audiences for such wide-ranging performers as the Talking Heads, pro wrestlers, Sesame Street Live, and the Ringling Brothers Barnum and Bailey Circus. Schedule information can be obtained by calling the 24-hour hotline at 615/862-6395. (Downtown)

RYMAN AUDITORIUM
116 Fifth Ave. N.
Nashville
615/889-6611

The Ryman presents an impressive lineup of nationally prominent concert performers, highly touted local musicians in styles from gospel to bluegrass, an annual theatrical perform-ance (Hank Williams, Patsy Cline, and the Everly Brothers have been subjects of extravagant stage shows at the Ryman over the past few years), and a classical series. See Chapter 6: Country-Music Culture. & (Downtown)

STARWOOD AMPHITHEATER
3839 Murfreesboro Rd.
Antioch
615/641-5800

Nashville's only regularly scheduled outdoor music venue, Starwood seats audiences both under an open, covered arena and on a grassy lawn outfield. Large rock and pop shows dominate the Starwood schedule. No coolers are allowed, and concessions are pricey. I recommend the covered seating for the best acoustics and ease of listening within what can be a large crowd scene. There is no real alternative to parking on the premises, which costs extra and can sometimes be a hassle. Ticketmaster has tickets for all Starwood events. (South Nashville)

TENNESSEE PERFORMING
ARTS CENTER
505 Deaderick St.
Nashville
615/741-7975 (information)
615/255-9600 (Ticketmaster)

Moonlighting Musicians

Vanderbilt University faculty members Mark O'Connor (violinist) and Edgar Meyer (double bassist) of the Blair School of Music play some of Nashville's finest traditional acoustic music on the side. They can be found some nights at the Station Inn playing with the likes of Maura O'Connell and Bela Fleck. They recently collaborated with cellist Yo Yo Ma to record a collection of traditional tunes entitled Appalachia Waltz *(Sony Classical, 1996), that is stunningly beautiful.*

The Tennessee Performing Arts Center (known as TPAC) is located in downtown Nashville in a large state office building that also houses the Tennessee State Museum on its basement level and supports an office tower above. Ticketmaster is located in the TPAC box office, and handles ticket sales for all companies performing on TPAC stages as well as many other events around town, including Vanderbilt University concerts and Great Performances series.

TPAC's three theaters, named after famous Tennessee politicians, run simultaneous performances, sharing a massive multileveled lobby. Refreshments including cocktails and a coffee bar are available. The Tennessee State Museum mounts a changing exhibit of contemporary art in the lobby spaces. (Andrew) Jackson Hall, the largest, is primarily a concert hall. Home to the Nashville Symphony, Jackson Hall hosts occasional pop music concerts, an annual schedule of Broadway musicals, dance, classical music, and opera. The (James K.) Polk Theater is a much smaller concert venue, designed for chamber music or dramatic productions. The (Andrew) Johnson Theater is a black-box theater, designed to house a variety of small-audience events, including theater, television shows, meetings, and trade-show exhibits. & (Downtown)

328 PERFORMANCE HALL
328 Fourth Ave. N.
Nashville
615/259-3288
Go West Productions runs this large music venue, one of Nashville's best. 328 features a variety of nationally known pop, rock, and alternative music acts, and occasional crossover country-music performers. Located

several blocks south of downtown, with ample free parking on nearby streets, 328 Performance Hall is a no-hassle, professionally run venue. Beer and soft drinks are available, and the staff is friendly. Seating varies from standing to general admission to reserved seats. For schedule and ticket information, check their Web site, *www.nea.net/328.html*, or look in *Nashville Scene*, where they regularly run advertisements. (Downtown)

VANDERBILT UNIVERSITY CONCERTS
402 Sarratt Center
Nashville
615/322-2471
Vanderbilt sponsors a wide variety of musical and performing arts events when the university is in session. The Vanderbilt Concerts Series appeals primarily to undergraduate students, with a range of pop, rock, and alternative bands appearing in Memorial Gym, Vanderbilt Stadium, and, on occasion, at the medical school's Langford Auditorium or in the cinema at Sarratt Student Center. Over the years, many famous bands have passed through Nashville courtesy of Vanderbilt concerts, not the least of which was the Rolling Stones on their most recent tour. Ticketmaster, which has an outlet at Sarratt Student Center, sells tickets for all events. (Midtown)

VANDERBILT GREAT PERFORMANCES SERIES
Langford Auditorium
402 Sarratt Center
Nashville
615/322-2471
The Great Performances Series, an annual subscription series that is one of the top attractions for the Nashville

community, features outstanding national and international dance, theater, classical, and avant-garde music performances. (Midtown)

BUYING TICKETS

Tickets to most of Nashville's cultural events are available by prior subscription through the following organizations: Nashville Symphony, Nashville Ballet, Nashville Chamber Orchestra, Tennessee Dance Theater, Darkhorse Theater, Tennessee Repertory Theatre, and Nashville Opera. Many companies allow members to refund unused tickets before shows, so a last-minute call or appearance at the time of performance may yield a good seat. Tickets are usually available at the door for Vanderbilt University campus events (except for big concerts, which draw a youthful audience from all over the region).

TICKETMASTER
505 Deaderick St. in Tennessee Performing Arts Center
Nashville
615/255-9600
Online: Citysearch
Serving the Tennessee Performing Arts Center and most other Nashville performing-arts venues, Ticketmaster also sells tickets to the Vanderbilt University concerts and Performing Arts Series. Outlets can be found at major department stores and Vanderbilt University's Sarratt Student Center.

Robin Hood

13

One of the pleasures of being in this city is that one can easily incorporate live music events into the course of everyday life. More often than not, Nashville nightlife features music in some form. Downtown, visitors can stroll into lower Broadway honky-tonks or seek out the once semisecret Printer's Alley night-clubs that offer dinner and a show every night of the week. All around the city are small bars and listening rooms that can make a performance by one or more solo songwriters, on any evening of the week, an intimate concert experience for less than $10. In this city of musicians, a concert venue can be any-thing from a large dance hall to a sandwich shop to a clothing store.

While major acts command the same high dollar as anywhere, you'll find incredible music listening bargains and once-in-a-lifetime opportunities to hear music as it should be heard. Scan the club listings for names of musi-cians you know—many times a widely acclaimed musician might be doing a one-night stand at a small club for an $8 to $10 admission fee. (Be sure to check Chapter 6: Country-Music Culture, for a rundown of country-only venues). If you pick the venue according to your musical inclinations and not by the name of the artist, you may be introduced to an exciting new act whose latest record is just days away from a national listing on the country, pop, gospel, new rock, or alternative charts.

For something entirely different, try staying home and listening in to WPLN (90.3) radio's Saturday night songwriters' showcase "Players and Poets;" to WRLT (100.1) radio's Nashville Sunday Night for a live performance from Third and Lindsley every Sunday night at eight; or attending a local song-writer's night at Davis-Kidd Booksellers while enjoying dessert and coffee.

If you're in the mood for a bar experience, with no cover and no schedule of performers to attend to, you'll find a nice assortment listed here. Nashville dance clubs run the full gamut, from trendy low-energy lounges to frenetic

TIP

Dancin' in the District takes place at Riverfront Park every Thursday night from May through September and features a wide range of pop and rock acts. The entertainers are top-notch, and food and beer are available. Seating is in a concrete amphitheater facing the river. It's a nice way to spend an evening. The free event is cosponsored by WRLT (100.1), Nashville's alternative radio station, where you can tune in for advance interviews with the performers.

techno music to two-steppin' country dance floors. Nashville's gay nightlife scene reflects the varied population of the town—from up-to-the-minute sophisticated clubs like The Connection to neighborhood restaurant/bars like the World's End—and visitors will find a good-sized, if fairly discreet, gay community here.

DANCE CLUBS

THE CANNERY
Cannery Row, off Eighth Ave. S.
Nashville
615/251-0979

This three-story brick building sits at the edge of the railroad tracks not too far from downtown. It used to be that concertgoers could hear an occasional train whistle and the creaking brakes of freight cars during lulls in the music. Under the current management, however, the Cannery has turned into a venue for young alternative pop and hard-rock bands. During these concerts or their regular weekend dance party for the retro set, the music sometimes emanates for blocks. A magnet for avant-garde music, the Cannery is also a venue for art exhibits and multimedia performances, so check the current listings. Cover charge, age 18 and over. Most events begin at 9 p.m. (Downtown)

THE CHUTE COMPLEX
2535 Franklin Rd.
Nashville
615/297-4571

Not far from downtown in an old strip of office buildings on Eighth Avenue (extended), this undistinguished-looking club has a dance floor, a nice outside patio, and a sports bar. Next door is the Silver Stirrup, a piano bar that serves food. Mixed gay crowd. Open daily. ♿ (South Nashville)

CLUB MERE BULLES
152 Second Ave. N., downstairs
Nashville
615/256-2582

Rock 'n' roll dance bands are highlighted Wednesday through Saturday. This club is located on the First Avenue side (lower level) of the brick warehouse building that houses Mere Bulles restaurant. Featured players reflect the range of Nashville musicians, such as the funk-based Wooten Brothers (up to five brothers perform, including solo bassist Victor and "Future Man," who plays with Bela Fleck). Doors open at 8:30 p.m. and music begins an hour later. (Downtown)

THE CONNECTION OF NASHVILLE
901 Cowan St.
Nashville
615/742-1166

Nashville's largest gay dance club offers several dance floors as well as special events and shows in what was once a boat-themed seafood restaurant just across the river from downtown. Stage shows featuring impersonators are usually on tap here in one room, but there is always continuous dance music for those who need to unwind after a hard day's traveling. Open every day but Mon. Cover charge. ఉ (East Nashville)

LAVA LOUNGE
1719 West End Ave., lower level
Nashville
615/329-3666
The Lava Lounge is as relaxed as the name implies and offers recorded swing, big band, and salsa music accompanied by martinis, cigars, and billiards. Disco with a disk jockey on Fri and Sat night. Live music after 9 on other nights. Cover charge. (Midtown)

176 UNDERGROUND
176 Second Ave. N.
Nashville
615/742-8909
176 Underground is a downstairs dance club right off Second Avenue in a long space as deep as the old brick warehouse block it occupies.

It's open nightly until 3 a.m., with theme-music nights for lovers of alternative music. Revisit industrial, techno, house, and rave on regularly scheduled disk jockey nights. Cover charge. (Downtown)

328 PERFORMANCE HALL
328 Fourth Ave. N.
Nashville
615/259-3288
Go West Productions runs this large music venue. 328 features a dance party with Johnny Jackson's Soul Satisfaction on Friday and Saturday nights at 9. Saturdays are 18-and-over nights. Located several blocks south of downtown, 328 Performance Hall is a no-hassle, professionally run venue. Ample free parking is available on nearby streets. Beer and soft drinks are available, and the staff is friendly. ఉ (Downtown)

JAZZ CLUBS

CAFFE MILANO
176 Third Ave.
Nashville
615/255-0322 (concert line)
615/255-0073 (reservations)
Housed in a beautiful renovation of a

Nashville's Jazz Scene

The Tennessee Jazz and Blues Society, which sponsors events around town, can be reached at 615/386-7500, or you can write them at P.O. Box 121293, Nashville 37212, to get a schedule of events in the area during your visit. WMOT (89.5), a public radio station at Middle Tennessee State University in Murfreesboro, broadcasts area jazz listings several times daily.

historic downtown brick storefront, Caffe Milano has been a very welcome entrant on the Nashville club scene. A stage within sight of all tables, good food, and nationally known jazz performers keep audiences coming back. Ticket prices ranging from $8 to $25 are paid happily by jaded music fans suffering from outdoor festival overload. Sitting down in a quiet space with good acoustics where music takes center stage is one of the true pleasures in life. See Chapter 6: Country-Music Culture. & (Downtown)

F. SCOTT'S RESTAURANT
2100 Crestmoor
Nashville
615/269-5861

This upscale restaurant has a pleasant bar where you can sip champagne, wine by the glass, or a well-made cocktail and enjoy live jazz before or after an evening event. Elegantly decorated, with warm caramel-colored walls and striped black and gray banquettes, this is a cozy spot for a romantic cocktail. They book a nightly ongoing series of easy-listening but serious jazz that is worth going out of your way to enjoy. The live music is piped in to the adjoining restaurant, giving it a subtly exciting supperclub atmosphere. & (West Nashville)

MANHATTAN'S
901 Second Ave. N.
Nashville
615/255-2899

This pleasant supper club is in the basement of Buddy Killen's Stock-Yard Restaurant. Tables on two levels surround a stage in the corner of a fairly large room. In some places the walls reveal a stacked limestone foundation (very characteristic in

this region), which adds to the cozy atmosphere. Live music, often solo vocals backed by a trio, brings in an after-work bar crowd daily 4–7 p.m., with a dinner set starting at 8. Recommended for jazz and cocktails. (Downtown)

MERCHANTS
Broadway at Fourth Ave.
Nashville
615/254-1892

Merchants, a cozy bar amidst honky-tonkin' lower Broadway, presents jazz on weekends. During the temperate months you'll find live music performed in their outside courtyard. Performers vary from good to superb. Located on the lower level of Merchants Restaurant, this club, housed in an old 1892 pharmacy building, is highly recommended for atmosphere alone. If you are lucky, though, you might encounter a Nashville session musician like pianist Matt Rollings, who is really a jazz musician at heart. No cover. & (Downtown)

MERE BULLES RESTAURANT
152 Second Ave. N.
Nashville
615/256-1946

Mere Bulles features nightly piano music during cocktail hour. Jazzy cover bands perform regularly in the large lounge area adjacent to the restaurant. There is also a club featuring rock and dance music on the lower level of Mere Bulles. No cover. & (Downtown)

BLUES CLUBS

BOARDWALK CAFÉ
4114 Nolensville Pike
Nashville
615/832-5104

The Boardwalk is a big, casual barroom that often has major blues acts on the bill on weekends. Weekend shows generally start around 9 p.m. Weekday shows at the Boardwalk feature jazz and blues jam sessions, songwriters' nights, and open-mike nights. The Sunday evening jam sessions start at 8. ♿ (South Nashville)

BOURBON STREET BLUES & BOOGIE BAR
Printer's Alley, between Church and Union Sts.
Nashville
615/242-5837
Bourbon Street features blues bands from around the country. This dark nightclub is open Mon–Fri 4 p.m.–3 a.m., Sat and Sun. 6 p.m.–3 a.m. Full bar, minimal cover charge. ♿ (Downtown)

3RD AND LINDSLEY BAR & GRILL
818 Third Ave. S.
Nashville
615/259-9891
Located just south of downtown in an industrial strip, this bar becomes a lively scene on weekends, when full bands play and dancing breaks out between the tables. There is a blues emphasis, but it's often up-tempo

blues with a nod to boogie-woogie and rock 'n' roll. Cover charge. ♿ (Downtown)

PUBS AND BARS

BLUEBIRD CAFÉ
4104 Hillsboro Rd.
Nashville
615/383-1461
For description, see listing in Chapter 6: Country-Music Culture. (West Nashville)

BOUND'RY
911 20th Ave. S.
Nashville
615/321-3043
This long, curved bar is always packed. Excellent martinis are the specialty, along with a beer list as long as your arm and lots of wines by the glass. Several televisions tuned to sports stations are suspended overhead, but the emphasis among the young power crowd always seems to be on socializing. A small side room near the pizza oven is a good spot for drinks and some of their fabulous tapas; outside seating is available in summer months. ♿ (Midtown)

BROWN'S DINER
2101 Blair Blvd.
Nashville
615/269-5509

Brown's is an old dining car with an addition built on. Saturday and Sunday afternoons find it filled with armchair quarterbacks lining the bar. It is voted as having the best hamburger in Nashville year after year. The bar serves beer only, no liquor or wine. (Midtown)

CAFE ONE TWO THREE
123 12th Ave. S.
Nashville
615/255-2233

A traditional long, wooden, mirrored bar with additional bar tables arranged in the front window area of the restaurant, Cafe One Two Three has bartenders who know how to make the perfect cocktail. Stop in for a drink, early or late, in "the gulch" (old industrial neighborhood) between downtown and West End. & (Downtown)

CHEZ COLLETTE
300 Hermitage Ave.
Nashville
615/256-9134

Chez Collette attracts a mostly female crowd in a bar run by a French woman of the same name. This place has been around for a long while and has a good following. (Downtown)

DOUGLAS CORNER CAFÉ
2106A 8th Ave. S.
Nashville
615/298-1688

Pinball machines, bar food, beer on tap, liquor, and friendly locals make Douglas Corner the closest thing Nashville has to a corner bar. Once you've settled in and watched the musicians set up for an "in the round" songwriter's night, you might even decide to stay for the music. Call ahead; the weekly schedule varies. Closed Sun. & (South Nashville)

GRANITE FALLS
2000 Broadway
Nashville
615/327-9250

A guitarist entertains the crowd at Bluebird Cafe

Meryl Truett

The bar seats around 10, but there is ample table space on the low-walled streetside patio. A nice place for a summer cocktail where the bartenders have traditionally been friendly. ♿ (Midtown)

HERMITAGE HOTEL LOBBY BAR/OAK BAR
231 6th Ave.
Nashville
615/244-3121

Nashville's only remaining historic downtown hotel, the Hermitage makes a lovely spot for a quiet drink either at cocktail hour or after supper. Piano music fills the air around the Lobby Bar at twilight, and light snacks are offered with cocktails. The lower-level Oak Bar, with its wood paneling and British club atmosphere, is a classic. It provides friendly service, a Beaux Arts decor, and is Nashville's quietest bar. ♿ Oak Bar only (Downtown)

McCABE PUB
4410 Murphy Rd.
Nashville
615/269-9406

McCabe's is a neighborhood bar and grill in the Sylvan Park area. Sports enthusiasts can always be found here. Beer on tap and good food make this a rallying point for after-softball summer evenings. ♿ (Midtown)

ROTIER'S
2413 Elliston Pl.
Nashville
615/327-9892

A true tavern, Rotier's, near the Vanderbilt campus, has a small bar area, vinyl booths, and Formica tabletops. Its decor includes neon beer signs in the window and television sets in full view from every seat. Rotier's has a good beer selection and good food. During the school year the place is usually so crowded with diners that it may not be conducive to lingering over a beer. (Midtown)

SAMMY B'S
26 Music Square
Nashville
615/256-6600

Right on Music Row, this popular restaurant has an outdoor courtyard and a nice inside bar. Customers tend to be music industry types. Good people-watching, but not the place for a quiet drink. (Midtown)

SÉANACHIE IRISH PUB
327 Broadway
Nashville
615/726-2006

Séanachie offers Harp and Guinness on tap, Irish food, live Irish music, and a happy hour when pints sell for half price. It's a big, barn-like place, with an overdone, theatrical decor, but the owners are Irish and the chef has his moments and the music and ambiance are just right. The pub now offers Celtic music and local variants

TIP

Club listings are best covered by the *Nashville Scene*, a weekly alternative paper available in racks all over town; and the *Nashville Music Guide*, another free monthly.

every night of the week. What more could you hope for as an escape from too much country music? & (Downtown)

SOUTH STREET
907 20th Ave. S.
Nashville
615/320-5555
Just down the street from Bound'ry and Granite Falls, South Street has a nice curved bar that is usually crowded. It is another good place to meet the locals and overhear friendly conversation. Whiffs from the smoker out back may make you want to stay for dinner. & (Midtown)

THE SUTLER
2608 Franklin Rd.
Nashville
615/297-9195
The Sutler is a friendly neighborhood bar with a regular crowd. The antique wooden bar is well worth a look. Beer, liquor, and good burgers are served, and when local musicians are playing, it becomes a musician's hangout. & (South Nashville)

3RD AND LINDSLEY BAR & GRILL
818 3rd Ave. S.
Nashville
615/259-9891
Located just south of downtown in an industrial strip of buildings, 3rd and Lindsley has a full bar and pretty good food. It is popular for lunch and is a

good place for drinks with live music because the cover charge is usually quite moderate. "Nashville Sunday Night," a radio program broadcast live on WRLT (100.1), comes from Third and Lindsley. Cover charge on Sun is always $5, often for some pretty major acts. & (Downtown)

TIN ANGEL
3201 West End Ave.
Nashville
615/298-3444
A quiet, neighborhood bar that never seems crowded, Tin Angel has a circular fireplace that makes it cozy in fall and winter. & (Midtown)

12TH AND PORTER
114 12th Ave. N.
Nashville
615/254-7236
12th and Porter has a good bar scene, where you'll see types ranging from grunge youth to well-heeled executives. The bar itself is a good place to wait for a show to begin next door at the Playroom, one of Nashville's top listening rooms. The moderately priced restaurant usually fills the bar-area tables, but you can carry your drinks next door if it gets too crowded. & (Downtown)

WOLFY'S
425 Broadway
Nashville
615/251-1621

Wolfy's well-appointed bar offers a spacious club-like atmosphere in decided contrast to the cramped honky tonks on either side. Music features a range of performers, from Brazilian-influenced to traditional country fiddle bands and once-famous country stars. & (Downtown)

WORLD'S END
1713 Church St.
Nashville
615/329-3480
One of Nashville's best bars, the World's End stays open late, serving good drinks and filling food like omelets and burgers to the dance crowd. The World's End has cozy booths and more seats at the bar than anywhere in town. The patrons are both gay and straight, the service is friendly, and the atmosphere is low-key. Dinner daily and Sunday brunch. & (Midtown)

YOUR WAY CAFE:
THE WOMAN'S CHOICE BAR
515 S. 2nd Ave.
Nashville

615/256-9682
Voted best place to get a bite to eat in the local gay paper *Xenogeny*, this friendly spot occupies the former site of Ralph's, a long-time-favorite women's bar. They also feature a variety of performances. Open daily 11 a.m.–3 a.m. (Downtown)

ROCK CLUBS

BAT BAR
207 Broadway
Nashville
615/244-8173
This dive bar has good prices on import beer and an upstairs room that is usually occupied by loud alternative rock bands. For the young crowd. (Downtown)

EXIT/IN
2208 Elliston Pl.
Nashville
615/321-4400
Nashville's original rock 'n' roll club has been through several incarnations since it opened in 1971. This

The Talk of the Town

Joan Tewkesbury, who wrote the screenplay for Robert Altman's Nashville, *talks about how Altman sent the actors out to work in some of the local establishments for several days so that they could not only observe the ambiance of the city, but also bring back real snippets of conversation and pronunciation they had overheard. At the Dusty Road, Tootsie's, and the Turf, you can do your own listening, because these little places have been attracting the same faithful clientele since long before Robert Altman ever set foot in this town.*

club played host to Taj Mahal, Chick Corea, Dire Straits, and many others in its heyday. It's worth a look if you want to check out up-and-coming bands on the alternative music scene and a variety of good local acts. ⅃ (Midtown)

SPRINGWATER
115 27th Ave. N.
Nashville
615/320-0345
You will not see any Music Row types at this divey neighborhood joint next to Centennial Park. Stop in for a beer at the closest thing on 27th Avenue to a lower Broadway honky tonk. ⅃ (Midtown)

DINNER THEATER AND COMEDY CLUBS

CHAFFIN'S BARN
DINNER THEATER
8204 Hwy. 100
Nashville
615/646-9977 (information)
800/282-2276 (reservations)

Chaffin's is an old Nashville tradition, with theater in-the-round on two stages. They vary their play selections widely and often. Chaffin's is the first dinner theater to have undertaken Shakespeare. It was a success, and they will be adding the Bard to their repertory in the future. Tue–Sat dinner at 6, shows at 8; tickets $30–$35. ⅃ (West Nashville)

ZANIES COMEDY SHOWPLACE
2025 8th Ave. S.
Nashville
615/269-0221
Zanies features the best national comedy acts in a very well-run club. Jay Leno performed here long before he hit the big time. Shows are nightly, Tue–Sun at 8:30. Wed is smoke-free and so is the early show on Fri nights. Fri and Sat shows are at 8 and 10:15; cover $5–$10. ⅃ (South Nashville)

MOVIE HOUSES OF NOTE

With the arrival of Regal Cinema's Hollywood 27, the movie malling of

Live music at Exit/In, p. 205

Exit/In

Nashville is complete. A number of more modest multiplex theaters, with up to eight screens, have heretofore been located only at the city perimeters. Soon to invade the sacrosanct Green Hills Mall area of West Nashville will be another Regal multiplex complex.

FRANKLIN CINEMA
419 Main St.
Franklin
615/790-7122

The Franklin Cinema is located on Main Street in Franklin's historic district. Its management has shown real class in the past few years by showing some first-run films with occasional nods to the masterpieces of film history. They also hold a weekly Friday and Saturday *Rocky Horror Picture Show* midnight vigil. You can quaff a beer and order a sandwich to take into the movie with you. Parking is nearby, and window-shopping the varied neighborhood storefronts before or after a film will make your evening complete. ♿ (South Nashville)

SARRATT CINEMA
Sarratt Student Ctr.
24th Ave. S. at Vanderbilt Pl.,
Vanderbilt University
Nashville
615/322-2471

The Vanderbilt University Student Center theater is open to the public year-round, presenting a well-orchestrated schedule of new and old films during the academic year. A special summer schedule features afternoon screenings. Film tickets cost $3–$4, and the popcorn is fresh. Parking can be very difficult on the Vanderbilt campus, so be prepared to walk several blocks and arrive early on nights coinciding with basketball games. The student center lobby also houses the excellent Sarratt Gallery, where early theater arrivals can spend the time viewing exhibits of contemporary art. Sarratt Student Center is a Ticketmaster outlet and can provide information about campus cultural events (concerts, dance, theater) that are open to the public. ♿ (Midtown)

SINKING CREEK FILM CELEBRATION, INC./NASHVILLE INDEPENDENT FILM FESTIVAL
Film House, Metro Center
P.O. Box 24330
Nashville 37202
615/742-2500

The Sinking Creek Film Celebration, which has changed the name of its annual event to the Nashville Independent Film Festival, is a 30-year-old festival named after a creek flowing through the East Tennessee farm of its founding director, Mary Jane Coleman. The festival is held for a week in June each year, attracting film and video entrants in both professional and student categories and awarding over $5,000 in prizes. Several well-known commercial filmmakers, as well as successful animators and award-winning documentarians, have gotten their start in independent film here.

The excitement of a festival like Sinking Creek/NIFF lies in seeing those works in original concept and meeting the artists before they become famous. The Sinking Creek Film Celebration also sponsors film premieres throughout the year and a Media Institute (offers week-long workshops in animation, screenwriting, etc.) in mid-June. Call to see if there are any events being held during your stay in Nashville or look up the schedule of events on the Web at *www.nashvillefilmfestival.org* or in the *Nashville Scene.* (North Nashville)

WATKINS-BELCOURT THEATER
2101 Belcourt Ave.,
in Hillsboro Village
Nashville
615/383-9140
The Belcourt has been Nashville's faithful art cinema through the years. With its recent purchase by Watkins Film School, the sagging seats have been replaced, the sound system improved, and the film schedule expanded to include more indie films. There are only two theaters and the movies generally run for just one week, but the popcorn is freshly popped, the staff is friendly, and the films are first-run and first-rate. It's worth going out of your way for if you long for the good old days of moviegoing. (Midtown)

Mary Entrekin

14

These one-day trips away from the city, radiating in every direction, offer opportunities to visit the wide variety of historic sites scattered around the Middle Tennessee area, to experience particular aspects of the cultural life of Middle Tennessee, or to make a foray into nature, often with the option of an overnight stay.

Day Trip: Appalachian Center for Crafts

Distance from Nashville: 65 miles, 1½-hour drive
A visit to the **Joe L. Evins Appalachian Center for Crafts**, 931/597-6801, Tennessee's only state-run craft school, located among low rolling hills surrounding Center Hill Lake, makes a perfect day out of the city. The **Appalachian Center**, which is affiliated with Tennessee Technological University in nearby Cookeville, offers a year-round schedule of classes in craft media: glass, metal, wood, ceramic and fibers, as well as innovative workshops with nationally known craft artists. It can be reached by several scenic routes that meander through small towns with central squares, railroad tracks, and running trains. The countryside around the center is pastoral, and **Center Hill Lake**, created by a TVA dam on the Caney Fork River, is ringed by the wooded forest of **Edgar Evins State Park**. The road to the center climbs for several miles before opening onto a hilltop campus containing rustic modern studio buildings, small cabins for artists-in-residence, and a large central office building with galleries, a craft store, and a dining room.

This rural setting, surrounded by hills, woods, and a large lake, inspires

NASHVILLE REGION

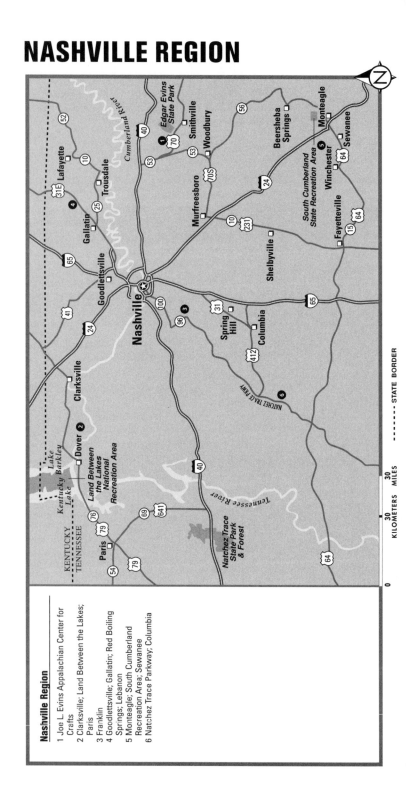

Nashville Region

1 Joe L. Evins Appalachian Center for Crafts
2 Clarksville; Land Between the Lakes; Paris
3 Franklin
4 Goodlettsville; Gallatin; Red Boiling Springs; Lebanon
5 Monteagle; South Cumberland Recreation Area; Sewanee
6 Natchez Trace Parkway; Columbia

many of the contemporary artists at the center to create works made from the materials of nature. The Craft Center's gallery consists of a large, cathedral-vaulted space with windows overlooking the wooded landscape, a small and intimate interior display area, and a large craft shop selling the work not only of center faculty and students, but of many other Tennessee craft artists. The public can visit daily from 9 to 5; a cafeteria-style lunch is available at moderate prices every day at Isabel's Pantry. Visitors can also walk around and peek in the studios to view the fibers, metals, wood, glass, and other materials used by the artists.

Nearby is the **Evins Mill Retreat**, 931/597-2088, a 14-room lodge and restaurant with a working gristmill. Evins Mill was built in 1939 by Edgar and Joe Evins, father and son Tennessee politicians for whom the nearby state park and the craft center were named. Call to see if they have any available rooms on the weekend. Evins Mills serves as a popular informal conference center for business clients during the week.

Smithville, six miles away from the center, is home to the **Old Time Fiddler's Jamboree**, 931/597-4163, held every year on the first weekend of July. This is the real thing, with Tennessee farmers in overalls standing alongside music journalists and apprentice musicians to hear live music on every corner of the town square.

Halfway back to Nashville on Highway 70 is tiny Watertown, where antique and junk shops line the railroad tracks. The **Depot** restaurant serves lunch and dinner, and there's a new bed-and-breakfast, the **Watertown Bed & Breakfast**, 931/237-9999, located in the historic Railroad Hotel. The **Broadway Dinner Train** runs here from Nashville several times a year.

Heading back toward Nashville along a southern route, Highway 53, the **Arts Center of Cannon County at Woodbury**, 800/235-9073 or 931/563-2787, is the place to get information on visiting the white-oak basket makers in the vicinity. The basket makers and chair makers in the area welcome drop-in visitors, especially during summer and fall, and there are lots of behind-the-house-type antique stores in this area. The annual **White Oak Country Craft Festival**, held the second week of August, is well worth the trip.

On the way from Woodbury to Murfreesboro on Highway 70 south is a sign pointing to **Readyville**. Just a mile or so off of the highway, Readyville is home to an operating gristmill. Stone-ground meal and flour from the mill are for sale.

Murfreesboro is a thriving small town with a historic past and beautiful homes lining its main street. Once the state capital, Murfreesboro still has a bustling courthouse square, but the major attractions here are a huge state university, a big outlet mall, and the **Uncle Dave Macon Days** celebration held in mid-July every year. This celebration is a three-day festival of banjo music, buck dancing, and clogging. For more information, call the Murfreesboro Chamber of Commerce, 615/893-6565. Murfreesboro is also the site of **Cannonsburgh Pioneer Village**, 615/893-6565, a reconstruction of a town from the early 1800s that has a log house, blacksmith shop, gristmill, and general store. The **Stones River Civil War Battlefield**, 615/893-9501, where 23,000 lives were lost in the worst battle of the western theater, and Fortress Rosecrans, a 200-acre Union supply depot, are linked by the Stones River Greenway, a three-mile walking and cycling trail. Some may be surprised to learn that the **International Grand Walking Horse Show**, 615/890-9120, is held here in early August. This event leads up to the better-known national celebration in Shelbyville, which is 23 miles south on Highway 231. A good place to stop for a bite to eat on the way to or from the Craft Center is **City Café**, a block off the courthouse square, featuring home-cooked "meat and three" meals that are hard to beat.

Getting There from Nashville: The most direct route would be to drive about 50 miles east on I-40, exit at Smithville/McMinnville (there is a sign for the craft center), and go south 15 miles on Highway 56. An alternate route, which goes through several small towns on the old highway (70) paralleling the interstate, would be to take the Watertown exit (about 30 miles from Nashville on I-40 East) to Highway 70 and drive east to Smithville. The center is located about six miles north of Smithville on Highway 56. Murfreesboro, exactly 30 miles southeast of Nashville, just off I-24 East, provides another gateway to the area, either coming or going. From Murfreesboro take 70 south to Woodbury, then Highway 53 north to Liberty, 70 east to Smithville, and Highway 56 north to the center.

Day Trip: Clarksville; Land Between the Lakes; Paris

Distance from Nashville: 45 miles, one-hour drive to Clarksville; 75 miles, 1½ to two-hour drive to Land Between the Lakes; 100 miles, 2½-hour drive to Paris

Although it would be possible to cover this scenic territory in a day without the addition of the excursion to Paris, this itinerary makes a good two-day ramble with an overnight stay at Land Between the Lakes (where the Cumberland and Tennessee Rivers meet). The route follows the Cumberland River out of Nashville to Clarksville, one of Tennessee's oldest towns, located at the juncture of the Cumberland and Red Rivers. The rich farmland along the way was once planted primarily in burley tobacco. At the turn of the century, Clarksville was home to the country's second largest tobacco market.

Heading up I-24 to Clarksville (45 miles from Nashville), take the Adams exit (Highway 256) to the **Port Royal** state historic area and walk across one of the few remaining covered bridges in Tennessee. Adams is the home of the "Bell Witch" legend, a story that kids will love about the ghost who plagued John Bell in the 1820s and 1830s. The **"Bell Witch" Flea Market** and **Opry** is a good place to find a copy of the tale. This antique/junk mall is open daily and is located in an old school. (The Opry designation refers to a local bluegrass music show held there on Saturday nights.)

From Adams, there are several ways to get to Clarksville, including a route through tiny Guthrie, Kentucky, where there are several antique shops as well as the boyhood home of writer **Robert Penn Warren** (*All the King's Men*), which is open to visitors. Aside from a number of lovely old houses, little remains to suggest Clarksville's former economic prominence except an eccentric Victorian post office (now the **Clarksville-Montgomery County Museum**, located at 200 Second Street, 931/648-5780, closed Monday) and relics of historic architecture such as one or two downtown brick storefront blocks and several "loose-floor" tobacco warehouses, where tobacco auctions still take place in late autumn. Lunch, dinner, or even an overnight at the well-known **Hachland Hill Inn**, 931/647-4084, will be worth remembering (reservations required). The **Dunbar Cave State Natural Area** at Clarksville is now just a nice place to take a hike, but in the '30s and '40s "the cave" was a private resort where Clarksville society came to play cards and sip iced tea in the rooms at the naturally cool mouth of the cave by day and dance to the sounds of Roy Acuff's Orchestra by night.

And, speaking of fiddling, Clarksville hosts the annual **Tennessee Old Time Fiddler's Championship** in late March. It's held on the campus of **Austin Peay State University**. Call the Clarksville Tourist Information Center, 931/648-0001, for details and a map of the city. Leaving Clarksville on Highway 79 takes one to Dover (31 miles), the site of **Fort Donelson**, a Confederate stronghold on the Cumberland River that was lost to Ulysses S. Grant in February 1862, opening the way for Union occupation of Clarksville, Nashville, and most of Middle Tennessee. A self-guided driving tour is available at the visitor's center and museum, which is open daily with free admission.

Crossing the Cumberland River at Dover signals entrance into the **Land Between the Lakes**, a 170,000-acre national recreation area with extensive wildlife observation areas and miles of little-traveled shoreline on the Barkley and Kentucky Lakes of the Cumberland and Tennessee Rivers. The vast open spaces are a nice contrast to the verdant hills of Middle Tennessee and make one feel a million miles away. LBL offers a variety of camping facilities, a mid-nineteenth-century working demonstration farm, a nature center, and a planetarium. As was once true in this part of the country, American bison roam the fields here, and efforts are also being made to restore the elk and the red wolf to their native habitat. This is one of the area's major boating and fishing areas, and restricted hunting is allowed with the requisite permits and licenses. There are no commercial lodgings within LBL, but **Tennessee's Paris Landing State Park** and **Kentucky's Kenlake, Kentucky Dam Village**, and **Lake Barkley State Parks** surround the area. Privately owned marinas with cabins and campgrounds can be found at every entrance route to the area.

For more information about LBL, which is operated by the Tennessee Valley Authority, write to: TVA LBL, Golden Pond, Kentucky 42211; or call 502/924-5602 or 502/924-1243. For information and reservations at Tennessee state parks, call 800/421-6683; for Kentucky state parks call 800/255-7275.

Thirty miles further on Highway 79 is Paris, Tennessee, whose claim to fame is **"The World's Biggest Fish Fry,"** held annually over five days in April. Paris is officially in West Tennessee (the Tennessee River, which one crosses when leaving LBL, forms the dividing line), and the fish in question are catfish. The large three-dimensional jumping catfish suspended over Paris is a once-in-a-lifetime photo opportunity. For information about food, lodging, and the WBFF, contact the Paris Chamber of Commerce at 901/642-3431.

Getting There from Nashville: Take I-24 north to Clarksville (45 miles), exit at Highway 256 north to Port Royal/Adams (10 miles). An alternate route into Clarksville is to travel west on Highway 41 to Guthrie, then south on Highway 79 to Clarksville. Leaving Clarksville: Continue south on Highway 79 to Dover (31 miles), Land Between the Lakes, and Paris. Leaving Paris: Take Highway 641 south to Highway 70 (22 miles). Cross the Tennessee River at New Johnsonville and pass through the towns of Dickson and Kingston Springs on the way into town (83 miles on Highway 70). Alternately, stay on 641 all the way to I-40 (36 miles) and head east back to Nashville (83 miles on I-40).

Day Trip: Franklin

Distance from Nashville: 18 miles, 40-minute drive
Just a short drive from Nashville, commuting distance for many, is historic **Franklin**, a charming town that has made historic preservation its byword. Restored Victorian homes line neighborhood streets adjacent to the downtown square. The entire 15-block area is listed on the National Register of Historic Places. Stop in at the **Heritage Foundation Visitor Information Center**, 209 East Main, open Monday through Friday from nine to four. Franklin also holds a highly acclaimed **Main Street Festival** on the last weekend in April and a lively **Jazz Festival** the first weekend of August. Both provide ample opportunity for the city to show off its talented craft artists, musicians, and chefs. For information on both festivals, which are held free of charge, call the Downtown Franklin Association at 615/790-7094.

There are two important historic homes in Franklin that figured prominently in the November 30, 1864, Battle of Franklin. Civil War history will come to life with visits to the 1830 **Carter House**, which stood in the center of the battlefield, and the 1826 **Carnton Plantation**, which was situated at the edge of the battlefield. Its main house served as a hospital, and its fields were converted into a 1,500-grave cemetery following the battle. (See Chapter 5: Sights and Attractions.)

Franklin is home to fashionable clothing stores, fine craft shops, good restaurants, and at least 17 antique stores (a printed list is available at stores and restaurants around town). There are choice bed-and-breakfast accommodations out in the country nearby. (See Chapter 3: Where to Stay.)

Getting There from Nashville: All roads leading south of town seem to head toward Franklin, so choose one for the departure and another for the return. Granny White Pike (12th Avenue), Hillsboro Road (21st Avenue), Franklin Road (Eighth Avenue), and I-65 south all converge at or near Franklin, which is located about 18 miles south of downtown. In fact, Hillsboro Road and Franklin Pike become two of the town's main streets. Driving through the countryside is preferable, since the roads are lined with horse farms, vegetable stands, nurseries, and a few beautiful old homes. If possible, avoid driving on either I-65 or any of the "inland" routes during rush hour in the commuting direction (to Nashville in the morning, from Nashville in the evening) as this side of town is the fastest growing in the area.

Day Trip: Goodlettsville; Gallatin; Red Boiling Springs; Lebanon

Distance from Nashville: 15 miles, 20-minute drive to Goodlettsville; 30 miles, 40-minute drive to Gallatin; 70 miles, 1½ -hour drive to Red Boiling Springs; 30 miles to Lebanon; 30 minutes to Nashville

This two-day tour winds through some of the prettiest countryside in the whole state. The trip starts by visiting some of the oldest settlements in the area, homesteads and stagecoach stops staked out along the Cumberland River, as it winds its way west through what is now Sumner County. Some of the homes in this area were built on land grants to Revolutionary War soldiers, and a driving tour to these substantial houses in very isolated locations gives a good sense of what it must have been like back then. After a day-long historic homes tour, staying overnight at a once-fashionable mineral spa will be welcome. An easy return passes through Lebanon, which is vying with Franklin to become Middle Tennessee's capital city of antique shops.

Goodlettsville, located about 15 miles northeast of Nashville, claims the area's oldest habitat at **Mansker's Station**, which is located in what is now **Moss-Wright Park**. The park is situated alongside the **Bowen-Campbell House**, which was built around 1787 and was the earliest brick construction in the region and the oldest residence in Middle Tennessee. Mansker's Station, dating to 1779 and a reconstruction of the original fortified settlement, was the first lasting refuge built by long hunters Henry Scaggs, Isaac Blesdoe, and Kaspar Mansker. These men had probably camped at Bledsoe's Lick (now Castalian Springs) with its founder, Thomas Sharpe Spencer, the year before.

At Hendersonville, about five miles east, visit **Rock Castle**, ca. 1790, the home of Daniel Smith, one of the first surveyors in the territory and author of the first map of the area west of the Cumberland Mountains. In Hendersonville, the **Center Point Pit Barbeque**, where you can order "Three Little Pigs" (three small minced-pork sandwiches) is located on Gallatin Pike (Highway 31 East) and makes a nice place to stop for lunch. Also on the way to Gallatin are places worth filing away for later: the **Sumner County Drive-In**, which must be one of the only operating outdoor theaters that shows first-run films, and the **Hancock House**, a bed-and-breakfast in a handsome log building that was once a stagecoach stop (see Chapter 3: Where to Stay).

Gallatin is a pretty town with a nice courthouse square that is home to the **Trousdale Place** (ca. 1813). Its owner, William Trousdale, became the 15th governor of Tennessee in 1849, and the house was continuously occupied by his descendants until fairly recently. Behind this well-preserved historic house is the **Sumner County Museum**, a repository of early artifacts from the region, including some stone tools thought to belong to Archaic Indian mastodon hunters.

East of Gallatin on Highway 25 is **Castalian Springs**, a mineral springs first called Bledsoe's Lick when it was found by the long hunters in 1772. Interesting in its own right as one of the earliest settlements in Middle Tennessee, it is also the site of **Wynnewood**, a long log structure built in 1828 as a stagecoach inn and later used as lodging for visitors to the mineral springs. Open year-round Monday through Saturday from 10 to 4, Sunday one to five; during the winter months, November through March, it's closed on Sunday. $3 adults, $2.50 seniors, $1.50 students, 50¢ for children, 615/452-5463. Close to Castalian Springs and almost directly across from Wynnewood is what appears to be the temple mound of an Indian village dating from the Mississippian period; and the Bledsoe Fort Historical Park, which marks the **Avery Trace**, one of the earliest Tennessee settlers' routes down from Cumberland Gap. A few miles down the road is **Cragfont**, a starkly impressive limestone house dating from 1802, which was the home of James Winchester, a Revolutionary War hero. Cragfont is open to the public as a museum for a small admission price, Tuesday through Sunday April 15 through November 1, 615/452-7070.

Drive east another 33 miles, taking Highway 25 then Highway 10, then take Highway 52 to **Red Boiling Springs**, once a popular mineral springs

Beautiful backcountry roads of Tennessee

National Park Service

resort that had as many as 25 hotels and boarding houses. There are still several pumps (sulphur water) around the town and a few operating hotels along Main Street. The **Donoho**, with a two-story wraparound porch, is the only one that's been in continuous operation. Its 32 clean and simple rooms open directly onto the porch, and the dining room serves delicious family-style food, 615/699-3141. **The Thomas House**, with 30 rooms, has a non–mineral water swimming pool, 615/699-3006. **Armour's Red Boiling Springs Hotel**, built in 1924, has 20 rooms, mineral baths, and meals by advance reservation, 615/699-2180. Red Boiling Springs puts on an annual **Folk Medicine Festival** in late July that features folk heritage demonstrations, medicine lore, and music, and there is a popular antique car show held every year on the first weekend after Labor Day. For information call the Sulphur City Association at Armour's Red Boiling Springs Hotel.

Leaving Red Boiling Springs on Highway 52 and turning south on Highway 141 is the most direct route to **Lebanon**, but one can head southwest toward Lebanon by driving south out of Red Boiling Springs on Highway 56 through Pleasant Shade, through Vice President Al Gore's hometown of **Carthage**, taking Highway 70N west into Lebanon. Lebanon, a former railroad town, has a central square ringed by antique shops. Friday nights in Lebanon often feature antique auctions, which are not only great entertainment but can also yield incredible unexpected bargains. Lebanon antique auctions are listed in the classified section of the Nashville *Tennessean* at least a week prior to the date. The James E. Ward Agricultural Center, which holds the annual Alliance for Native American Indian Rights Pow Wow every year in late September, features a reproduction Indian village named TANSAI, through which visitors can take a self-guided tour May through August. For information about the Pow Wow call 615/444-4899; Ward Center can be reached at 615/443-2626. Lebanon is home to the Cracker Barrel chain of restaurants. Bar-B-Cutie, on Highway 231 heading out to I-40 on the way back to Nashville, is rated best Q around in this writer's informal taste tests against most of the Nashville barbeque joints, and is another good choice for lunch.

Getting There from Nashville: Taking I-65 north is the fastest way to get to the Goodlettsville/Hendersonville area. Exit at Two Mile parkway toward Goodlettsville and follow the signs to Moss-Wright Park to find Mansker's Station and the Bowen-Campbell House. Then follow Gallatin Pike (Highway 31 East) to Hendersonville and on into Gallatin. From Gallatin, take Highway 25 east to Castalian Springs, then Highway 10 north to Lafayette, and Highway 52 east into Red Boiling Springs.

Day Trip: Monteagle; South Cumberland Recreation Area; Sewanee

Distance from Nashville: 85 miles, 1½-hour drive to Monteagle; 110–120 miles, 2½-hour drive to Stone Door or Savage Gulf Park entrances
People all over the South used to pack up their families and head for the

hills when temperatures rose every summer. Tennesseans drove south-east toward the Cumberland Mountains and stayed in summer homes, hotels, and cabins in the heights of Monteagle, Beersheba Springs, and Sewanee. Families today still do.

Monteagle, one of the only Chatauquas in the South, has a resident summertime population comprised primarily of Nashvillians. Featured speakers and special programs are still presented on many evenings for the resident guests. Up on the mountain it's at least 10 to 15 degrees cooler on most days, and the dense woods and waterfalls of the **South Cumberland Recreation Area** surrounding Monteagle help keep it that way. The spectacularly beautiful South Cumberland natural area is quite large, spanning over 12,000 acres in seven separate areas in a 100-square-mile region. It includes: **Savage Gulf**, a canyon-like gorge; the **Stone Door**, a tall, narrow passage down into the gorge; **Greeter Falls**; the 60-foot-high **Foster Falls**; **Grundy Forest State Natural Area**; and the **Sewanee Natural Bridge**. The entrance to the Stone Door is located at **Beersheba Springs**, a Methodist retreat center and another popular old summer community where most family cabins are occupied all summer and on many spring, fall, and winter weekends. Unfortunately, there are no public accommodations at Beersheba. Primitive camping is allowed in several locations of the South Cumberland Recreation Area. The **South Cumberland State Park Visitor Center** is located on Highway 56, between Monteagle and Tracy City, 931/924-2980. Not officially part of the South Cumberland Recreation area but located very nearby is **Franklin Forest**, a favorite retreat for mountain bikers, which has a lake where primitive camping is allowed.

A several-day visit to this area could include a stay at the luxurious 100-year-old **Adams-Edgeworth Inn**, 931/924-4000, on the Monteagle assembly grounds; or at the nearby, highly recommended **North Gate Inn B&B**, 931/924-2799. The annual **Monteagle Crafts Festival**, a small show featuring a great selection of local wares, is held at Monteagle Elementary School on the first weekend in August.

The neighboring town of Sewanee is home to the **University of the South**, a well-known private undergraduate university and Episcopal seminary. Sewanee, as the school is known, hosts the excellent **Sewanee Summer Music Festival** in late July, part of an annual instrumental music teaching seminar. Many Nashvillians drive to Sewanee for the performances, which are held throughout the day and evening on the final weekend of the seminar, and for other outstanding music events held throughout the year. Tickets to the festival are under $10 for adults, and performances are held at Guerry Hall, 931/598-1225. **Pearl's Foggy Mountain Café**, 15344 Sewanee Highway, is an elegant one-story cedar building in a woodland glade that serves scrumptious New American cuisine, including trout and salmon smoked on the premises. Open for dinner only, closed on Monday, bring your own wine, 931/598-9568.

Getting There from Nashville: I-24 south towards Chattanooga is the most direct route to Monteagle (approximately 85 miles) from Nashville.

Both Highway 50 and Highway 56 north/east from Monteagle lead to Beer-sheba Springs, the Stone Door, and Savage Gulf State Natural Area. Se-wanee is located about eight miles south of the Monteagle exit from I-24 on Highway 64.

Day Trip: Natchez Trace Parkway; Columbia

Distance from Nashville: 15 miles, 25-minute drive to Natchez Trace Park-way; 60 miles, one-hour drive to Columbia
As preparation for a day out in beautiful natural surroundings, make reser-vations the day before, then rise early and head out to the **Loveless Motel and Café**, 8400 Highway 100, 615/646-9700, for a hearty breakfast of eggs, biscuits, and country ham. After breakfast, embark on a trip down the Natchez Trace Parkway. By car, bicycle, motorcycle, or on horseback, this trip, on an uncrowded, smoothly paved road through miles of billboardless landscape is a visual delight. The northern entrance to the Trace, mapped as an Indian trail by the French as early as 1733, and a well-traveled route into what was considered the "southwest wilderness" by the turn of the nineteenth century, is at Highway 100 and Highway 96, just a few miles be-yond the Loveless Motel. An amazing new highway bridge of white con-crete, which is really quite beautiful, spans the valley and lifts the road off and on its way. The Trace can also be entered at **Leiper's Fork**, a pretty community 25 miles or so from downtown Nashville that contains several bed-and-breakfasts (see Chapter 3: Where to Stay).

The Natchez Trace is a national parkway whose construction began in the 1930s. It runs from Natchez, Mississippi, to Nashville, with frequent mile markers at hiking, camping, and horseback riding trailheads, picnic spots, and historic sites. About 40 miles down the Trace is the **Meriwether Lewis National Monument**, where one of America's best-known early ex-plorers is buried. Lewis died of gun shot wounds in 1809 while staying at Grinder's Inn, formerly at this location on the Trace. There are campsites, picnic areas, and hiking trails here as well as a pioneer cemetery and a small exhibit about Lewis.

It might be fitting to exit the Trace at this point and embark on one's own adventure, driving 15 or 20 miles west to one of several canoe outfitters on the Buffalo River. (See Chapter 11: Sports and Recreation for listings.)

An exit east of the Trace leads through **Mount Pleasant**, once the center of a thriving phosphate mining operation, and home to a quirky small museum on the public square (closed Wednesday and Sunday), and on to **Columbia** (25 miles), a center of antebellum wealth where one can visit some of the most impressive plantation houses in Tennessee. The Maury County Visitor's Bureau, which also serves the town of **Spring Hill** (home to GM's Saturn plant), offers a self-guided driving tour of Ten-nessee's "Antebellum Trail." Route maps giving directions to homes with names such as Rattle and Snap, the Athenaeum, and Rippavilla can be

White-tail fawns at Land Between the Lakes, p. 213

obtained at the visitor's bureau on the public square in Columbia. In late September the **Majestic Middle Tennessee Fall Tour** opens additional homes and historic churches for viewing (for more information call 931/381-4822 and get directions to the Athenaeum, where you can also stop in for tea). The home of James K. Polk, Tennessee congressman, governor, and 11th president of the United States (1845–1849), is located in downtown Columbia on West Seventh Street and is open to the public for a small admission fee.

Columbia is perhaps best known in the region for its annual **"Mule Day"** celebration, honoring the working man's beast that once populated the cotton plantations and tobacco farms of Tennessee. Held in early April, this is Columbia's heritage festival, complete with a parade, a mule-pull, and a knife show. Call the Mule Day office at 931/381-9557 for information.

Getting There from Nashville: Highway 100 (Broadway–West End–Harding Road, extended) leads to the Natchez Trace terminus at Highway 96, 12 miles from Leiper's Fork. Meriwether Lewis National Monument is located at mile marker 385.9 (about 38 miles south of the Trace's northernmost entrance). Exit the Trace east on Highway 412 to Mount Pleasant and Columbia (25 miles) and return to Nashville via Highway 31 north to Spring Hill or by continuing on 412 to I-65 north (about 45 miles).

EMERGENCY PHONE NUMBERS

Police, Fire, Ambulance
911

Nonemergency Police Assistance
615-862-8600

Poison Control
615/936-2034

Suicide Prevention/Crisis Intervention
615/244-7444

Tennessee Highway Patrol (Emergency)
615/741-2060

HOSPITALS AND EMERGENCY MEDICAL CENTERS

Baptist Hospital
2000 Church St.
615/329-5114
Emergency, 615/329-5555

Centennial (Columbia Health System Hospital)
2300 Patterson St.
615/342-1000
Emergency, 615/342-1500

Hendersonville (Columbia Health System Hospital)
355 New Shackle Island Rd.
615/264-4000
Emergency, 615/264-4144

Nashville Memorial (Columbia Health System Hospital)
612 Due West Ave.
615/865-3511

Emergency, 615/865-3485

Southern Hills (Columbia Health System Hospital)
391 Wallace Rd.
615/781-4000
Emergency, 615/781-4600

Summit (Columbia Health System Hospital)
5655 Frist Blvd.
615/316-3000
Emergency, 615/316-3600

Metropolitan General Hospital
72 Hermitage Ave.
615/862-4000

St. Thomas Hospital
4220 Harding Rd.
615/222-2111
Emergency, 615/222-6733

Vanderbilt University Medical Center
1211 22nd Ave. S.
615/322-5000
Emergency, 615/322-3391

RECORDED INFORMATION

Time and Temperature
615/259-2222 or 615/737-1111

Weather
615/244-9393

Tennessee Highway Patrol
615-741-2060
(Road Conditions Hotline)
800/858-6349 or 800/342-3258

POST OFFICES

Main branch
525 Royal Parkway, Donelson
615/885-1005
Downtown
901 Broadway
615/255-9447 or
The Arcade
615/255-3579

VISITOR INFORMATION

Nashville Convention and Visitors
Bureau
161 4th Ave. N.
615/259-4700 or
Corner 5th and Broadway
615/259-4747

Tennessee Department of Tourist
Development
P.O. Box 23170
615/741-2158 or 2159

CITY TOURS

(For walking tours, see Chapter 5:
Sights and Attractions)

COMMERCIAL
TOUR COMPANIES

Country & Western/Gray Line Tours
615/883-5555

Grand Ole Opry Tours
615/889-9490

Johnny Walker Tours
615/834-8585

Orion Charters & Tours
615/244-0234

CAR RENTAL

Alamo
800/327-9633
Airport, 615/275-1050

Avis
800-831-2847
Airport, 615/361-1212

Budget
800/527-0700
Airport, 615/366-0800

Dollar
800/366-5000
Airport, 615/275-1005

Enterprise
800/325-8007
Airport, 615/872-7722 or Downtown,
615/254-6181

Hertz
800/654-3131
Airport, 615/361-3131

National
800/227-7368
Airport, 615/361-7467

Thrifty
800/367-2277
Briley Parkway Area, 615/361-6050

DISABLED ACCESS

Disability Information Office
25 Middleton St.
615/862-6492

COMMUNITY
ORGANIZATIONS

African American Cultural Alliance
615/227-7258 or 615/299-0412

Gay and Lesbian Switchboard
615/297-0008

The National Conference for
Community and Justice (NCCJ)
615/327-1755

CHILDCARE

Duck Duck Goose Drop In Child
Care
615/352-4343

Duck Duck, Too
615/377-1122

Kids & Company Drop in Child Care
615/269-6114

Kids Stop
615/591-0865

NEWSPAPERS

In Review (free, bimonthly,
    alternative business and
    entertainment)
Metropolitan Times (free, weekly,
    African American)
Nashville Business Journal (weekly)
Nashville Music Guide (free,
    monthly, club listings and live-
    music promotion)
Nashville Parent (free, monthly)
Nashville Pride (weekly, African
    American)
Nashville Scene (free, weekly,
    alternative)
Nashville Woman (free, monthly)
The Tennessean (morning, Sunday)
Tennessee Tribune (monthly, African
    American)

ON-LINE

CitySearch
www.nashville.citysearch.com
(magazine, guide, and Web sites for
Nashville arts, entertainment, news,
events, restaurants, hotels, shopping, and Ticketmaster outlet)

RADIO

WKDF 103.3, Album Rock
WLAC 105.9, Adult Rock
WMOT 89.5, Public, Murfreesboro
WPLN 90.3, Public, Nashville
WQQK 92.1, Urban
WRLT 100.1, Alternative/Rock
WSIX 97.9, Country
WSM 650 AM & 95.5 FM, Country

TELEVISION STATIONS

WDCN-8, Public
WNAB-58, WB
WKRN-2, ABC
WSMV-4, NBC
WTVF-5, CBS
WZTV-17, Fox

BOOKSTORES

Barnes & Noble
1701 Mallory Lane, Brentwood
615/377-9979
Books-a-Million
1789 Gallatin Pike, 615/860-3133
Bookstar
4301 Harding Rd., 615/297-2994
Bookworld
Harding Mall, 615/834-1862
Brentano's
Bellvue Ctr., 7620 US 70 S.
615/662-1913
Davis-Kidd
4007 Hillsboro Pl., 615/833-9192

Doubleday Book Shop
7620 Hwy. 70 S., 615/646-7195
Media Play
100 Oaks Mall, 615/383-5114
5435 Bell Forge Ln. E., Antioch,
915/731-4345
2101 Gallatin Park N., Madison,
615/851-1586
Tower Books
2404 West End Ave., 615/327-8085
Waldenbooks
217 Church St. Ctr., 615/244-9320
Rivergate Mall, 1000 Two Mile Pkwy.,
Goodlettsville, 615/859-3387
Hickory Hollow Mall, 5252 Hickory
Hollow Pkwy., 615/731-2159
Stadium Square, 386 W. Main St.,
Hendersonville, 615/824-9044
Winston-Derek Booksellers
101 French Landing, 615/321-0535

INDEX

You'll Feel like a Local When You Travel with Guides from John Muir Publications

CiTY·SMaRT™ GUIDEBOOKS

Pick one for your favorite city: *Albuquerque, Anchorage, Austin, Calgary, Charlotte, Chicago, Cincinnati, Cleveland, Denver, Indianapolis, Kansas City, Memphis, Milwaukee, Minneapolis/St. Paul, Nashville, Pittsburgh, Portland, Richmond, Salt Lake City, San Antonio, St. Louis, Tampa/St. Petersburg, Tucson*

Guides for kids 6 to 10 years old about what to do, where to go, and how to have fun in: *Atlanta, Austin, Boston, Chicago, Cleveland, Denver, Indianapolis, Kansas City, Miami, Milwaukee, Minneapolis/St. Paul, Nashville, Portland, San Francisco, Seattle, Washington D.C.*

TRAVEL✦SMART®

Trip planners with select recommendations to: *Alaska, American Southwest, Carolinas, Colorado, Deep South, Eastern Canada, Florida Gulf Coast, Hawaii, Illinois/Indiana, Kentucky/Tennessee, Maryland/Delaware, Michigan, Minnesota/Wisconsin, Montana/Wyoming/Idaho, New England, New Mexico, New York State, Northern California, Ohio, Pacific Northwest, Pennsylvania/New Jersey, South Florida and the Keys, Southern California, Texas, Utah, Virginias, Western Canada*

Rick Steves' GUIDES

See *Europe Through the Back Door* and take along guides to: *France, Belgium & the Netherlands; Germany, Austria & Switzerland; Great Britain & Ireland; Italy; Russia & the Baltics; Scandinavia; Spain & Portugal; London; Paris; or the Best of Europe*

ADVENTURES IN NATURE

Plan your next adventure in: *Alaska, Belize, Caribbean, Costa Rica, Guatemala, Honduras, Mexico*

JMP travel guides are available at your favorite bookstores. For a FREE catalog or to place a mail order, call: 800-888-7504.

John Muir Publications ✦ P.O. Box 613 ✦ Santa Fe, NM 87504

ABOUT THE AUTHOR

Susan Williams Knowles has been active in the culture and arts of the Middle Tennessee area for over 20 years. She has held curatorial positions at the Country Music Hall of Fame, Cheekwood Museum of Art, and directed gallery programs for the Metro Nashville Arts Commission, Middle Tennessee State University, and the Nashville International Airport. She writes regularly on art and restaurants for City Search Nashville (an on-line guide to the city). Her published essays on artists can be found in art papers and regional gallery and museum catalogues. As an independent curator, Knowles directed "From the Mountains to the Mississippi: Contemporary Tennessee Artists" for the National Museum of Women in the Arts, and co-produced an interactive video project entitled "Southern Voices: English in the American South" for the Tennessee Humanities Council. She lives in the Cumberland Mountains, two hours east of Nashville, on a small farm with her husband, artist Andrew Saftel.